THE CENTRAL AMERICAN
PEACE PROCESS, 1983–1991

THE CENTRAL AMERICAN PEACE PROCESS, 1983–1991

SHEATHING SWORDS, BUILDING CONFIDENCE

JACK CHILD

LYNNE RIENNER PUBLISHERS ▪ BOULDER & LONDON

Published in the United States of America in 1992 by
Lynne Rienner Publishers, Inc.
1800 30th Street, Boulder, Colorado 80301

and in the United Kingdom by
Lynne Rienner Publishers, Inc.
3 Henrietta Street, Covent Garden, London WC2E 8LU

Library of Congress Cataloging-in-Publication Data
Child, Jack.
  The Central American peace process. 1983–1991 : sheathing swords,
building confidence / by Jack Child.
    p.   cm.
  Includes bibliographical references and index.
  ISBN 1-55587-343-X
  1. Central American—Foreign relations—1979; 2. Diplomatic
negotiations in international disputes.
F1439.5.C525   1992
327.728—dc20   92-10645
                                              CIP

British Cataloguing in Publication Data
A Cataloguing in Publication record for this book
is available from the British Library.

Printed and bound in the United States of America

The paper used in this publication meets the requirements
of the American National Standard for Permanence of
Paper for Printed Library Materials Z39.48-1984.

For the helpful fixers

CONTENTS

ILLUSTRATIONS

MAPS

FIGURES

TABLES

PREFACE

When I retired from the U.S. Army in 1980 after a relatively brief and unspectacular career as a lieutenant colonel, Latin American area specialist, I felt that I had left things military behind me. As I began my civilian academic career at the School of International Service and the Department of Language and Foreign Studies of the American University, I concentrated on teaching the Spanish language, translation, and Latin American area studies. Geographically, I focused on that part of the Western Hemisphere that is physically, culturally, and politically as far from Central America as one could imagine: South American Antarctica and the islands of the far South Atlantic.

But somehow Central America and things military interrupted my concentration on the far South Atlantic. As the Central American crisis heated up in the early 1980s, the army asked me to consider returning to active duty to serve in that area. (They dropped the request when I said I would return only if I could abstain from shaving and shining.) At the same time, it seemed as though almost every Latin Americanist I knew was devoting increasing time and attention to Central America, and I felt I too had to weigh in. The question was what contribution I, as a non–Central Americanist, could make in an increasingly crowded field. After a brief flirtation with activist peace groups, I settled on a very satisfying and productive working relationship with the International Peace Academy (IPA), a nongovernmental educational organization closely associated with the United Nations that stresses conflict resolution techniques, mediation, third-party neutral intervention, peacekeeping, and confidence building. Through most of the decade of the 1980s, I consulted for the IPA, wrote papers and edited books for them, and attended numerous conferences, workshops, and off-the-record sessions sponsored by them, which eventually involved most of the important actors in the Central American peace process. General (retired, Indian Army) Indar Jit Rikhye, the founding president of the IPA, and Richard Millett, the IPA's principal Central American consultant, were friends, colleagues, and inspiration in these fascinating years, when the IPA quietly worked to help the parties to the conflict, the Contadora representatives, and numerous other "helpful fixers" to understand the potential, and the limitations, of military peacekeeping and confidence building.

These two concepts, "peacekeeping" and "confidence building," appealed to me because they provided practical ways in which the military could make an important positive contribution to peace. A third concept, "zones of peace," was especially interesting to me because it had a Latin American origin and provided a bridge between my Central American and Antarctic interests (the Antarctic Treaty is in effect the constitution for the largest zone of peace in the world).

In 1989 a generous grant from the United States Institute of Peace (USIP) permitted me to bring my involvement in the military aspects of the Central American peace process under more systematic research and study. For two-and-a-half years, the USIP grant provided me with funds for two research assistants, some release time from my university duties, and the opportunity to travel to Canada and Central America. In June 1991 I joined the Latin American Studies Association's "Nicaragua Field Seminar," led by the indefatigable Tom Walker of Ohio University, in an opportunity to interview Nicaraguans from all walks of life as well as key international-organization officials in Managua and the hinterland. I am very grateful for the assistance provided by Lieutenant Colonel Dermont Early (UN Headquarters), as well as Fernando Castañon and Colonel Gustavo Lazcano of ONUCA and Santiago Murray and Juan Castagnino of CIAV-OAS.

This book, along with several articles and conference papers, is the culmination of this decade of work with the IPA and the USIP. (The ideas and opinions expressed here are, of course, my own and do not necessarily reflect those of the IPA or USIP.) The book would not have been possible without the steady support of these two institutions, and of many friends and colleagues along the way. Chief among these are my two principal research assistants, Jonathan Darling and Sarah Howden. My work-study assistants in these years did much of the thankless work of chasing down and photocopying materials; they include Shelly Sweeney, Fernando Alvarez-Tabío, Dauri Sandison, Jill Kzewina, Nadja Reger, Kelly Bundy, Joe Clougherty, Julio Medina, Flora Calderón, Ramona Bock, Ivelisse Bonilla, and Marcela Ghiggeri. As in the past, Salvador Vélez and Gioconda Vallarino of the Inter-American Defense College were most helpful.

The USIP grant permitted me the luxury of sending the manuscript to a number of unsuspecting volunteers who graciously accepted my pleas for comments and corrections. They richly deserve recognition: Pope Atkins, Covadonga Fuertes, Gregg Higgins, Tom Dodd, Amy Oliver, Dan Masterson, Dave Johnson, Herb Huser, Mary Vanderlaan, David Pion-Berlin, Gabriel Marcella, Harold Klepak, Indar Rikhye, Larman Wilson, Chris Coleman, Dave Petreman, Cynthia McClintock, Vadim Medish, Nina Serafino, Carol Sparhawk, Phyllis Walker, Liisa North, and Michael Gold. I also owe special thanks to the publisher, Lynne Rienner, who has been a constant source of good advice ever since she worked with me on my first book a decade ago, as well as her able editors Gia Hamilton and Steve Arney.

Finally, Leslie Morginson-Eitzen, *colega, compañera, y amiga,* contributed with her usual careful editing, patience, and understanding, as did Evita Canal de Beagle and La Perrichola. The word processing was done with the help of María Macarena and María Mactusi.

Jack Child

Key Sites in the Central American Peace Process

(See Chronology, Appendix 1)

1. Contadora Island, Panama
2. Cancún, Mexico
3. La Palma, El Salvador
4. Esquipulas, Guatemala
5. Sapoá, Nicaragua
6. Costa del Sol (Tesoro Beach), El Salvador
7. Tela, Honduras
8. San Isidro de Coronado, Costa Rica
9. Tocontín Airport, Honduras
10. Montelimar, Nicaragua
11. Yamales, Honduras
12. Antigua, Guatemala
13. Puntarenas, Costa Rica
14. Alajuela, Costa Rica

PART 1
INTRODUCTION

1
THE SETTING AND THE
INSTRUMENTS OF THE PEACE PROCESS

The Contadora process from its inception in 1983, and its evolution to the Arias/Esquipulas peace plan, was not only an important contribution to the resolution of a specific conflict in Central America, but also a watershed for the Inter-American System and the U.S.–Latin American relationship. Moreover, it led to significant changes in the roles and presence of two international organizations in the Western Hemisphere: the United Nations (UN) and the Organization of American States (OAS). Furthermore, the Contadora/Arias/Esquipulas process left a rich legacy in the field of peacekeeping, peace verification, and confidence-building measures. It also contributed to the steadily growing body of materials supporting the notion of "zones of peace" in the Western Hemisphere.

This book analyzes the process of verifying the Central American peace accords and the building of confidence among the various parties involved. The principal focus is on security aspects, although many of the concepts and developments discussed are also applicable to political, economic, and diplomatic facets. Because of the prominent role they played, considerable attention is paid to the UN and the OAS, as well as Canada. The focus on security aspects necessarily implies more emphasis on the military side of treaty verification and confidence building, and less on election monitoring, human rights protection, and the encouragement of democracy.

The long and painful process of searching for peace in Central America has emphasized two concepts—"peace verification" and "zones of peace"— with a distinctly Latin American flavor. This book argues that the special use of these two concepts in the context of the Central American peace process is an important addition to the field of conflict resolution, and goes beyond the specific situation in Central America to influence the search for peace in other areas.

The use of the term "helpful fixer" throughout the book merits a brief explanation. The peaceful resolution of the Central American conflict in the 1980s required outside helpful fixers. The traditional OAS machinery for conflict resolution in the hemisphere was incapable of achieving peace, and the hemisphere's superpower was directly involved in the conflict and was thus hardly a credible fixer of the problem. The Canadians contributed enormously, directly and indirectly, to mounting an effective UN peacekeeping and peace-verification mission in the Western Hemisphere for the first time. "Helpful fixers" has been consistently used in the Canadian literature to reflect that nation's modest but important contribution as a middle power with strong links to the United States and a fundamental commitment to the use of the global organization in military peacekeeping missions.[1]

BASIC IDEAS

The verification of peace accords and the building of confidence involve two different sets of concepts taken from the general field of conflict resolution and prevention. The verification of peace accords is a form of third-party neutral presence or interposition, in which the two sides in a conflict agree to request help from a third party that has earned their trust through its neutrality and competence. The second set of concepts seeks to resolve the basic causes of the conflict through mediation, conciliation, or arbitration ("peacemaking") then solve the underlying socioeconomic roots of conflict ("peace building"), while establishing a set of steps that make it less likely that conflict will result from misunderstanding or misreading of another's intentions ("confidence building").

Peacekeeping involves the prevention and termination of hostilities through the peaceful presence of a neutral third party. The peacekeeping contingent, which can include military and civilian personnel, does not seek to enforce peace or impose solutions to the conflict by sheer power. Instead, it attempts to create the conditions that lead to dialogue and eventual resolution of the conflict. In short, its mission is to create space and time in which to allow the combatants to cool off and permit the diplomats to do their work. Peacekeeping, under this definition, is *not* the settlement of a dispute by an overwhelming supranational force intent on imposing an outside solution to a conflict. Nor does it stem from collective security sanctions in which an alliance's military response is triggered by an act of aggression. This definition of peacekeeping, based on the peaceful presence of a third-party neutral, is more specific than the rather loose usage under which almost any military action intended to produce peace is called "peacekeeping." In recent years this looser definition has included such things as the intervention in Liberia by a group of neighboring countries (ECOMOG, the military arm of the Economic Committee of West African States), the ill-fated U.S. Marine presence in Lebanon in 1983, and the naming of an intercontinental ballistic missile "the Peacekeeper."

Peace observing has the same basic purpose as peacekeeping but is usually a much smaller effort, which in turn affects its techniques and functions in the field. Peacekeeping contingents may range from several hundred to several thousand troops, but peace-observer missions are much smaller, and may in fact consist of only one or two persons whose function is to serve as the eyes and ears of the international organization or ad hoc group that sent them to the scene of the conflict. Their ability to interpose themselves between the opposing sides is obviously very limited, and their function is usually only to investigate, observe, and report back.

Peacemaking, which is frequently called "peaceful settlement of disputes," is that collection of techniques and institutions that are available to resolve conflicts through negotiation, mediation, amelioration, arbitration, and conciliation. This field belongs more to the diplomat and international jurist than to the military or civilian peacekeeper in the field.

Peace building is the development effort that attempts to reduce conflict by improving social and economic conditions and meeting fundamental human needs. The assumption is that economic and social injustices must be addressed in order to provide the basis for a permanent solution to conflict. Although peace building has traditionally focused on economic and social conditions, it also has a security dimension (military, political, and diplomatic) in the sense that cooperative development efforts will increase mutual trust, build confidence, and thus make future conflicts less likely.

Confidence-building measures (CBMs) are certain techniques designed to lower tensions and make it less likely that a conflict will break out through a misunderstanding, mistake, or misreading of the actions of a potential adversary. CBMs emerged from attempts by the Cold War superpowers and their military alliances (NATO [North Atlantic Treaty Organization] and the Warsaw Pact) to avoid nuclear war by accident or miscalculation. However, as several authors have noted, CBMs also exist at other levels of conflict situations, and in different regions of the world, including Latin America, although they might not have been called CBMs.[2]

Jonathan Alford has proposed a useful metaphor for CBMs in terms of the actions of two swordsmen with weapons raised to strike: neither one wants the conflict, but neither one is willing to let his guard down.[3] The process of avoiding the conflict involves a slow and formal ritual in which the adversaries slowly back away until outside striking range, slowly lower their swords, then sheath the weapons (which are still at hand if the adversary moves aggressively). Finally, they unbuckle their scabbards and reach out to each other to shake hands. Each step in the process involves caution and verification that the other side is making an equally significant move away from the conflict. Alford notes that this simple analogy is imperfect because in international relations the asymmetries of doctrine, power, and force postures make the creation of this ritual framework an extremely difficult process. The process involves a great deal of imagination as the adversaries search for small but meaningful ways to build up verifiable steps toward peaceful resolution of their differences. The role of CBMs is to provide some of these steps.

The Contadora/Arias/Esquipulas peace process in Central America from 1983 to date has emphasized two additional concepts stemming from the Latin American response to this regional problem. These concepts have become so integral to the diplomatic search for a Central American peace, as well as to the academic analysis of that process, that they merit consideration as Latin American contributions to conflict-resolution theory and practice. These two concepts are "peace verification" and "zones of peace."

Peace verification is the effort by a third-party neutral contingent to assure an international organization or ad hoc group of peacemakers that the conditions of a signed peace treaty are being complied with. The scope of peace verification and monitoring is broader than simple peace observing because of the magnitude and complexity of the geography and forces involved; it is also a more aggressive process than peace observing, which passively reports on events. Peace verification implies frequent and unpredictable movement and patrolling, supplemented by technological means to broaden the area and the targets of the process. It is less than traditional peacekeeping, however, because there is no effort to physically interpose the contingent between the possible adversaries, and the size of the verification and monitoring group is substantially smaller than a traditional peacekeeping group. The Latin American sensitivity to the terms "peacekeeping" and "peacekeeping force" made the use of "peace verification" a much more attractive concept, and helps explain why this usage predominated in much of the debate over the Central American peace process.

Zones of peace are extensive geographic areas in which explicit confidence-building measures have reached a point where the various parties in the region have significantly lowered their levels of arms, while external military powers have been persuaded to reduce their military influence in the area to a minimum. The concepts of "disarmament," "interdependence," and "integration" are closely related to the notion of a "zone of peace," as is keeping external influences out and letting the nations of the region work out their own destinies. Zones of peace can be considered "CBM regimes" because of the way they rely on CBMs as their foundation. Metaphorically, creation of the Central American zone of peace has been described as seeking to build "peace dominoes," in pointed contrast to "conflict dominoes."[4] The hemisphere already has two other zones of peace: one established by the Tlatelolco Treaty proscribing nuclear weapons, and the second created by the

Antarctic Treaty, which has succeeded in keeping that continent (one-quarter of which is closely associated with South America) demilitarized for over thirty years. The 1982 Anglo-Argentine war over the Malvinas/Falkland Islands led to several proposals, including UN General Assembly resolutions, that the South Atlantic be declared a zone of peace; but this was more hortatory than real, and was opposed by the United States on the grounds that such a zone would be inconsistent with generally accepted principles of freedom of navigation and innocent passage.[5]

Recently, there has been some very original Latin American strategic thinking focusing on building new security arrangements based on zones of peace. These new geopolitical concepts would give the region greater autonomy in its own defense based on disarmament, withdrawal of outside powers, and confidence-building measures. Although primarily stemming from the work of an unofficial South American Peace Commission, this new strategic thinking has also focused on Central America and a proposal to make the Caribbean a "Sea of Peace."[6]

The Conflict Resolution Spectrum and the Causes of Conflict

These semantic considerations involving peacekeeping and associated concepts can perhaps be better appreciated by representing them graphically. Figure 1.1 shows a spectrum of third-party interposition roles with historical examples: a minimal one-person peace observer, a larger peace verification mission, a traditional peacekeeping mission, and finally a massive peace enforcement intervention. It should be noted that there is a quantum leap (indicated by the broken line) when one crosses over into peace enforcement. At this point the peace enforcers become adversaries in the conflict, and the chances for long-term peaceful resolution diminish markedly.

Figure 1.2 illustrates the different levels at which one can address the basic causes of conflict once the keepers, verifiers, or observers of peace have been interposed to act as third-party neutrals. At the surface level, the process of peacemaking is used to find a diplomatic solution to the specific conflict at hand. At the intermediate level, confidence-building measures are used to make conflict through misunderstanding or accident less likely. And at the most profound level, the development process of peace building is used to get at the fundamental socioeconomic causes of injustice and conflict.

Basic Principles of Peacekeeping, Observing, and Verification

Regardless of whether the international third-party neutral contingent is involved in peacekeeping, peace observing, or treaty verification, there are certain basic principles that, if respected, considerably increase the chances of success of the operation. One source has compiled a list of these generally accepted principles, based on an analysis of a number of United Nations

Figure 1.1   A Conflict Resolution Spectrum

Peace Enforcement
Imposition of a temporary end of conflict by major force
  Example: UN in Korean War; IAPF in the
  Dominican Republic, 1965 (14,000 troops)

Peacekeeping
Third-party neutral interposition by a substantial contingent
  Example: UNFICYP in Cyprus (6,400 troops)

Peace Verification
Third-party neutral presence by a significant
  contingent, possibly unarmed, to verify and monitor
  compliance with a treaty
  Example: ONUCA in Central America (1,100 troops)

Peace Observation
Small "eyes and ears" group sent to a conflict to report back
  Example: two men sent to Belize-Guatemala, 1972

Figure 1.2   Addressing the Basic Causes of Conflict

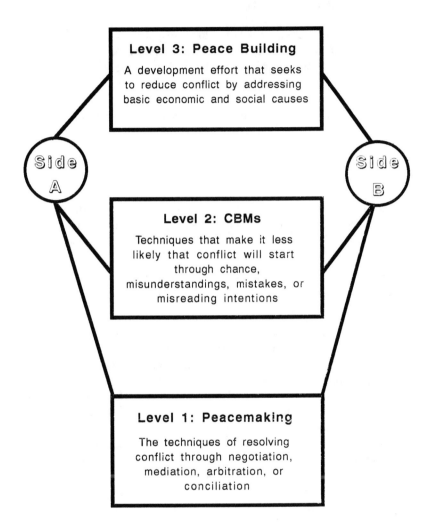

experiences.[7] These principles, which will be used in our subsequent analysis
of peacekeeping in the Western Hemisphere, include:

- *Consent* of the principal parties to the dispute.
- *Impartiality and neutrality* of the peacekeeping contingent.
- *Balance* in the national and political makeup of the force.
- *Approval* by the major regional (or global) powers.
- *Freedom of movement* within the area of conflict.
- *Non-use of force* except in very clear cases of self-defense.
- *Voluntary participation* by a broad representation of states that are
  members of the international organization involved.
- *Simultaneous peacekeeping and peacemaking* so that the time gained
  by the peacekeepers can be used by the peacemakers to resolve the
  underlying causes of the conflict.
- *Centralized management* of the administrative and logistical aspects
  of the peacekeeping mission by a single element of the international
  organization's secretariat.

PEACEKEEPING, OBSERVATION,
AND VERIFICATION IN LATIN AMERICA[8]

At first glance, the Inter-American System possesses a highly complex,
comprehensive, and integrated set of institutions and procedures for peaceful
settlement, peacemaking, and peacekeeping. There is, after all, a collective
security treaty (the Rio Treaty of 1947), a detailed Treaty on Pacific
Settlement (Bogotá, 1948), and a charter (Bogotá, 1948), all with a strong
commitment to finding peaceful solutions to disputes. However, a series of
special circumstances peculiar to the Inter-American System limit this
imposing juridical structure and make its operating reality considerably less
than meets the eye. In terms of national power, the 35 sovereign states of the
Western Hemisphere include a single global superpower, the United States, a
half-dozen mid-level nations, and a number of small states with limited
resources. Moreover, the United States historically has not hesitated to
intervene unilaterally to protect its own strategic, economic, or political
interests, especially in the sensitive Caribbean–Central American area.

Given these realities, it is understandable that the Latin American
nations in the system have sought juridical and legal means to limit
intervention by the United States. Furthermore, they view with great
suspicion the establishment of peacekeeping forces or arrangements that
might serve as a "fig leaf cover" for unilateral U.S. actions. Thus, the Inter-
American System has an overriding commitment to nonintervention and
national sovereignty, which frequently has blocked or severely restricted
effective peacekeeping efforts. As a result, the emphasis has been on

peacemaking, not peacekeeping. Peace observing has been employed effectively at times, but usually on a mixed military-civilian basis and with clear subordination of the observers to the politico-diplomatic organs.

The permanent military organs of the Inter-American System have been kept weak deliberately and isolated from the diplomatic and decisionmaking elements. Attempts to formalize the role of the permanent military organs in preparations or support of peacekeeping or peace-observing missions have been consistently blocked. Yet the Inter-American System has not hesitated to tap military resources (troops, equipment, expertise) on an ad hoc basis when required for peacekeeping or peace-observing purposes.

The most successful peacekeeping efforts in the Inter-American System have been at the lower end of the scale. They have usually involved limited peace observing with a strong peacemaking component in terms of mediation and arbitration on the part of the peace observers, and the most effective efforts have involved small-state border conflicts. The limited military resources of these smaller nations preclude extended combat, and the nature of the disputes are usually territorial, nonideological, and therefore more conducive to neutral third-party dampening. The larger nations tend to settle their differences through direct negotiations or outside arbitration; their more sophisticated diplomatic experience seems to require less help from the system's peacemaking or peacekeeping assets.

In the 1980s the OAS's conflict-resolution mechanisms and the Inter-American Security System (IASS) continued to lose their ability to function effectively due to the impact of several crises: the Malvinas/Falklands conflict of 1982, the Grenada invasion/rescue effort of 1983, the 1989 invasion of Panama, and the continuing Central American crisis. Furthermore, the traditional success of the OAS was due largely to the influence of the United States and the logistical, administrative, and diplomatic support that the United States provided to OAS efforts at conflict resolution. For any number of reasons, the United States could not credibly play this role in the Central American conflict environment of the 1980s, and the effectiveness of the OAS suffered as a result. As we shall see in subsequent chapters, the OAS did play a role in the implementation of certain aspects of the Esquipulas accords, but in a form quite different from its historical peace-observing and peacemaking role.

THE CENTRAL AMERICAN
CONFLICT/PEACE ENVIRONMENT

Because of sensitivities to the term "peacekeeping"—to say nothing of "peace force" or, worse yet, "inter-American peace force"—these terms had to be used cautiously in connection with the Central American peace process. Any contingent placed on the ground would be more readily accepted if it were called a "peace-observing mission," a "technical group," an "international verification group," or some other term that stressed a limited observation and verification function and made it clear that there was no intent to insert large numbers of troops. It would also seem advisable to keep the military side of the contingent as small as possible and make the civilian and diplomatic side as large as possible, to further stress that the group had an observation and verification function and not one involving force or large-scale interposition.

The physical environment of Central America presents severe challenges to any verification, peace-observing, or peacekeeping mission. The terrain is varied, ranging from swamps to relatively open agricultural areas to mountainous tropical rain forests. Distances are substantial: the Honduran-Nicaraguan border is about 350 miles long, while the Nicaraguan–Costa Rican border and the Honduran-Salvadoran border are about 175 miles each. The key Gulf of Fonseca, where El Salvador, Honduras, and Nicaragua come together, is about 25 miles across at its narrowest point.

A multitude of trails and paths cross these borders, and for centuries they have been porous to people on foot or burros. Over the years these paths have provided ample opportunity for border crossings by smugglers, gunrunners, political refugees, immigrants, cattle rustlers, and guerrillas. Yet there are relatively few roads across these borders, making wheeled or tracked transportation difficult and suggesting that any peace-observing contingent would have to make heavy use of helicopters. A useful, although limited, precedent can be found in the experiences of the OAS peace-observer team that patrolled the border between Honduras and El Salvador using helicopters for a number of years after their 1969 war.

An important factor in the Central American peace equation was the way in which the United Nations, and especially its peacekeeping activities, "came back into fashion," as the Secretary-General expressed it, in the late 1980s.[9] This was dramatically demonstrated when the UN peacekeepers won the 1988 Nobel Peace Prize, and was further emphasized when a number of conflict situations were mentioned as possible candidates for new UN peacekeeping missions, including Iran-Iraq, Angola, Namibia, Cambodia, Yugoslavia, and Central America. Many of these operations were welcomed by the Security Council, and by the United States and the former Soviet Union in particular. The latter went so far as to suggest the creation of a permanent standby UN peacekeeping force and the strengthening of the largely symbolic UN Military Staff Committee.[10] But despite promises by the United States and others to fulfill past financial obligations and to provide new funds for such operations, the increasing popularity of UN peacekeeping has raised the issue of how these new missions would be financed because their cost could conceivably rise to several times the regular budget of the United Nations. In September 1990 the UN Secretary-General pleaded for authority and funds for standby peacekeeping forces, noting that the UN peacekeeping operations were greatly overextended and that funds were available for only 24 further days of operation. He cited a shortfall of over $1 billion for regular dues and for peacekeeping operations, of which the United States owed about half. A year later the Secretary-General asked private corporations and wealthy individuals (as well as governments) to contribute voluntarily to a $1 billion Peace Endowment Fund to help pay for UN peacekeeping missions.[11]

The enthusiasm for UN peacekeepers gave rise to thoughtful analyses of the relative advantages of UN versus non-UN peacekeeping missions in terms of the politics, the logistics, and the finances involved.[12] Pertinent examples were taken from the UN experience, ad hoc arrangements such as the Multinational Force and Observers (MFO) between Egypt and Israel, and peacekeeping by regional international organizations such as the OAS and the European Community (in the Yugoslavian civil war). The use of the term "peacekeeping" to mask non-neutral third-party intervention has continued unabated, as evidenced by the peace-enforcement role played by the Economic Committee of West African States (ECOWAS), which in 1990 sent 4,000 troops to restore peace in Liberia and promptly got involved in military actions with the various factions in that civil war.

We turn now to an analysis of how these various approaches to peacekeeping, peace observing, treaty verification, and confidence building gradually became significant elements in the Central American peace process from 1983 to 1991.

NOTES

1. See Ichikawa, *The "Helpful Fixer."*
2. See, for example, the following works: Macintosh, *Confidence (and Security) Building Measures*; Palma, "Confidence Building"; Child, "A Confidence-Building Approach to Resolving Central American Conflicts," in Child, *Conflict in Central America*; Palma, "Medidas de Confianza Recíproca" and "Co-operation and Confidence-Building Measures."
3. Alford, *Confidence-Building Measures.* See also Child's chapter on CBMs in Child, *Conflict in Central America.*
4. The idea of "peace dominoes" is used by Cepeda in *Democracia y Desarrollo.*
5. *Washington Post,* 15 November 1988, A27.
6. Somavía and Insulza, *Seguridad Democrática*; Varas, *La Política de las Armas*; Portales, "Zona de Paz."
7. These principles are adapted from those suggested by the International Peace Academy in its *Peacekeeper's Handbook.* For another perspective on the application of basic concepts, see Leary, "Principles of Peace Observation."
8. This section draws on Child, "Peacekeeping and the Inter-American System."
9. For commentary on UN peacekeeping, see *Washington Post,* 26 July

1988, A1; 25 September 1988, A31; 30 September 1988, A1, A20; 5 October 1988, A27; 10 January 1989, A18; 27 August 1990, A1; and *New York Times,* 5 August 1990, 3. See also the Secretary-General's "Foreword" in United Nations, *Blue Helmets.*

10. *Washington Post,* 4 November 1989, A23; and 19 September 1990, A14.

11. *New York Times,* 25 November 1991, A3.

12. Fouquet, "Counting the Cost of UN Peacekeepers"; Houghton, *Multinational Peacekeeping,* 33–37, 77–81; Allen, "Peacekeeping," 61; *Washington Post,* 5 September 1991, A23.

PART 2

THE CONTADORA PROCESS, 1983–1987

2

THE EARLY CONTADORA
MEETINGS AND DOCUMENTS

THE FIRST CONTADORA MEETING, 8–9 JANUARY 1983

The Contadora process formally began with a two-day meeting on the Panamanian island of the same name. The meeting, called by Mexico, involved the foreign ministers of Colombia (Rodrigo Lloreda Caicedo), Mexico (Bernardo Sepúlveda Amor), Panama (Juan José Amado), and Venezuela (José Alberto Zambrano). The stated purpose was to discuss threats to regional peace and security stemming from the ongoing crisis in Central America. Unstated was their concern that the Reagan administration's policy of emphasizing military solutions was leading the region to war.

The Contadora Declaration made an urgent appeal to the countries of Central America "to engage in dialogue and negotiation so as to reduce tension and lay the foundations for a permanent atmosphere of peaceful coexistence and mutual respect among states."[1] The ministers also expressed their deep concern regarding foreign interference and called on all states to refrain from action that might aggravate the situation. They also reviewed the various peace initiatives and emphasized the importance of having other Latin American countries become involved in the peace process; this was an appeal for broad regional support, which later evolved into the Lima Group (Argentina, Brazil, Peru, and Uruguay) and the participation of several Latin American nations in the peacekeeping and peace-observing effort. In a fundamental disagreement with the United States, they indicated that they regarded the basic causes of conflict as stemming from socioeconomic injustices in the region, not from East-West tensions.

The verification issue was not addressed at the first Contadora meeting, which produced a general statement of principles calling for dialogue and negotiation as the best paths to peaceful settlement. However, this first meeting can be seen as a confidence-building measure in the sense that it called for greater trust, contacts, and involvement.

THE CONTADORA OBSERVER MISSION TO THE NICARAGUAN–COSTA RICAN BORDER, APRIL–MAY 1983

This rather modest effort at peace observing was significant because it was the first one that the Contadora group attempted. The situation that led to it generated a three-way pull among those who favored either Contadora, the UN, or the Organization of American States as the multilateral organization to provide the peace-observing presence. The experience also showed the actors involved the possibilities and problems involved in peace observing, not to mention peacekeeping. It consequently marked the beginning of a slowly growing realization that any meaningful effort at peace observing—and certainly peacekeeping—would require more technical expertise and prior experience in this area than any of the Contadora nations possessed.

The causes of the tension involved one more iteration, albeit a potentially far more dangerous one, of the perennial problem of strain along the Costa Rican–Nicaraguan border. In late April 1983 Costa Rica complained that Nicaraguan troops had crossed the border onto Costa Rican soil. Even though the Contadora process was available, Costa Rica chose to take the case to the OAS and requested a multinational peace force, based on the assumption that in the OAS Costa Rica could count on the United States (and the Rio Treaty) to defend its borders.[2] The Contadora nations, however, correctly interpreted Costa Rica's move as a challenge to them and succeeded in persuading the OAS not to take any action on the case but to refer it to the Contadora group. Mexico, which had always taken a firm position against any OAS peace force, was especially adamant that if the matter were not handled by the Contadora group, it would severely weaken their efforts.

Meeting in Panama on 11–12 May, the Contadora nations discussed the Costa Rican request to establish a peace force strong enough to monitor the area of Costa Rica bordering on Nicaragua. The Contadora nations agreed to send an observer commission (not a "peace force" as requested) to study the situation and make recommendations. In their discussion there had been some internal differences, with Venezuela supporting a peace force while the other three Contadora nations, led by Mexico, argued that an observer commission was all that was required. The commission was to include two civilians and one military observer from each of the four Contadora countries, for a total of twelve; however, Mexico, showing its extreme sensitivity to military intervention in any form, declined to send a military observer, and the final size of the group was thus eleven.

A further complication was created by the Nicaraguan preference for the

UN as the source of any multinational verification mission along its borders. On 9 May 1983 the *New York Times* reported that the Nicaraguan government would be asking the UN to send a peacekeeping force to patrol its borders in the face of incursions by Nicaraguan Contras from Honduras. But the UN Security Council demurred, suggesting that the Contadora Group had the situation well in hand.

In mid-May the eleven Contadora observers visited several sites along the Nicaraguan–Costa Rican border where the Costa Ricans had reported border crossings by the Nicaraguan security forces. Part of their visit involved flying over areas where fighting had been reported between the forces of Edén Pastora and the Ejército Popular Sandinista (Sandinista People's Army—EPS), but the observers saw no actual combat. Their trip included visits to Managua and San José, where President Luis A. Monge reminded the observers of Costa Rica's commitment to permanent neutrality.[3] The observer commission's report was an internal one delivered to the Contadora foreign ministers at their 28–30 May 1983 meeting in Panama City. There was little to report, but Contadora's first try at peace observing had shown them the problems involved in verifying anything along a 300-kilometer border with a handful of inexperienced observers.

Even though the Contadora observer mission had neither accomplished much nor impressed many with its thoroughness, the Costa Rican government pressed for a permanent observer mission that would be available to patrol its sensitive border area with Nicaragua. The Contadora nations were unwilling to launch such a permanent group but did raise the possibility in discussions with the UN Secretary-General in New York.[4] There were also bilateral contacts between Costa Rican and Nicaraguan authorities along the border in which coordination between each other's border posts was discussed. In May 1984 these contacts were formalized in an agreement to create a bilateral Commission of Supervision and Prevention for border inspection, which was largely ineffectual.

THE CANCÚN SUMMIT, 17 JULY 1983: THE CANCÚN DECLARATION

The meeting was held at the Mexican resort of Cancún and included the presidents of the four Contadora nations. It produced the Cancún Declaration, which called for renewed efforts to continue the peace process and laid out principles and recommendations to be considered in an eventual agreement. These recommendations included several that embodied basic confidence-building measures and established the foundations for international peacekeeping and peace observing.

The Cancún Declaration,[5] although short (three pages), took the

Contadora statement of January 1983 and fleshed it out with more specific proposals, establishing the pattern in 1983–1984 that each subsequent meeting would provide increasing details. Security was a major concern of the Cancún Declaration, which focused on effectively controlling the arms race, ending arms trafficking, eliminating foreign military advisors, creating demilitarized zones, prohibiting the use of one state's territory to destabilize another's, and prohibiting other forms of interference in the internal affairs of countries in the region. The issue of verification was also given greater specificity in that the declaration mentioned the need to establish appropriate supervisory machinery in order to verify several of the security commitments.

Confidence-building measures also appear in the Cancún Declaration in the form of recommendations for joint boundary commissions and direct communications between governments, and in the need to give prior notice of troop movements near frontiers when the contingents exceed certain limits. The use of the phrase "commitment to promote a climate of détente and confidence" also reflects an increasingly specific appreciation of the utility of confidence-building measures.

The U.S. response to the Cancún Declaration was, predictably, ambiguous. President Reagan expressed support for its general objectives, but in a letter to the Contadora country presidents, he called for "comprehensive, fully adequate verification" and suggested that the Organization of American States would be the suitable verifier of agreements. The excessively general nature of the Contadora statements to date, and the apparent unwillingness to deal with the specific mechanisms of control and verification, were cited unofficially as the principal obstacles to greater U.S. support for the Contadora process.[6] The president's suggestion that the OAS should be the appropriate mechanism for verification and compliance was revealing in that this was the forum in which the United States could exercise greatest influence.

A few days after Reagan's letter to the Contadora presidents, on 26 July 1983, the U.S. announced the Big Pine II military maneuver with Honduras, with over 16,000 troops and 19 ships involved. In an interesting attempt at transferring NATO–Warsaw Pact confidence-building measures to the Central American arena, Honduras invited Nicaragua to send observers to the maneuver, but the Sandinistas declined, saying that the maneuvers were an obstacle to a peaceful solution to Central America's problems.

PANAMA FOREIGN MINISTERS' MEETING, 7–9 SEPTEMBER 1983: THE 21 OBJECTIVES DOCUMENT

This gathering was significant in that it involved the four Contadora countries plus the five Central American countries, and produced the first document agreed on by all nine.[7] The 21 Objectives document should be viewed as the foundation on which subsequent draft treaties were built. The security objectives were the most controversial and were fairly specific. They included stopping the arms race (and the initiation of negotiations for the control and reduction of weapons and troops), eliminating foreign bases and foreign military advisors, establishing internal mechanisms to control arms trafficking, and preventing the use of national territory to destabilize other states or support acts of terrorism, subversion, or sabotage.

The problem of effective verification remained unsolved by the 21 Objectives document. However, during the meeting the text of the internal agenda for the earlier 29–30 May 1983 meeting was released,[8] and this agenda mentioned a Multilateral Oversight Committee that would be charged with supervising the fulfillment of the commitments dealing with security and political issues in any eventual treaty or agreement. The composition of this committee was unspecified in the agenda, although it was described as "technical" in nature, and under the control of a "higher body" made up of the Central American foreign ministers. There was no indication of the role of any third-party neutrals or international organizations, although the Contadora nations were beginning to realize that verification might require outside help.

UN involvement was also becoming necessary. Under the provisions of UN Resolution 530, the Contadora nations formally informed the Security Council, through the Secretary-General, of the Panama meeting and the 21 objectives. In his transmittal letter to the Security Council, the Secretary-General pointedly noted the increase of tensions in Central America and the charges and countercharges of military pressures and arms buildups. He added that he was "unable to make definitive judgments" on these charges because "the Secretary-General has no way of reliably verifying each and every one of the components of this situation."[9] Shortly afterward, representatives of each of the Contadora nations spoke at the UN General Assembly strongly supporting the Contadora initiatives and asking for unspecified UN support; a similar set of speeches was made at the annual OAS General Assembly in November.

Reaction and developments moved swiftly in late 1983. Hard-liners within the Reagan administration, such as Under Secretary of Defense for Policy Fred Iklé, called for a military victory in Central America, and the U.S. invasion of Grenada in October persuaded many observers that a similar event could occur in Nicaragua. The covert mining of Nicaraguan harbors and the possible revival of CONDECA (Central American Defense Council) added to the tensions. But despite the Contadora nations' call for a prompt agreement on a treaty, the attempts to translate the 21 Objectives document into something acceptable to all five Central American nations made little progress.

ATTEMPTS TO REVIVE CONDECA IN LATE 1983

CONDECA had been created at the instigation of the U.S. government in the early 1960s as part of the attempt to invigorate the Inter-American Military System as a weapon against Cuban-inspired insurgency. CONDECA had the peculiarity of being an agreement between defense ministers, not heads of state, and thus was more of an understanding of mutual support than a formal treaty. Under the strong tutelage of the U.S. Southern Command in Panama, it was active in holding maneuvers and planning and coordinating the activities of the Central American military until it fell into disrepair in the wake of the 1969 war between El Salvador and Honduras. The final blow for CONDECA came with the fall of Somoza and the coming to power of the revolutionary government in Managua in 1979.

In late 1983, and especially after the invasion of Grenada and the mining of Nicaraguan harbors, any talk of reviving CONDECA probably would have been interpreted by most Central American governments and other interested actors as a U.S.-led alliance of conservative military establishments aimed at pressuring the Sandinistas and possibly setting the stage for a Grenada-style invasion of Nicaragua. As one Panamanian diplomat put it, "at that time [late 1983] CONDECA was the antithesis of Contadora."[10]

Nevertheless, in October 1983 a CONDECA meeting was held in secrecy on a farm owned by President General Oscar Mejía Victores outside of Guatemala City. Attending were the defense ministers of Guatemala, El Salvador, and Honduras and the U.S. Southern Command's General Paul Gorman. Nicaragua was not invited to attend the Guatemala meeting, and Costa Rica refused to go, saying that such a meeting would jeopardize the Contadora effort and the moves to create a peacekeeping presence. After the meeting a U.S. spokesperson said that CONDECA could mount joint border patrols, including naval patrols in the Gulf of Fonseca, to prevent arms flows from Nicaragua. The United States indicated it might also step up training for CONDECA troops at its bases in Honduras.[11]

The most likely scenario for a CONDECA invasion of Nicaragua would have involved either a border crossing by the Sandinistas, which would have been labeled a provocation, or the "intervention by invitation" option whereby the Nicaraguan Contras would have attempted to hold a piece of territory on the border with Honduras, proclaimed themselves the legitimate government of Nicaragua, invoked the CONDECA agreement, and requested military assistance from the CONDECA nations and the United States. The parallels to the Grenada invasion and the request for help under the obscure security provisions of the Treaty of the Organization of Eastern Caribbean States made this latter possibility quite credible. Indeed, Lieutenant Colonel Oliver North was later to cite this as one of the contingencies that had been considered in the Reagan White House.[12]

Despite the best efforts of General Gorman and key allies in the military establishments of El Salvador, Honduras, and Guatemala, CONDECA was not revived, even though the possibility was mentioned numerous times in the following months and years by both U.S. and Central American hard-liners who favored a military victory, as opposed to a Contadora peace process.

PANAMA FOREIGN MINISTERS' MEETING, 8–9 JANUARY 1984: THE "PRINCIPLES FOR IMPLEMENTATION"

The foreign ministers of the Contadora Group and Central American nations met in Panama in early January 1984 (the first anniversary of Contadora) to continue the process of moving from the early Contadora documents toward a treaty. The intermediate step taken in Panama took the form of "Principles for the Implementation of the Commitments Undertaken in the Document of Objectives,"[13] which contained greater specificity on issues of verification and confidence building. Principles involving security issues—including inventories of arms, bases, and troops, their subsequent control and reduction, and a census of foreign military advisors ("with a view toward elimination")—were the most controversial. One item that was dropped was a call for a moratorium on new arms acquisitions. There were several confidence-building measures, some carried over from prior documents. One of them called for the establishment of "direct communications mechanisms for the purpose of preventing and resolving incidents among states."

The technical group established at Panama was an important innovation. It was to be an advisory body to the joint meeting of the Contadora and Central American nations and would have no enforcement powers. The technical group was charged with following up on the measures provided for by the "Principles" in three areas: security, politics, and socioeconomics. There were also three working commissions for each area with each Central American country having two members on each commission. The agreement also provided for external advisors, who could be experts in their individual capacities or representatives of international organizations; their use was to be approved in advance by consensus. In this technical group was the germ of the idea of tapping expertise from outside the Contadora and Central American nations, a possibility that was to be sorely needed when it came to the specifics of realistic verification and monitoring.

U.S. RESPONSE AND ACTIONS; THE KISSINGER COMMISSION

The U.S. approach to the Contadora search for peace—specifically the aspects of verification and confidence-building measures—in late 1983 can be seen in both the work of the Kissinger Commission and hard-line U.S. responses in early 1984.

The Kissinger Commission (formally the National Bipartisan Commission on Central America) took testimony and deliberated throughout 1983, during Contadora's first year, and delivered its report to the president on 10 January 1984. The most noteworthy feature of the commission's report with regard to the Central American peace process was how little attention it paid Contadora and its various documents and initiatives. Contadora is addressed only three times in the report, and the most extensive treatment is barely one page in a document of well over one hundred pages. It is hard to avoid the conclusion that the Kissinger Commission was following the Reagan administration's lead of paying lip service to Contadora, but did not really take it seriously. Effective verification of any Central American peace agreement is stressed in the chapter "The Search for Peace," with the passing comment that the Contadora countries could play a role in this process. Indeed, this secondary verification role appears to be the main contribution the Kissinger Commission felt could be made by Contadora.

The one-page assessment of Contadora noted the weaknesses of the Contadora Group in terms of their divergent interests, their lack of experience in working together, and the fact that they had not been tested in the key area of "crafting specific policies to provide for regional security."[14] The same paragraph included a telling comment: "Thus the United States cannot use the Contadora process as a substitute for its own policies." And, in a condescending comment that many Latin Americans found annoying, the report observed that "experience has shown that the [Contadora] process works most effectively when the United States acts purposefully. When our policy languishes, the Contadora process languishes. When we are decisive, the Contadora process gathers momentum."

The Kissinger Commission report listed as an issue that required attention the possibility of a strengthened role for the Inter-American Defense Board (IADB).[15] This presumably reflected the participation of Ambassador-at-large General Gordon Sumner, a former chairman of the IADB and one of the commission's advisors. The possibility of the board's involvement in verifying a Central American peace accord was to be floated only a few months after the Kissinger Commission's report. The commission did not deal with any specific matters of peace verification or confidence-building measures, nor was testimony in this area met with any interest by the commission.[16]

Criticisms of the Kissinger Commission focused on its heavy emphasis on the traditional instruments of U.S. Central American policy: military buildup, economic assistance driven by geopolitical considerations rather than basic human needs, hostility to the Sandinistas, containment of Soviet-Cuban–inspired insurgencies, and other aspects seemingly defined by Central

America's place in an East-West confrontation.[17] A biting commentary by a British parliamentary opposition group that traveled to Central America about the same time as the Kissinger Commission questioned the moral authority of the United States because of its support for the Contras and covert actions against Nicaragua. Their report suggested that the supervision of Central American demilitarization could best be handled in the framework of the UN.[18]

The criticism that the United States was paying lip service to the Contadora process but was blocking it by establishing impossible verification standards began to gain prominence in this period. According to critics, this ploy allowed the Reagan administration to have it both ways: it could avoid international opprobrium by verbally supporting the Contadora process, and yet could insure that it would never come to pass by insisting on impossibly high verification standards. Perhaps to counter this criticism, the United States made a modest effort to involve itself in strengthening Contadora verification early in 1984 by sending a team of security specialists to friendly governments in Central America to provide expertise on compliance with security aspects of international agreements. There was also an indication that the United States was willing to fund compliance verification, and an estimate of $20–25 million a year was mentioned.[19]

CANADA'S INCREASING ROLE

The change from Canada's long-standing distant attitude toward Latin America and its contribution to the Contadora/Esquipulas process are watershed events in the international relations of the hemisphere. During the Contadora/Esquipulas years, Canada re-evaluated its role in the hemisphere, joined the Organization of American States, was a major influence in the shaping of the Contadora/Esquipulas verification instruments, and participated directly and substantially in the first UN peacekeeping operation in the Western Hemisphere, the UN Observer Group in Central America (ONUCA). Many of these steps are probably now irreversible, and thus one of the lasting effects of the Contadora process was to get that historically distant nation much more involved in hemispheric affairs.

An important factor in the awakening of Canadian interest in Latin America, and in its increasing involvement in the Central American peace process from 1983 on, was the lobbying done by a loose coalition of Canadian church, Third World development, academic, and human rights groups. These organizations, and their members, would contact individual members of Parliament or government offices with reports of their travel to Central America, their meetings, and their policy suggestions.[20] There had also been some contact with Latin American delegations at the UN through the Canadian official who had traditionally been a member of the permanent staff of the International Peace Academy (an independent organization involved in education and training for peacekeeping and conflict resolution associated with the UN). These contacts notwithstanding, the Canadian government was always sensitive to the possibility that a more active role in Central America might place it on a collision course with the United States because Canadian public opinion (reflected in the Parliament and government) generally held the view that the root causes of the Central American crisis lay in historical socioeconomic problems, and not in the export of revolution by a Moscow-Havana axis. The memory of Canadian-U.S. strains over Vietnam and Cuba was still fresh in the minds of many in Ottawa and Washington, as were the problems caused by Canadian participation (military and civilian) in the Indochina International Control Commission.[21]

In Canada's first policy statement regarding Contadora (at the UN General Assembly on 27 September 1983), External Affairs Secretary Allan MacEachen expressed support for Contadora and offered Canadian backing to the Contadora proposal "to stop the process of militarization and to verify and monitor the progressive withdrawal of all foreign military personnel from the region."[22] In early October Deputy Foreign Minister Jean-Luc Pépin clarified the meaning of this statement, saying that Canada was ready to send observers to monitor a Contadora peace agreement. "That's the price you pay for being involved, you can't expect to be just in the cheering section."[23]

Canadian advice was ongoing and effective from this point on. There were numerous contacts with different actors in the Central American peace process, culminating with formal input on verification in the various draft Contadora Acts. The Canadians were also involved in the process of enlightening the Latin American nations on the nature, expense, problems, and promise of UN-sponsored peacekeeping, which was of a fundamentally different nature than that experienced to that date in the hemisphere.

Secretary MacEachen's trip to Central America in April 1984 not only demonstrated Canada's willingness to help, but also demonstrated its concern over being caught between the Central American crisis and a U.S. policy of which it disapproved. Shortly before his trip, the Canadian secretary visited Secretary of State George Shultz, who asked for greater Canadian backing for U.S.-supported governments in the region and pressured him to visit El Salvador instead of Nicaragua. But MacEachen, holding to Ottawa's wish to distance itself from the U.S. vision of Central America as an East-West crisis, continued to argue that Canada believed that "the roots of the evils are economic, social and political frustrations."[24] On his trip MacEachen informed his Central American hosts of Canada's willingness (if asked) to put its unique 35 years of experience in international peacekeeping at the service of Contadora, although there was no commitment to provide people on the ground. He specifically offered to help the Contadora nations in the design of what was to be the Control and Verification Commission of the early Contadora Treaty drafts.[25]

On MacEachen's return the Canadian Departments of National Defence and External Affairs began to take a serious look at Central America and the verification and peacekeeping problems associated with any peace treaty. Professor Harold P. Klepak of the Canadian Royal Military College at Saint-Jean was asked to look into the specifics, and his monographs published by the Canadian government are some of the best sources of detailed information on the verification and peacekeeping problems.[26] There apparently was also some thought given in early and mid-1984 to the possibility that Canadian assistance might take the form of a peacekeeping force, but that possibility was rejected by Mexican President Miguel de la Madrid in his May 1984 visit to Canada, reflecting the traditional Mexican suspicion of substantial peacekeeping forces.

Canadian officials were also making use of their UN delegation and their presence in the International Peace Academy (located across the street from the UN) to make contacts with various Latin American government representatives. The IPA became more active in Central American peacekeeping and confidence-building measures in this period, responding in several cases to inquiries from key countries.[27]

PANAMA FOREIGN MINISTERS' MEETING, APRIL–MAY 1984, AND POSSIBLE IADB INVOLVEMENT

This was the sixth meeting of the "Contadora four" and the "Central American five." There had been hopes that a treaty draft could be finalized at this meeting, but it turned out to be one of the more polarized and rancorous of the series, with little agreement despite an official report that tried to put a favorable gloss on the event.[28] The polarization had El Salvador, Honduras, and Costa Rica on one side accusing Nicaragua of intervention, while the Contadora nations (to varying degrees) felt that these three nations were acting suspiciously in concert in supporting U.S. goals. Guatemala was aloof, and Nicaragua played the sympathies of the four Contadora nations to its advantage. There were also suspicions that U.S. Special Envoy to Central America Harry Shlaudeman was lobbying hard (especially among the three closest allies of the United States in Central America) to delay the signing of any draft treaty. Security issues were the most contentious, especially when El Salvador, Costa Rica, and Honduras challenged Nicaragua to agree to a proposal under which they would all disclose military information and reduce troop strength, weapons, and the number of international military agreements, weapons sources, and foreign advisors.

The three nations also proposed that the IADB verify these proposed military reductions. Considering the high U.S. profile in the board's key leadership posts, they could hardly have chosen a more provocative, and less impartial, verifier. Suspicions that this was all a plan to derail the meeting were strengthened when it became known that the three countries had decided on this joint approach regarding the IADB at a private meeting held the week before. At that 25 April meeting, they had agreed to ask the IADB to send a special inspection commission to verify the various categories of troop levels, weapons, and foreign military influence in Central America. All the Central American countries would also agree to inform the IADB of any new arms and munitions deliveries, and to publish the number and location of all foreign military personnel for verification by the board.[29]

Not surprisingly, the three nations' proposal was quickly and emphatically rejected by Nicaragua, with the tacit support of the four Contadora nations. The official communiqué on the meeting diplomatically stated: "Lastly, various proposals concerning the most appropriate means and instruments of verification and monitoring were discussed; in that connection, the need to insure the impartial constitution of the mechanism concerned became apparent." Officials on the board itself were disappointed but not surprised since the Nicaraguan delegate to the IADB had frequently voiced his government's preference for UN, not OAS or IADB, involvement in any verification process.[30] Shortly afterward, an unidentified senior Mexican diplomat accused the three Central American nations of sabotaging the Contadora effort and in so doing increasing the chances of war in the region.[31] The specific vehicle for this sabotage, he charged, was the 25 April meeting (which violated the understanding that all such discussions should be within the Contadora framework) when the three of them agreed on the approach they took at the Panama meeting.

NOTES

1. UN Document A/38/599 27 January 1983, 1.
2. Calloni, La "Guerra encubierta," 78.
3. San José, Radio Reloj, 26 May 1983, in Foreign Broadcast Information Service (FBIS), 31 May 1983, P-1.
4. San José, Radio Reloj, 22 June 1983, in FBIS, 22 June 1983, A-2.
5. For text, see UN Document A/38/303, 19 July 1983; or FBIS, 18 July 1983, A-4.
6. Falcoff, "Regional Diplomatic Options," 60.
7. For text, see UN Document S/16041, 18 October 1983; or FBIS, 11 October 1983, P-1.
8. La Prensa, Panama, 9 September 1983, in FBIS, 13 September 1983, A-1.
9. Note by Secretary-General, part of UN Document S/16041, 18 October 1983.
10. Ortega Durán, Contadora y su Verdad, 44.
11. La Nación, San José, 13 October 1983.
12. Roy Gutman, "US Is Holding Cards to Invade Nicaragua," Newsday, 31

October 1983. See also Calloni, *La "Guerra encubierta,"* 147–152, 176–178, 207.

13. For text, see UN Document A/39/71, 10 January 1984; and FBIS, 9 January 1984.

14. *Kissinger Commission Report,* 120.

15. Ibid., 103.

16. The author testified before the commission on this subject in September 1983 and can attest to the lack of interest in this area.

17. For typical criticisms, see Rico, "La Experiencia de Contadora," 106; Lernoux, *Fear and Hope,* 14; and Méndez Asensio, *Contadora: las Cuentas,* 145–161.

18. Holland, *Kissinger's Kingdom,* 70–71.

19. U.S. Department of State, *US Efforts to Achieve Peace in Central America,* special report no. 115, 15 March 1984; *New York Times,* 3 March 1984; *Baltimore Sun,* 2 December 1984. See also Serafino, "The Contadora Initiative, the US and the Concept of a Zone of Peace," 197, 213.

20. Baranyi, *Canadian Foreign Policy,* 24.

21. Treleaven, "Canada, U.S., Vietnam, and Central America." The author also recalls conversations in Vietnam in 1963 with Canadian officers serving on the International Control Commission in Southeast Asia.

22. Canada, House of Commons, *Peace Process in Central America,* 8.

23. "Canadian Offer to Monitor Peace Arrangements," *International Canada,* October–November 1983.

24. *Maclean's,* Canada, 16 April 1984, 32. See also "Ministerial Visit," *International Canada,* April–May 1984, 14–15.

25. See Canadian Ambassador John W. Graham's chapter, "Canada and Contadora," in McDonald, *Canada, the Caribbean, and Central America.*

26. Discussions with Canadian military officers (Directorate of International Policy), Toronto and Ottawa, 1986, 1987, 1989. See also Klepak, *Security Considerations* and *Verification of a Central American Peace Accord.* For comment on the Mexican rejection of Canadian peacekeeping forces, see Schmitz, *Canadian Foreign Policy,* 26.

27. Communication from IPA President General Indar Jit Rikhye, 7 November 1988. See also several IPA publications in these years dealing with Central America. The author was involved in numerous workshops and off-the-record meetings sponsored by the IPA from 1983 to 1989, attended by diplomatic and military officials from a wide range of interested nations.

28. For the text see UN Document A/39/226 and S/16522, 2 May 1984. For accounts of the tensions, see *La Nación,* San José, 3 May 1984; *Washington Post,* 2 May 1984, A16; and *Latin American Index,* 1 May 1984, 32.

29. U.S. Department of State, current policy no. 572, 2 May 1984, 7.

30. Discussions with senior officers of the IADB, Washington, D.C.

31. *Washington Post,* 13 May 84, A32.

3

THE DRAFT CONTADORA ACTS

This chapter examines the series of draft Contadora Acts between mid-1984 and mid-1986, which, even though they failed, set the stage for the successful Arias/Esquipulas peace plan in 1987. Consistent with the scope of the book, the emphasis is on the peacekeeping, peace-observing, and confidence-building aspects of the process.

THE FIRST DRAFT CONTADORA ACT, 9 JUNE 1984

Although there was a strong feeling that the time was not propitious, the Contadora four presented the Central American five with the first draft Contadora Act at their 8–9 June 1984 meeting. Their action was precipitated by a belief that the diplomatic process was stagnating, and that it was necessary to put a draft on the table for discussion, even though there was little likelihood of it being accepted. The draft was presented with a request for comments and amendments by 15 July.

The first draft Act for Peace and Cooperation in Central America, was the product of the Contadora Group's internal technical commission and the three working groups, with little input from outside sources and with minimal coordination with the Central American five or other key actors such as the United States. The reaction of the United States and its three key Central American allies was identical: the draft treaty was seen as too favorable to Nicaragua, especially because the provisions for verification and compliance were weak and would allow the Sandinistas to violate the act with ease.[1] The other major objection was that the draft was merely a general and vague statement of goals already appearing in the 21 Objectives document, with little to convert these ideas into concrete measures. Furthermore, under the draft act the negotiations on arms and

29

troop levels and the presence of foreign military advisors would be deferred until after the treaty was signed. The United States was especially concerned that it would be required to end support to the Contras as of the date of signature; U.S. military assistance to El Salvador and Honduras would also be stopped, allowing Nicaragua to keep its military advantage over its neighbors.

The Contadora Group's request for Canadian input on security and verification aspects came soon after the meeting. It was clear that to be acceptable to El Salvador, Honduras, and Costa Rica (and by implication also to the United States), the verification instrument had to be made more credible, and for this Canadian help was needed. The formal request came in July, and the Canadians replied in August with basic criteria for establishing a Control and Verification Commission (CVC), including recommendations on fundamentals such as funding, composition, communications, and structure.[2] The Canadian recommendations were not specifically tied to the Central American or Contadora context and reflected general Canadian experience with UN peacekeeping and peace observing. This was the first of four formal written inputs provided by the Canadians in the Contadora treaty drafting process through 1986; there were also three meetings with detailed discussions.

THE REVISED CONTADORA ACT, 7 SEPTEMBER 1984

The Contadora four and the Central American five met in Panama in early September 1984 to present a revised act amidst ominous signs: tensions between the United States and Nicaragua were high and increasing, and the Contadora Group was showing cracks in its earlier, seemingly united approach to peace. There was much disagreement between Nicaragua, on the one hand, and El Salvador, Costa Rica, and Honduras on the other, with Guatemala maintaining its customary aloofness. To make matters worse, shortly before the meeting, Costa Rica's president, Luis A. Monge, said that although Contadora had made an extraordinary effort, it had reached the end of its possibilities, and it was now time to move the issue of Central American conflict to the Organization of American States.

The revised Contadora Act of 7 September 1984 was presented to the Central American five in Panama in an attempt to incorporate a variety of objections and comments that had been made in response to the June 1984 first draft; it also reflected Canadian input on security and verification matters.[3] The revised act included most of the provisions of the previous Contadora documents, and continued the trend of increasing detail and specificity that had characterized each successive document. The security provisions continued to be a major element of the act and included the prior general framework on arms limitations and ending arms trafficking and the use of foreign military advisors and bases. One crucial issue was timing. The act would require an immediate freeze on new arms, military maneuvers, and support to insurgents, but did not set definitive limits on the quantity of arms or troops; this was to be negotiated after the treaty was signed, but with no date specified. This was seen by the United States and its regional allies as favoring Nicaragua because the act would cut off immediately U.S. military assistance (mainly to El Salvador and Honduras) and aid to the Contras (thus easing the pressure on Nicaragua), but would not press Nicaragua to reduce its large military establishment. Despite this problem, the initial reaction to the revised act seemed to be positive on the part of the Central American five, with Nicaragua showing the greatest enthusiasm.

The provisions for verification and confidence-building measures of the revised act were far more detailed and specific than in any previous Contadora document, and showed the impact of Canadian input as well as an attempt by the Contadora four to satisfy the verification concerns so frequently expressed by the United States and its regional allies. There was also an attempt to involve both the UN and OAS in order to satisfy those nations that favored a UN role in verification (mainly Nicaragua) and those that preferred the OAS (the United States, El Salvador, Costa Rica, and Honduras); details of the involvement by these two international organizations were not specified beyond the fact that they would be observers.[4]

The Canadian input to the revised act was evident in the increasing specificity of verification provisions. Canadian suggestions on the composition, funding, structure, and communications aspects of the CVC were submitted to the Contadora Group in August, but only the more general suggestions were included in the act, with the understanding that a more detailed treatment would be prepared after the commission was established. The Canadians expressed concern over the lack of "tightness" in the draft,[5] and this was clearly a problem for the United States and its three principal allies. As a result, a more detailed provision for the CVC was prepared, with considerable Canadian input, and released in March 1985.

The worst fears of the United States and Central American countries that mistrusted the Sandinistas were confirmed two weeks after the Panama meeting when Nicaragua announced that it was willing to sign the revised act, but on the condition that there be no further changes and that the United States sign the act's protocol, which would commit it to ending aid to the Contras and military assistance to its Central American allies. The Reagan administration's reaction was summed up by one of its principal spokespersons on Central America, who said: "The draft of the treaty as it stands right now contains all of the right categories of issues, but quite frankly it does not have adequate verification mechanisms to ensure Nicaraguan compliance."[6] He added that the development of specific verification measures should not be left until after the draft is signed.

In mid-October Secretary of State Shultz made a hurried trip to Central America to explain the U.S. objections to the act, and shortly afterward, the Costa Rican, Salvadoran, and Honduran governments were expressing their dissatisfaction with the provisions for verification. Speaking at the UN, Honduran Foreign Minister Edgardo Paz Barnica suggested that the Contadora plan should include a calendar of proposed actions, and that the mechanisms for control and verification needed to be "polished," a reaction that was similar to the State Department's objection.[7] He added that a group such as the Inter-American Commission on Human Rights was needed, with the power to conduct on-site inspections to monitor both military reductions and political standards. A similar position was taken the same day at the UN by the Costa Rican foreign minister, who said that the verification mechanism should be improved and strengthened to include setting arms limits before imposing a freeze.

THE CONTADORA TEGUCIGALPA DRAFT

On 20 October 1984 the foreign ministers of Costa Rica, Honduras, Guatemala, and El Salvador met in Tegucigalpa to discuss the 7 September Contadora draft and issue the Revised Tegucigalpa Draft of the Contadora Act. (Guatemala abstained and Nicaragua did not attend.) This revision strengthened the verification and enforcement aspects, which made it more acceptable to the United States. It should be noted that this revision was the product of four Central American nations (with considerable U.S. input) and did not involve either the Contadora nations or Nicaragua.

The Tegucigalpa draft clearly reflected the U.S. position regarding Contadora and, given the circumstances of the Tegucigalpa meeting, was almost certain to be rejected by Nicaragua. The U.S. strategy of attempting to isolate Nicaragua and work with the so-called core four (actually three, since Guatemala's support for the United States was very tentative) was revealed in a secret U.S. National Security Council memo dated 30 October 1984, which stated: "We have trumped the latest Nicaraguan/ Mexican efforts to rush signature of an unsatisfactory Contadora agreement." In contrast, the Tegucigalpa draft was described as "a document broadly consistent with U.S. interests."[8] At about the same time, National Security Advisor Admiral John Poindexter was summarizing his views on negotiations in a memo to his assistant Robert McFarlane: "Continue active negotiations, but agree on no treaty, and agree to work out some way to support the Contras, either directly or indirectly. Withhold true objectives from staffs."[9]

The verification provisions of the Tegucigalpa draft show how this issue was the key to U.S. objections to the earlier Contadora drafts, especially the lack of specific standards and procedures. In particular, the Tegucigalpa draft provided for an ad hoc disarmament group and an international inspectorate staffed by four outside nations, which would be authorized to conduct roving inspections to ensure compliance. There were suggestions that the Inter-American Defense Board might be involved, an idea that a Panamanian diplomat involved in the Contadora process labeled unacceptable.[10]

The negative reaction from Nicaragua and the Contadora four was predictable and swift. The Contadora Group (meeting in Madrid to receive the Prince of Asturias Peace Prize) did indicate that there could be some accommodation with regard to the makeup of the proposed CVC (such as getting the UN involved), but only as the specific procedures and composition of the CVC were determined. Moreover, it would not change the basic text of the September draft. There was no Contadora support for the notion of the Tegucigalpa ad hoc disarmament group and international inspectorate, especially if it involved the IADB. The Tegucigalpa meeting also led to the greater independence of Guatemala from the core four. In part, this reflected resentment at U.S. efforts to control the Tegucigalpa draft, but it was also a reaction to long-standing strains between Washington and Guatemala over human rights issues, as well as Guatemalan anger over the cutoff of U.S. military assistance.[11]

THE CONTROL AND
VERIFICATION COMMISSION, APRIL 1985

The Contadora and Central American representatives met in Panama in April 1985 to discuss the mechanisms for verification and execution of a Contadora treaty. They agreed to create a CVC for security matters (contained in the Statute of Verification and Cooperation) and ad hoc political, social, and economic groups. In general, the documents were an attempt to bridge the differences between U.S. and Nicaraguan approaches, especially on issues of verification and control.

One issue that was beginning to emerge was that of peacekeeping versus peace observing. The issue could be framed in terms of the notion of a "corps" of international inspectors (a substantial peacekeeping presence) or a "group" of international treaty verifiers (a small peace-observing mission). At the Panama meeting, Víctor Hugo Tinoco, the Nicaraguan deputy foreign minister, said his government was disappointed because the Nicaraguan proposal for a broad plan put forward by the Contadora Group was rejected by El Salvador, Honduras, and Costa Rica. A basic problem, he said, was that these three countries wanted a major peacekeeping force of a military nature, something that Nicaragua could not accept.[12]

Canadian inputs on the verification issue were becoming increasingly significant. Although operating with a low profile, and taking little public credit for their contribution, the Canadians had provided the major input to the detailed statute for the CVC and International Inspector Corps (IIC).[13] This input included a tentative organizational structure, including a headquarters (with a secretariat), an operations division, a support division, and a regional headquarters for each of the five Central American countries, with enough personnel to undertake inspections.[14]

The Canadians continued to be troubled by the lack of a clear mandate and a permanent political body that would supervise the activities of the CVC and the IIC and make the sensitive decisions if treaty violations were found and documented. Canadian representatives at various conferences made it clear that any active participation by their nation in the CVC or IIC, which was being actively discussed from 1985 on,[15] would depend on getting a clear mandate from such a permanent international body. Their preferences were consistent: the UN over the ad hoc Contadora or the OAS, especially if the IADB was involved.[16]

Canadian involvement in peacekeeping and peace observing in Central America had the support of substantial sectors of that nation's political spectrum. The Left backed it because it permitted Canada to play a role independent of the United States, while involvement had the support of the military and its constituency on the Right because of the technical and operational facets of a peacekeeping role. Because of its humanitarian aspects, it had the general support of the political center and public opinion, which relished the role of Canada as a helpful fixer in a situation the United States was becoming mired in. The only sector left out of this constituency was the Canadian anti-Communist far Right, which was not a significant element in the political spectrum.

THE CONTADORA SUPPORT GROUP, JULY 1985

At the inauguration of President Alán García of Peru, the Lima Declaration was signed, which resulted in the forming of the Contadora Support Group (Argentina, Brazil, Peru, and Uruguay). An all-Latin peace force to act as a military security cordon was suggested, and Uruguayan President Julio Sanguinetti offered peacekeeping troops.[17] The Support Group nations were concerned about Washington's policy of military pressure and a possible invasion of Nicaragua. There was also the need to present a common Latin front to ease the strains on the Central American states that were perceived to be under excessive U.S. influence (Costa Rica, El Salvador, and Honduras). The four Support Group nations were in the forefront of the redemocratization process in Latin America in the early 1980s, and their moral authority was considerable. When added to the four Contadora nations, the combination included most of Latin America's population. When the Central American nations (plus Canada as a silent ally of the Lima Group) were added to the negotiating group, the end result was a constellation of hemisphere nations that tended to isolate the United States more than ever before in the Central American crisis.[18]

Contacts with Canada were soon made by the Support Group. External Affairs Minister Joe Clark quickly issued a statement of congratulations and encouragement to the group, which in turn announced that they were in agreement with the Canadian proposals for verification of Contadora proposals and would discuss them in detail at their forthcoming Cartagena meeting. There was talk of forming a Northern Contadora Support Group centered on Canada and European countries interested in helping the process move along and possibly willing to supply inspectors and observers for the CVC and IIC.[19]

THE SECOND DRAFT
CONTADORA ACT, SEPTEMBER 1985

The Panama meeting of Contadora and Central American nations produced the second draft Contadora Act, which was an attempt to bridge the differences between the revised draft presented by the Contadora nations on 7 September 1984 and the Tegucigalpa draft of 20 October 1984 prepared by El Salvador, Honduras, and Costa Rica under heavy U.S. influence.[20] The second draft Contadora Act devoted much more attention to problems of implementation, verification, and enforcement, reflecting the Canadian inputs and the refinement in the Contadora nations' thinking on this matter in the intervening year.

Specifically, the second draft act tried to satisfy Washington, and its three Central American allies, by allowing some international military maneuvers while negotiations on final troop strengths were carried out. The restrictions on foreign military advisors were broadened to include personnel "capable of participating in military, paramilitary and security activities within six months of signature," presumably to allay U.S. concerns about Cuban and Soviet-bloc advisors in Nicaragua. The verification provisions were strengthened by allowing the CVC to make on-site inspections on its own initiative.

Nicaragua felt that this draft tilted too much toward the U.S. side and rejected it, mainly because it did not require the United States to end support to the Contras, nor prohibit foreign military maneuvers. Nicaragua was in favor of a neutral zone on its borders monitored by a multinational peacekeeping force. This was supported by the Lima Group but opposed by the United States because such a buffer zone would take pressure off Nicaragua.

NICARAGUAN ARRANGEMENTS
WITH HONDURAS AND COSTA RICA, EARLY 1986

In February 1986 Costa Rica and Nicaragua agreed to form a permanent multilateral inspection group to operate on their border. This was the third body the two nations had set up for this purpose. The group would include members from Contadora and its Support Group, as well as Nicaragua and Costa Rica, and would have about 50 support personnel and technical experts, some of them military, who would operate from several locations on both sides of the border. Funds would be raised to provide for the necessary equipment, including helicopters, patrol boats, and jeeps. Many observers said they doubted the group could really stop the operations of guerrillas, especially since the Reagan administration apparently planned on expanding the Contras' southern front against the Sandinistas. During the meeting, when the Sandinistas called for demilitarization of their mutual border, Costa Rican President Luis A. Monge replied that he would welcome this, inasmuch as the Costa Rican side of the border had been demilitarized "since 1948."[21] Little was heard from this Nicaraguan–Costa Rican inspection group, and its functions were eventually absorbed into the Arias peace plan and ONUCA.

A similar attempt in March to demilitarize Nicaragua's border to the north was equally unsuccessful. President Daniel Ortega appealed to the Contadora nations to consider creating a force of supervision and control along the Honduran-Nicaraguan border; its mission would be to ensure that all border crossings would be made through regular immigration posts. The proposal foundered on the reality that the Hondurans exercised very little control of the border in areas where the Contras held sway. However, the contacts did produce a basic confidence-building measure: a hot line between the two presidents and an agreement to exchange information on known illegal border crossers.[22]

U.S. VIEWS ON PEACEKEEPING AND CONFLICT

In May 1986 a serious internal split developed in the Reagan administration over the possibilities for Central American peace versus conflict. The president, in typical fashion, attempted to stay above the fray and made concessions to both the pragmatists in the State Department and the hard-liners in the Defense Department and the National Security Council (NSC).

The State Department weighed in first with its vision of what a Contadora–Central American peacekeeping effort would look like and cost.[23] State estimated that policing a Central American peace would involve 1,300 observers and cost $40 million a year. The peace-observing effort was described as a jungle version of the Sinai MFO (Multinational Force and Observers). The department's document, "Essential Elements of Effective

Verification," was based on the Sinai MFO and noted that what made it work was that there were only two nations involved, and both wanted it to work. Based on the Sinai effort, the Central American observers would have a headquarters staff of about 25 civilians in each of the five capitals. They would supervise inspection teams of 25 people who would conduct random surveys and be available on call to verify any violations. There would also be sector command posts and special observation posts manned by military personnel at key locations such as ports, airports, major border crossings, and military installations. One key feature of the verification process was the separation of the observation process, conducted by the people in the field, from the process of resolving disputes, adjudicating them, and deciding on sanctions. The State Department document noted that one of the weaknesses in the Contadora treaty draft was that these two very different functions were still merged in one body.

The Defense Department countered with a publicly released 12-page document, "Prospects for Containment of Nicaragua's Communist Government," written by a group headed by Fred Iklé and supported by the NSC. It started with the assumption that a Contadora treaty along the lines of the September 1985 draft would be signed, and that while the United States and its allies would abide by it, the Sandinistas would not. Based on historical analogies to Communist violations of treaties in Korea, Cuba, and Vietnam, the document argued, the Sandinistas could be counted on to exploit every avenue for violations. The document concluded that present Contadora proposals would be difficult to monitor and would permit Nicaragua to cheat. As a result of such a weak Contadora agreement with inadequate verification provisions, the United States would have to stop Nicaraguan aggression by direct military means involving 100,000 troops, which, along with supporting air and naval forces, would cost perhaps $9.1 billion and many lives.

It seemed clear that the Defense Department document was a major effort to discredit Contadora, and reflected the views of hard-liners at the top civilian levels, such as Iklé, and their like-minded colleagues in the NSC and intelligence agencies. The uniformed military were a great deal more restrained in their views, and in fact believed that if the verification provisions could be strengthened, then something like Contadora was the best available course of action.[24] The hard-liners dismissed these pro-Contadora views as the misguided product of the "Vietnam syndrome," which drove the military to fear any armed intervention.

THE FINAL DRAFT CONTADORA ACT, JUNE 1986

At the last meeting of "The Thirteen," the Contadora and Support groups presented the Central American nations with the final draft Contadora Act, with the clear implication that the Contadora process had run its course, and that if this version were not acceptable, then another forum would have to be found. This draft did attempt to include some of the points raised in objection to the second draft (September 1985), but there was probably no way to bridge the gaps between the various positions in the present climate. There was a general feeling that the final draft favored Nicaragua (which was confirmed when Nicaragua agreed to sign it), and this paved the way for a rather quick and decisive rejection by Costa Rica, Honduras, and El Salvador, supported by the United States.[25]

Verification and confidence-building aspects were considerably more detailed than in the second draft and continued the trend of increasing levels of specificity (almost minutiae) as each Contadora document gave way to the next.[26] With the final draft, Contadora produced the most detailed of all the verification documents in the entire eight-year Contadora/Esquipulas process, to the point where the barriers of common sense and good judgment finally seemed to have been breached. In their zeal to provide the most exhaustive possible verification and control structure, the Contadora countries outdid themselves, proving the relevance of the old saying, "*lo perfecto es enemigo de lo bueno.*" ("The perfect is the enemy of the good.") The most notable example of this trend was a highly complicated, and unrealistic, attempt to give precise quantitative weights to each type of offensive and defensive weapon in order to achieve parity by having each nation eventually reduce their forces so as to have the same number of "points." The total number of points for each country was set at 100,000 "units of military strength," with certain categories of offensive weapons worth more than defensive ones; each country would be free to establish its own mix, as long as it did not exceed the limit of 100,000.[27] The end result of this process, if carried to its literal conclusion, would resemble nothing as much as a board game of the war-simulation variety.

There was a general feeling among the Central American nations that they no longer needed the Contadora (and Support Group) nations' somewhat paternalistic recommendations on what was good for Central America. The old perception that the larger nations of Latin America looked down on the smaller nations of Central America was coming to the fore again at the end of the long, frustrating road Contadora had traveled. Reflecting this, a week after the Panama meeting Salvadoran President José Napoleón Duarte said: "Contadora's function has ended, because the document it presented at Panama does not satisfy the region's hopes for peace. . . . No more tutelage, no more manipulation . . . from now on we will have the meetings we ourselves want, and they will be held in the place and at the time we want. . . . If the Contadora countries want to join us, that is their responsibility."[28]

Disillusionment with Contadora was accompanied by rumors that the military commanders of El Salvador, Honduras, and Guatemala were once again talking about reviving CONDECA. Costa Rica carefully distanced itself from the idea, and it was not clear whether this was to be the "old" anti-Nicaraguan version of CONDECA, which the United States would favor, or whether it might include Nicaragua, in which case it would appear to be more of a confidence-building measure than an anti-Communist alliance. In any case, little was heard of this idea after the Arias peace plan began to take shape in early 1987.[29]

ATTEMPTS TO REVIVE CONTADORA, LATE 1986, EARLY 1987

With the failure of the final draft Contadora Act, it was clear that Contadora was dead, and that something would have to replace it if the momentum for a peaceful settlement was to be maintained. The vacuum was eventually filled by the Arias/Esquipulas plan in mid-1987, but the transition from Contadora to Esquipulas was provided by an unexpected source in late 1986 and early 1987: an unprecedented and creative joint effort by the Secretaries-General of the United Nations and the Organization of American States.[30]

The process began with informal meetings at the UN General Assembly in the fall of 1986. It moved into the glare of publicity in November 1986 when the Secretaries-General of the UN and OAS offered their good offices to the Contadora Group. This was an unusual step because in security matters these two international civil servants are traditionally somewhat subordinated to their Security Council and Permanent Council, respectively. Another unprecedented aspect was that their initiative was a joint one between the global organization and the regional one, which had in the past experienced some strains in dealing with each other. The fact that the Secretaries-General were both Latin Americans whose countries of origin were active in the Contadora Support Group also helped, as did the fact that they were constantly kept informed, formally and informally, of all the major developments in the Contadora process.

The December 1986 formation of the Rio Group, consisting of the original Contadora four plus the Support Group four, helped back up this initiative when it was made clear that the Rio Group would be working closely with both the UN and the OAS. Meeting in Rio de Janeiro, the Contadora and Support Group foreign ministers condemned outside intervention and announced their decision to convert the Contadora process into a mechanism to discuss significant broader issues. They also decided to convert their meetings into a more formal Rio Group, which would meet three times a year to discuss common problems. They assured outsiders that this was not the start of "an OAS without the U.S.," a clarification they apparently felt they had to make in the face of recent calls by Peruvian President Alán García for a "Latin-only" regional body.[31] They also proposed to make an "urgent" visit to the capitals of the region in the company of the

Secretaries-General of the UN and OAS. It was clear that this involvement of
the heads of the two key international organizations, linked as it was to the
Rio Group, was creating a dramatically new opening on the ashes of
Contadora. The end result was an unprecedented effort in the hemisphere that
was not only to move Central American peace forward, but was also to
deeply involve other actors (Canada and Spain) and change the role of the UN
and the OAS on security matters in the Western Hemisphere. In all of these
changes the U.S. role was secondary.

Washington's displeasure was taken out on the two Secretaries-General.
In early January 1987 the United States called a special meeting of the
Organization of American States to question Secretary-General Baena Soares
about his efforts to deal directly with the Rio Group and Contadora and thus
bypass the United States. U.S. UN Ambassador Vernon Walters also had
conversations in New York with the UN Secretary-General on the same
topic. The Reagan administration was by now deeply embroiled in the Iran-
Contra scandal, and the distractions created space and moral authority for the
Secretaries-General to act more independently in this matter. Sniping at the
Secretaries-General and the Rio Group by figures such as Elliott Abrams,
assistant secretary of state, was met with rejections. A Mexican diplomat
commented that Abrams's statements were a "clumsy expression of political
arrogance."[32]

The Secretaries-General of the United Nations and the Organization of
American States made their historic visit to the five Central American
capitals on 19–20 January 1987 in the company of the eight foreign
ministers of Contadora and the Support Group, now forming the Rio Group.
They discussed, among other things, the measures that might contribute to
the peaceful solution to the crisis, and laid the groundwork for the
collaborative aspects they would later carry out under Arias/Esquipulas.

NOTES

1. Aguilar Zinser, "Central America and Contadora," 105.
2. John W. Graham, "Canada and Contadora," in McDonald, *Canada, the
Caribbean and Central America*, 91–2, 95.
3. For text of the revised act, see UN Document A/39/562, 9 October 1984;
also in Child, *Conflict in Central America*, 167–204.
4. Ortega Durán, *Contadora y su Verdad*, 102–103.
5. *International Canada*, October–November 1984, 18–19. See also
Cepeda and Pardo, *Negociaciones*, 32.
6. The spokesperson was L. Craig Johnstone, the deputy assistant
secretary of state for Central America. *New York Times*, 3 October 1984.
7. *La Nación Internacional*, San José, 18 October 1984.
8. *Washington Post*, 6 November 1984, A1; Sklar, *Washington's War*,
304. See also Gomariz, *Balance*, 43–44.
9. Gutman, *Banana Diplomacy*, 317.

10. Ortega Durán, *Contadora y su Verdad*, 130.
11. *Washington Post*, 10 November 1984, A17.
12. *Washington Post*, 14 April 84.
13. Conversation with Lt. Col. Gerry Donahue, director, Directorate of International Policy, Canadian Department of National Defence, Toronto, January 1986. See also *Rumbo Centroamericano*, 11 April 1985.
14. York University, *Central America*, 26.
15. See, for example, the reports of various conferences and workshops, such as in North, *Negotiations for Peace*, and Roundtable on Negotiations, *Interim and Confidence-Building Measures*.
16. Discussions, York University conference on Central American peacekeeping, 29 January 1986.
17. Council on Hemispheric Affairs (COHA), *Washington Report on the Hemisphere*, August 1985.
18. Rico, "La Experiencia," 163–165; Cepeda and Pardo, *Negociaciones*, 42.
19. Schmitz, *Canadian Foreign Policy*, 30; *Excelsior*, Mexico, 22 August 1985; North, *Negotiations for Peace*, 36–37.
20. Gomariz, *Balance*, 44–45; Rico, "La Experiencia," 179–182.
21. Wall, "Costa Rica and Contadora: A Narrative," 6; *Miami Herald*, 25 February 1986.
22. *New York Times*, 31 March 1986; *Christian Science Monitor*, 13 May 1986.
23. *Washington Post*, 11 May 1986, A4.
24. Gutman, *Banana Diplomacy*, 276; Leogrande, "Rollback," 105.
25. Méndez Asensio, *Contadora*, 208–210; *Strategic Survey*, 1986/87, International Institute for Strategic Studies (London): 203; *La Nación Internacional*, 13–19 June 1986, 8.
26. For extracts of the extensive verification provisions, see Klepak, *Verification of a Central American Peace Accord*, 55–68. See also Goldblat, "Zone of Peace," 401–403.
27. COHA, *Washington Report on the Hemisphere*, 25 June 1986, 6.
28. "Seis Meses de Gestaciones," *Estudios Centroamericanos*, May–June 1986, 470.
29. *Excelsior*, Mexico, 19 June 1986; *Latin American Index*, 1 June 1986; *Miami Herald*, 30 May 1986; COHA, *Washington Report on the Hemisphere*, 23 July 1986.
30. Méndez Asensio, *Contadora*, 197–198; Center for International Policy, "Contadora Eludes U.S.", January/February 1987, 2. The comment that they were both concerned because they were Latin Americans was made by Alvaro de Soto, executive assistant to the UN Secretary-General, at a press briefing on 18 November 1986.
31. Communiqué by Rio Group, 18 December 1986 (published by Embassy of Mexico, Washington, D.C.). *New York Times*, 22 December 1986, A-19.
32. *Washington Post*, 20 January 1987.

PART 3
THE ARIAS/ESQUIPULAS
PEACE PLAN, 1987–1989

4

THE ARIAS PLAN AND
THE 1987–1988 SUMMITS

In analyzing the Arias peace proposal and the Esquipulas agreement that formalized it, one must keep in mind the continuity with the Contadora documents that preceded them, since perhaps three-quarters of the language in the Arias/Esquipulas documents had already appeared in Contadora documents. The origins of the Arias/Esquipulas plan are to be found in the Central Americans' frustrations with Contadora, and the feeling in early 1987 that something had to be done to activate the now-stagnating peace process. In the United States, the Congress—and public opinion generally—was becoming disenchanted with the Contras, and it was clear that Contra aid could not be continued indefinitely. Encouraged by discussions with Senator Christopher Dodd in December, President Oscar Arias of Costa Rica took the lead in drafting a preliminary plan based on Contadora. This plan would attempt to span the seemingly unbridgeable gap between the U.S. and Nicaraguan positions by giving something to both: a U.S. commitment to slowly end aid to the Contras and a Nicaraguan commitment to allow verified free elections. These ideas were floated to key congressmen and State Department functionaries by Costa Rican diplomats in January 1987, with generally positive results.[1] Arias was encouraged, and prepared a formal proposal for the February meeting of the presidents of Costa Rica, El Salvador, Guatemala, and Honduras (the core four).

At the 15 February 1987 summit meeting in Costa Rica, President Arias presented his colleagues with the plan labeled *"Una hora para la paz"* ("A time for peace"). It differed from Contadora Act drafts in that there was more emphasis on internal democratization, and it was to be the product of the Central Americans themselves. The principal verification aspect of the proposal called for the formation of an oversight committee in 60 days. This committee would consist of the Secretaries-General of the United Nations and

45

the Organization of American States and the foreign ministers of the Contadora and Support Group countries.[2]

In presenting the document, which was an outline of general steps to be taken, Arias tactfully stated that his proposal was certainly subject to modification because it would not be reasonable to expect that a proposal agreed to in a few hours could achieve what Contadora had not been able to achieve in four years. Instead, he simply was suggesting the major steps, which would constitute "a harmonic and indivisible body," that could lead to a "procedure for the establishment of solid and lasting peace in Central America." Although building on Contadora, and requesting the Contadora nations' help in verification, Arias made it clear that this was not a plan to be molded or changed by the Contadora nations. Instead, it was to be a starting point agreed on by the core four nations, who would then present it to Nicaragua for comments and hopefully quick approval. Democrats in the U.S. Congress, especially key senators who were enjoying their recently regained control of the Senate, received the plan with enthusiasm. They saw it as a Democratic alternative to both the defunct Contadora process and the slowly dying Reagan project to keep supporting the Contras to the bitter end.[3]

Arias's travels to Europe and Washington in May and June of 1987 were to prove crucial. In Europe he visited eight countries and was generally successful in lining up support. Two key countries were Spain and Germany, which later under the Esquipulas plan would help make up the first UN peacekeeping group on the ground in Central America. In Spain he made an emotional appeal in a speech to the Parliament, asking that the nascent Iberian democracy help its counterparts in Central America.[4] His Washington trip was more harrowing. Arriving at the White House, Arias was ushered into the Oval Office to find President Reagan flanked by a retinue of eight high-powered advisors, including Vice President George Bush, Chief of Staff James Baker, and Assistant Secretary of State Elliott Abrams. Arias was told by Reagan that the Sandinistas had to move toward verifiable and genuine democratization before any pressure could be taken off them by reducing or ending aid to the Contras. Arias responded that it was the other way around: the Contras gave the Sandinistas an excuse not to allow freedoms and democracy. One of Arias's aides was later to describe the meeting as "very scary stuff. The Oval Office was filled with all the big boys, and Oscar appeared like Spartacus going before the Roman generals."[5]

One of the events in late July 1987 that caused the jelling of the Arias/Esquipulas plan was the knowledge that the Reagan administration was moving ahead with its own version of a bipartisan peace plan for Central America, known as the "Reagan-Wright plan." The plan was announced on 5 August, only two days before the scheduled Esquipulas Summit. The peace plan agreed on by President Reagan and Speaker of the House of

Representatives Jim Wright set out the basic elements that needed to be included in any regional peace accord. The proposal called for an immediate cease-fire, non-use of territory for aggression against neighbors, a simultaneous suspension of U.S. aid to the democratic resistance (the Contras) and Soviet-bloc assistance to the Sandinistas, the withdrawal of foreign military advisors from Nicaragua, and national reconciliation, democratization, and respect for basic human and political rights in Nicaragua. In some quarters, especially in Latin America, the Reagan-Wright plan was interpreted as a last-ditch administration effort to kill any attempt at an Arias plan at the summit.[6] However, Arias had been forewarned, and was the only one of the five presidents who knew the full scope and significance of the U.S. plan. He was able to adroitly use this knowledge to persuade his four colleagues to go along with his plan lest they be co-opted by the Reagan administration. In turn, the Reagan administration found itself outfoxed by Arias and the other four presidents on 7 August when they signed the plan and in effect gave the divided Reagan administration a fait accompli they had little choice but to accept.[7]

ESQUIPULAS II, AUGUST 1987

The plan agreed to in Esquipulas, Guatemala, on 7 August 1987 called for a cease-fire, national reconciliation, amnesty, democratization, an end to aid to insurgent movements, and free elections (see Appendix 4 for text). One analyst from Central America described it as "changing everything without changing anything."[8] By this he meant that although Esquipulas made no major structural changes to what had gone before in Contadora, it had the virtue of creating mutual confidence to such a degree that forward progress could be made. And once begun, that progress would lead to greater trust and communication, and even greater progress. It is important to note that Esquipulas was not technically a treaty, but rather a commitment to abide by "procedures for establishing a stable and enduring peace in Central America." In effect, it was a collection of confidence-building measures and a commitment to use them to create greater mutual trust and confidence.

The International Commission for Verification and Follow-up (CIVS for its Spanish initials: Comisión Internacional de Verificación y Seguimiento) was the key instrument for verification. Esquipulas specified its general composition but left its procedures and authority vague. In part, this reflected the haste with which Esquipulas was drafted, but it was also a reaction to the excessive detail on verification contained in the final Contadora documents. The approach taken in Esquipulas was to allow neutral third-party outsiders, especially the UN, to determine the most appropriate verification methods, procedures, organization, and operations. As we shall see below in the section dealing with the initial actions of the CIVS, this was a key commission charged with entering into highly sensitive areas that had not been fully worked out before the signing of Esquipulas.

The first CIVS was formally constituted at a meeting held in Caracas late in August 1987 with the attendance of the five Central American, four Contadora, and four Support Group nations, with representation from the two international organizations mentioned in the Esquipulas agreement, the UN and OAS. The initial organization of CIVS is shown in Figure 4.1. It had considerable authority and prestige because it brought together thirteen Latin American foreign ministers and representatives of the Secretaries-General of the OAS and UN. They were to report directly to the Central American presidential summit, with powers to create ad hoc subcommittees (such as the December 1987 UN-OAS technical commission), and with links to the old Contadora Security Commission and the National Reconciliation Commissions.[9]

THE UN-OAS TECHNICAL COMMISSION

In October 1987 the UN announced it was sending an advance peace-observer team of six people to Central America to see how the UN could monitor compliance with the Esquipulas peace plan. The Secretary-General was responding to a request from the 13-nation CIVS established by the plan, and the UN team was joined by an OAS contingent responding to the same request. For the OAS this was an opportunity to change its relationship to both Latin America and the United States. The United States had not been pleased with the OAS Secretary-General's involvement with Contadora, and had a similar reaction to seeing him send a preliminary peace-observing reconnaissance team to the field alongside the UN's. But the two international organizations, and their Secretaries-General, reinforced each other and made it difficult for the United States to openly oppose their involvement without seeming to be against the peace process. For many Latin Americans the Organization of American States was redeeming itself with this emerging role, changing the old perception that it was an instrument of U.S. policy, and was in fact recovering from the inaction it had demonstrated during the Falklands/Malvinas war and the invasion of Grenada.[10]

The technical commission traveled to several Central American countries in late 1987 and provided the CIVS with two reports that stressed the difficulties of conducting a rigorous verification effort on the ground in Central America. There were two major problems according to the UN-OAS team when it reported back to the CIVS at UN headquarters.[11] The first was the lack of clarity concerning what was to be verified; the Esquipulas plan, after all, was vague, and it was not clear how much of the old Contadora text was applicable. The second problem was technical and dealt with the physical

Figure 4.1   The Original CIVS

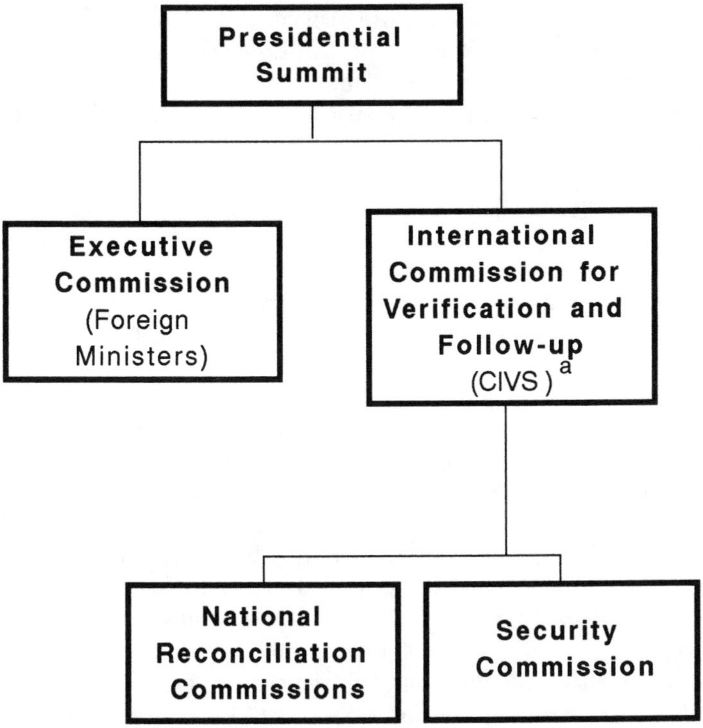

```
              ┌─────────────────────┐
              │    Presidential     │
              │      Summit         │
              └─────────────────────┘
         ┌─────────────┴───────────────┐
┌─────────────────┐         ┌─────────────────────┐
│   Executive     │         │   International      │
│   Commission    │         │   Commission for     │
│   (Foreign      │         │   Verification and   │
│   Ministers)    │         │   Follow-up          │
└─────────────────┘         │   (CIVS) a           │
                            └─────────────────────┘
                       ┌────────────┴────────────┐
              ┌─────────────────┐     ┌─────────────────┐
              │    National      │     │    Security     │
              │  Reconciliation  │     │   Commission    │
              │   Commissions    │     │                 │
              └─────────────────┘     └─────────────────┘
```

Note: a. CIVS was made up of the foreign ministers of the five Central American countries (Costa Rica, El Salvador, Guatemala, Honduras, and Nicaragua), the four Contadora countries (Mexico, Panama, Venezuela, and Colombia), and the four Contadora Support Group countries (Peru, Argentina, Brazil, and Uruguay), plus representatives of the Secretaries-General of the UN and OAS.

and logistical problems of actually doing the verification in the geography of
Central America. In effect, the verification teams would be asked to verify a
cease-fire that had not yet been implemented, and would be exposing
themselves to the possibility of getting caught between various armed groups
that might or might not have accepted the cease-fire.

The UN-OAS technical commission also defined four minimum
requirements to be satisfied before verification could begin:

1. A clear definition of the peace observers' roles;
2. A cease-fire that would be respected by all parties in the conflict,
   including irregular forces;
3. Agreement on the details of disarmament; and
4. Guarantees of freedom of movement and physical security for the
   observers.[12]

Canadian activities related to Central America increased dramatically in
this period as the UN became more involved. External Affairs Minister Joe
Clark made a well-publicized trip to Central America in November 1987
amidst criticism at home that Canada was not taking concrete steps to help
the Esquipulas process beyond moral support and technical advice on
peacekeeping and verification. He was accompanied on his trip by two
Canadian military officers with considerable experience in international
peacekeeping, one of whom was Colonel Don Ethell. In reporting to the
House of Commons after his trip, Clark stressed the "practical challenges of
designing and operating verification and peacekeeping systems," and indicated
that Canada was now prepared to go beyond simply providing advice when he
said that "Canadian expertise would be available for all or part of that work,
if the five presidents agreed unanimously that they wanted Canadian help."[13]
The reaction from Nicaragua was clear: during a trip to Ottawa in October,
Nicaraguan Vice President Sergio Ramírez said that his country was counting
on Canadian help to keep the United States from meddling in the peace
process.[14]

Colonel Ethell's observations after his Central American trip showed the
need for realism on both sides. He said that he was a little surprised by the
ruggedness of the terrain and the problems it would cause in peacekeeping or
peace observing: "The terrain is very, very severe. You could fly over this
with a helicopter at night, and beneath you there could be 1,000 men and you
wouldn't see them."[15] Another major problem would be financing the
international contingents from European and South American nations because
the latter probably would not be able to fund their own troops' participation.
Colonel Ethell estimated that the peacekeeping group would require about
300 people and perhaps 11 helicopters, along with sophisticated equipment
such as radar. Moreover, he found Central American officers and functionaries

somewhat complacent about setting up a peacekeeping operation: "They don't understand the complexity of organizing an observer-group mission."

Furthermore, any such mission had to have a clear mandate and terms of reference in order to be viable. Minister Clark was quoted as saying that he found the Central American leaders eager to discuss the philosophy of peace but unwilling to get bogged down in details. For example, President Arias stated that the priority was getting cease-fire agreements; the rest, he said, would fall into place. Mr. Clark concluded: "That kind of vagueness was useful in getting agreement on the peace plan in the first place, but it is not good enough now. The regional presidents should be encouraged as loudly as possible to decide what they mean by peace, and just exactly how they propose to go about maintaining it."

The loose lobby supporting Canadian involvement in Central American peacekeeping was getting stronger as direct involvement seemed nearer. The coalition was being called, somewhat facetiously, the "ecclesiastical-academic-military complex."[16] A series of workshops involving these academics, clergy, politicians, and military officers involved in peacekeeping was held in this period, including workshops whose major theme was the use of confidence-building measures in connection with any peacekeeping or peace-observing effort. In early and mid-1988 the House of Commons held hearings and sent a select group of its members on a trip to Central America in connection with Canadian involvement with peacekeeping and confidence-building measures in the Esquipulas process.[17]

THE FIRST CIVS AND THE
ALAJUELA SUMMIT, JANUARY 1988

The first CIVS—made up of the foreign ministers of the thirteen Contadora, Support Group, and Central American nations and the Secretaries-General of the UN and OAS—had a brief and stormy existence that revealed the delicacy of the verification issue and the sensitivity of the Central American nations to interference by the larger nations of South America and by Mexico. Part of the problem was that the Central American nations were outnumbered and outpowered on the commission, which tended to reflect the views of Mexico, Venezuela, Colombia, and the South American nations recently returned to democracy. The CIVS had been set up this way under the August 1987 Esquipulas agreement as a calculated risk. It was recognized as unwieldy, and probably unmanageable, due to its size, its level, and the diversity of opinions it embraced. On the other hand, Arias and the other Central American presidents felt it necessary to bring this many Latin American nations into the verification process in order to give Esquipulas credibility in the face of opposition from the Reagan administration.

From the beginning, the CIVS was seen as representing Contadora, and as a continuation (or interference, depending on the viewpoint) of Contadora in the Esquipulas process. It had been created as part of Contadora, with considerable Canadian input, and was a comprehensive instrument with detailed statutes governing operations, organization, and procedures. The CIVS was able to establish close contacts with the National Reconciliation Commissions in each country, which had strong representation from human rights groups with an ax to grind against each of their governments. The CIVS was understandably interested in hearing complaints of abuses from these groups and included much of this material in its extensive final report. Unfortunately, this proved fatal for the CIVS.

President Daniel Ortega greeted the CIVS with enthusiasm in Managua. Interviewed on Radio Sandino during the commission's visit, Ortega accused the United States of prolonging the Central American conflict and described how he presented the commission with mutilated children wounded by the Contras. He argued that the CIVS "is proof that Esquipulas continues to work," and added that the CIVS should be allowed to make surprise visits *in situ* anywhere in Central America.[18] The commission's visits to El Salvador and Honduras were more difficult. President Duarte was outraged when the commission allowed his government's representative only 10 minutes to lay out the official view, and then gave opposition and human rights groups more than 12 hours of interview time. "That seemed infantile to me, a lack of respect, and at the same time a lack of impartiality in what the Commission was doing."[19] Duarte denied that Contras were operating out of El Salvador (as stated by some of the opposition), while accusing the Sandinistas of supporting the Frente Farabundo Martí de Liberación Nacional (FMLN). In Honduras the CIVS wanted to visit the U.S. bases, presumably to check on alleged activities that supported the Contras. President José Azcona said that the CIVS could visit the Palmerola and Aguacate bases, which had a heavy U.S. presence, but would have to announce their arrival ahead of time "because one does not storm into a military zone."[20]

The report of the first CIVS, dated 12 January 1988, was lengthy, detailed, and spared none of the five Central American nations, although it tended to focus on the information it had obtained from human rights and opposition groups and thus came down heavily on Guatemala, El Salvador, and Honduras.[21] It presented the case that Nicaragua was complying more fully with the Esquipulas agreement than any of the other Central American countries, and was therefore seen as overly inclined toward Nicaragua by the core four Central American nations and the United States. The report was the main business of the Alajuela Summit of Central American presidents, 15–16 January 1988, which has been described as "the most traumatic event to date in the implementation of Esquipulas II."[22] The reaction was predictable, with El Salvador, Honduras, Guatemala, and Costa Rica criticizing the report and Nicaragua defending it. Duarte was especially bitter, saying that "this business of creating commissions who wander around investigating like policemen is an insult; it's like telling us presidents that we are liars or sly little cheats ('pícaros')." His security minister put it this way: "The report is biased and partial to Nicaragua. . . . With this report the CIVS has finished its work; there is nothing left but to say thank you very much and goodbye."[23]

Which was indeed what happened at Alajuela. In polite diplomatic language, the Central American presidents expressed appreciation to the CIVS for its work, announced that its task had been completed, and assigned its verification responsibilities to the Executive Committee made up of their own representatives. The end result was to shut the Contadora nations out of the Esquipulas process and, in a sense, "Centralamericanize" the peace process, a road they had been traveling since the stagnation of Contadora in June 1986. Others saw the decision not as a "Centralamericanization" of Esquipulas, but rather as an overreaction to an honest but blunt and undiplomatic report by the CIVS. Furthermore, by excluding the larger Latin American nations and the Secretaries-General of the OAS and UN from the verification process, the Central American nations lost credibility. There were also serious, and very valid, doubts as to whether the Central American nations had the technical competence and means to conduct verification, to say nothing of the unbiased political will.[24]

By abolishing the first CIVS, the Central American nations ran the risk of alienating their Latin American colleagues and the Secretaries-General of the UN and OAS. But no one took major offense, and the response from those who might have felt injured by this action was low-keyed. What did happen was that the Esquipulas process went into stagnation for over a year until bilateral agreements between the Contras and the Sandinistas, and a new administration in Washington, helped create the conditions that allowed the impasse to break up in early 1989. The lack of an effective verification mechanism created by the death of CIVS was not filled for some time and contributed to the stagnation of Esquipulas. However, when a new instrument for verification was created, it involved outside actors (Canada, Spain, Germany, and Venezuela, under a UN flag) in ways that were totally unprecedented in Latin America.

THE SAPOÁ AGREEMENT, MARCH 1988

Central America came close to regional war with U.S. troop involvement in March 1988, ironically during the traditional lull of Easter week. Fighting broke out along the Nicaraguan-Honduran border between Contras and Sandinista forces, who had entered Honduras in hot pursuit, chasing the Contras to their camps along the border. After some heavy-handed, behind-the-scenes persuasion by U.S. diplomats, President Azcona asked for U.S.

assistance, and President Reagan sent 3,200 U.S. Army combat troops to Honduras. After Sandinista forces crossed the border to hit the Contra base near Bocay, Honduran jet aircraft attacked Sandinista targets inside Nicaragua. At one point, President Azcona claimed that 2,000 Sandinista troops were occupying 36 square miles of Honduran territory, and he threatened air strikes deep into Nicaragua unless they withdrew. After 11 days, the Sandinistas announced they had ended their offensive against the Contras and pulled back.

Nicaragua requested that the UN confirm their withdrawal, and UN Secretary-General Javier Pérez de Cuéllar announced on 19 March that a small team (two military observers and two political officers) would be visiting the Nicaraguan-Honduran border. The military observers turned out to be Uruguayan army officers transferred from the Kashmir UN observation mission, and the two civilians were UN staffers of Peruvian and Brazilian nationality.[25] The group was in Central America for only a brief period and had limited capabilities since it only operated on the Nicaraguan side of the border. The conflict, and the UN response to it, pointed out the potentially serious nature of clashes between Sandinistas and Contras and the way in which such clashes could quickly involve Honduras and the United States. At the same time, the very limited UN response was clearly only symbolic, and could hardly do much more than verify the obvious.

Despite, or perhaps because of, the clashes along the Honduran border in March, the off-again, on-again talks between the Sandinistas and Contras were restarted and reached a major breakthrough in a historic meeting at the small border town of Sapoá on 21–23 March 1988. The two sides agreed to a three-day truce during the period of their talks, which ended with an agreement to expand this to a 60-day cease-fire, to be monitored by Cardinal Obando y Bravo and OAS Secretary-General Baena Soares, acting as individuals. Other provisions, some of which only emerged after subsequent talks, included the regrouping of the Contras within Nicaragua in secure zones (zones of peace) to be guaranteed by the verifiers, and amnesty, dialogue, repatriation, and elections.[26] The significance of Sapoá was understood by all involved: there would be no enduring peace in Central America, and no fulfillment of Contadora or the Arias or Esquipulas peace plans, unless the Nicaraguan Contras and the Sandinistas made peace with each other. Although there had been numerous contacts of one kind or another between these two antagonists, Sapoá marked the beginning of the end of the Nicaragua civil war and of U.S. support to the Contras.

As part of the Sapoá Agreement, the Contras insisted on guarantees of continued humanitarian aid from the U.S. Agency for International Development (USAID). But the Sandinistas insisted that this aid be channeled through a neutral third party or international organization, which turned out to be the Organization of American States. This was the beginning of the USAID-OAS-Contra link that was to eventually finance

CIAV-OAS (the OAS half of the International Commission of Support and Verification), and which led to tensions in late 1990 and 1991. It did not take long for the Organization of American States and the United States to disagree on the details of implementating this aid. In late April 1988 the *Washington Post* reported that the process was being delayed by a dispute between the OAS and USAID over how the $10 million for the verification commission was to be spent (this money was part of the $50 million nonlethal aid package approved by the Congress). The dispute was finally settled in May, but it was only the first of many problems presented to the Organization of American States by its involvement in humanitarian and resettlement aid to the Contras in the 1988–1991 period.[27]

CREATION OF THE NEW CIVS WITH ITS TAG

Almost lost in the attention being paid to the Sandinista-Contra talks and the Sapoá Agreement was a meeting of the Esquipulas Executive Commission, made up of the Central American foreign ministers, held in Guatemala on 7 April 1988. This meeting was to have major significance in the verification process because it created what became known as the new CIVS in the shape of a Technical Advisory Group (TAG) made up of Canada, the Federal Republic of Germany, Spain, and an unspecified Latin American country, which later turned out to be Venezuela. This TAG was in essence the forerunner of ONUCA (the UN Observer Group in Central America). Although a number of sources called this group the "new" CIVS, this was something of a misnomer since the "old" (or "first") CIVS still existed on paper, but without any meaningful functions.

When the first CIVS (consisting of the Contadora four, the Support Group four, the Central American five, and the Secretaries-General of the UN and OAS) was disbanded at the January 1988 Alajuela Summit, the five Central American presidents gave more authority to the Executive Commission under their direct control, consisting of their own foreign ministers. This was done with the obvious intent of avoiding any embarrassing verification reports such as the one that had caused such anguish at Alajuela. This Executive Commission had been meeting on a regular basis since then, but had produced few results until their 7 April meeting when they announced the creation of this Technical Advisory Group, which would be charged with the task of preparing the verification plan for Esquipulas.[28] (See Figure 4.2.) The three nations involved had obviously been approached for their acquiescence, but the April announcement was the first public indication that the process was moving toward fruition.

In theory, the arrangement also included a Security Commission, but no one seemed very clear as to its function. It met once in early 1988 but did not accomplish anything noteworthy. It was not until 1990 that this

Figure 4.2 The New CIVS and Technical Advisory Group

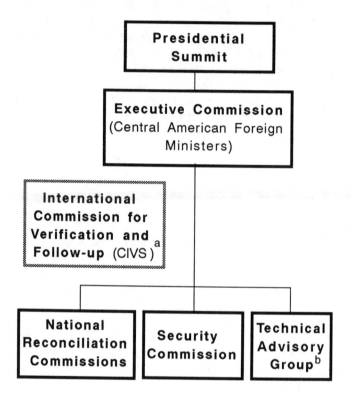

Notes: a. This old CIVS was left without any meaningful functions after April 1988.

b. The Technical Advisory Group was made up of Canada, Spain, Germany, and an unspecified Latin American country (eventually Venezuela), plus representatives of the Secretaries-General of the UN and OAS. In mid-1988 it assumed the functions of the old CIVS.

commission would begin to play an important (although frustrating) role in attempting to place caps and eventually reduce the levels of arms and troops in Central America.

The composition of the TAG was important. Canada was the most obvious member, inasmuch as Canadian officials had been involved in the "real" world of Central American peacekeeping and peace observing from the very beginning of the Contadora process. Canada had made important contributions by consistently pointing out that peacekeeping and peace observing were not going to be as simple or easy as they seemed, and that things would not fall into place unless a lot of careful planning was done first. President Ortega had mentioned Canada (the only specific country he named) in February as a participant in the verification body that he predicted would eventually be formed.[29] Canada's willingness to participate had been conditioned on a number of premises, most importantly that its presence be acceptable to all the parties involved, and that there be a clear mandate from some reliable international organization. The routing of the Esquipulas Executive Commission's request through the UN was a promising step in this process,[30] although nothing was firmed up until November when the UN Secretary-General was formally requested by the Esquipulas Executive Commission to ask the nations involved to join the TAG. Despite the delays, there were reports that Canadian peacekeeping troops were being alerted for possible Central American duties as early as May 1988.[31]

Spain was in one way an obvious choice because of its history in the region and its cultural affinity, but was somewhat of a liability because of a lack of peacekeeping experience. However, Spain had been playing a growing role in Central American affairs over the past decade and was seen as being uniquely qualified to participate. In backing Spain for a role in verification, Daniel Ortega said that "Spain has a great deal of independence and enjoys the confidence of every Central American government."[32] Germany was a less obvious candidate, but it too had been taking a greater interest in the Central American conflict and had been involved in the region, especially Guatemala, for many years. Germany faced a constitutional problem of prohibitions against sending any troops in a peacekeeping mission outside of its borders. There was talk that this could be overcome by sending police officers, but eventually this difficulty meant limiting Germany's role in ONUCA to logistical support in the form of civilian aircraft crews and medical teams.

There had been rumors of also including a Latin American nation (Venezuela, Colombia, Uruguay, and Brazil had all been mentioned at one time or another), but it was not possible to get approval of the nation concerned in time for the April announcement. The IPA continued to play a role in preparing the way for a peace-observing mission. The chairman of the IPA and several of his staff held consultations in Central America in early and mid-1988 at the request of the Central American countries, and briefings were given to UN and OAS personnel involved in the advance work. Portions of the IPA's basic *Peacekeeper's Handbook* were being translated into Spanish for use by the Central Americans and other Spanish-speaking personnel involved in peacekeeping or peace observing.[33]

NOTES

1. Gomariz, *Balance*, 51.
2. Escalante Herrera, *La Propuesta de Paz*, 37–49; Rojas Aravena, *El Proceso de Esquipulas*, 11; Center for International Policy, "Arias Primer," June 1987.
3. Aguilar Zinser, "Central America and Contadora," 113; *Washington Post*, 17 February 1987.
4. Arias, *El Camino de la Paz*, 234–237.
5. Arias advisor John Biehl quoted in Sklar, *Washington's War on Nicaragua*, 375.
6. Frohman, *De Contadora al Grupo*, 405; "Crónica de un Difícil Consenso," *Pensamiento Propio*, October 1987, 3.
7. Gutman, *Banana Diplomacy*, 346–351.
8. Rojas Aravena, *El Proceso de Esquipulas*, 11–12.
9. Gomariz, *Balance*, 73–76; *New York Times*, 24 August 1987.
10. Centro de Estudios Internacionales, *Working Papers*, no. 1, 21.
11. Gomariz, *Balance*, 94–99; FLACSO, *Informe Blanco*, vii–xi.
12. *Central American Report*, 18 December 1987, 386.
13. *Toronto Globe and Mail*, 27 November 1987. Purver, *Guide to Canadian Policies*, 1987, 234.
14. *International Perspectives*, Canada, January–February 1988, 8–10.
15. Paul Knox, "Keeping the Peace Wouldn't Be Easy," *Toronto Globe and Mail*, 1 December 1987.
16. Roundtable on Negotiations, *Interim and Confidence-Building Measures*.
17. Canada, House of Commons, *Peace Process in Central America*.
18. Managua, Radio Sandino, 6 January 1988, in Foreign Broadcast Information Service (FBIS), 7 January 1988, 13.
19. *Washington Post*, 15 January 1988.
20. Panama, ACAN, 12 January 1988, in FBIS, 15 January 1988, 14–15.
21. For summary text of the report, see Gomariz, *Balance*, 372–381. An English version is in FBIS, 19 January 1988, 20–24.
22. Canada, House of Commons, *Supporting the Five*, 13.
23. *Diario Latino*, 14 January 1988, in FBIS, 15 January 1988, 11; Baradini, "Otro Año," 17.
24. For commentary on the various interpretations of doing away with CIVS, see Herrera Cáceres, *Democracia*, 31–37; Klepak, *Security Considerations*, 49; and Rojas Aravena, *Política Exterior*, 173.
25. FBIS, 20 March 1988, 30; 24 March 1988, 11; Gomariz, *Balance*, 149.
26. For documentation on Sapoá, see U.S. Department of State, *Regional Brief: Central America*; and Center for International Policy, "Cease-Fire Primer," July 1988. For analysis, see Alvarez, "El Proceso de Esquipulas."

27. See *Washington Post,* 6 April 1988, A7; 29 April 1988, A26; 19 May 1988, 29.

28. *Central America Report,* 15 April 1988, 110.

29. Managua Domestic Service, 4 February 1988, in FBIS, 5 February 1988, 22.

30. Discussion with Richard Gorham, Canadian ambassador-at-large for Central America, Ottawa, 6 May 1989.

31. *International Perspectives,* Canada, April–May 1988, 40–41.

32. *New York Times,* 25 January 1988, A-14.

33. Communication from Maj. Gen. Indar Jit Rikhye, chairman of the IPA, 20 June 1988.

5
BRINGING PEACE VERIFICATION
TO ESQUIPULAS, 1988–1989

ATTEMPTS TO REVIVE ESQUIPULAS, LATE 1988

On its first anniversary, prospects were not bright for the Esquipulas process. The fundamental element of the process, the forging of peace between the Sandinista regime in Managua and the Contras, had stalled when the talks broke down in June 1988. The Reagan administration attempted to place the blame on Nicaragua, but in early August Secretary of State Shultz, on a Central American tour, was unable to persuade the core four Central American presidents to publicly condemn the Sandinista regime. In an apparent effort to preempt criticism, Ortega contacted Arias asking for the reactivation of the International Verification Commission. Arias, seeking to revive the peace plan, responded by asking Ortega to stop taking measures against the opposition and to try and reach a permanent cease-fire. Arias's efforts continued at the inauguration of President Rodrigo Borja of Ecuador on 10 August, where he asked Fidel Castro to support his plan.

Throughout these developments, and especially after Arias's concerted attempt to get things moving, there was a general feeling that there would be no progress until the inauguration of the new U.S. president. Contra aid and U.S. policy toward Nicaragua and Central America lay at the heart of the peace process, and uncertainties about a possible major policy shift in January 1989 kept the Esquipulas process from accomplishing much in this period.

Another obstacle for Esquipulas was a suit taken to the International Court of Justice (ICJ) by Nicaragua that accused Honduras of allowing its territory to be used by the Contras. The government of President Azcona denied that this was happening and, in retaliation for the Nicaraguan suit, managed to block any decisions in the Esquipulas Executive Commission, including the formal request to the UN to ask Spain, Germany, and Canada to set up peacekeeping machinery in Central America. But by late 1988 the Hondurans were getting increasingly nervous over the U.S. abandonment of the Contras, which would leave Honduras with the unpleasant situation of having somewhere between 10,000 and 12,000 well-armed Contras in its territory. With the end of U.S. support, these Contras might very well take to banditry inside Honduras if they could not return to Nicaragua. Thus, there were increasing incentives in late 1988 for Honduras to promote the Esquipulas process, and a peacekeeping mission along the Nicaraguan-Honduran border was one promising avenue. In September President Azcona accepted the possibility of an international peacekeeping force such as the one proposed by Ortega, on the condition that this would be a quid pro quo for Nicaragua's withdrawing its ICJ suit against Honduras.[1]

About the same time Azcona was warming to the Nicaraguan suggestion of a peacekeeping mission on their border, the notion of third-party involvement by international organizations received a significant boost when the Nobel Peace Prize was awarded to UN peacekeepers. Just as the award to President Arias had improved prospects for his peace plan the year before, the 1988 prize also had its political purpose: it served to highlight the increasing importance of the UN in the late 1980s and was a message of encouragement to those who might be interested in inviting or supporting UN peacekeeping operations.

A Contra peacekeeping proposal was also floated in September as a counter to the Sandinista suggestion of a peacekeeping group on the Honduran-Nicaraguan border. It was made by Contra leader Enrique Bermúdez, who asked the Nicaraguan government to turn power over to an inter-American peacekeeping force until a government of national salvation could be formed.[2] He denounced the Sandinista request for military observers on the Nicaraguan-Honduran border as a way of blocking the Nicaraguan Resistance, and thus allowing the Sandinista government to allocate more troops for repressing the population. As an officer in the Somoza Guardia Nacional, Bermúdez had served with the Inter-American Peace Force (IAPF) in the Dominican Republic and had something like this in mind when he made his September 1988 proposal. In the circumstances of 1988, such a peace force was a strong reminder of the Dominican Republic's IAPF in 1965 and the aborted 1979 U.S. attempt to create an OAS "peace presence" to save the remnants of the Somoza regime in Nicaragua. Although nothing came of the Bermúdez proposal, it was a reminder that peacekeeping was not universally considered a positive thing in much of Latin America.

With these elements as background, the Hondurans formally launched their peacekeeping proposal at the UN General Assembly in October 1988. Speaking in New York, Honduran Foreign Minister Carlos López Contreras called for a United Nations military peacekeeping contingent on the Nicaraguan-Honduran-Salvadoran border, to include elements from Spain,

West Germany, and Canada, and with the power to relocate the Contras by force if necessary. This latter possibility seemed unlikely, and the proposal was interpreted as a way of expressing Honduran concern over the possible U.S. abandonment of the Contras in Honduras.[3] The Nicaraguan government supported the Honduran proposal, but the other Central American countries had reservations. Two of the countries that would provide troops, Spain and Canada, said they were prepared to help, but only if the five Central American countries reached an understanding on the Honduran proposal. The third country, the Federal Republic of Germany, had constitutional provisions against allowing troops outside its borders and might not be able to provide the support requested. There was also criticism that the Honduran proposal was premature and not fully coordinated with the governments involved in providing troops. A San Pedro Sula, Honduras, newspaper noted that this proposal created serious problems for the UN Secretary-General, and that its discussion tended to undermine the Esquipulas International Security Commission, which had almost become reality.[4]

The UN General Assembly spent an unprecedented portion of its 1988 session dealing with the Central American crisis. In addition to the Honduran peacekeeping proposal, the assembly approved a resolution strongly supporting the peace process and exhorted the Central American nations "with the utmost urgency, to promote and supplement the agreed verification machinery, with the co-operation of regional or extra-regional States and bodies of recognized impartiality and technical capacity, which have shown a desire to collaborate in the Central American peace process."[5]

Peacekeeping in Central America was also a major topic behind the scenes at the inauguration of Mexican President Carlos Salinas de Gortari in early December 1988. The Central American foreign ministers were, of course, all present, and by prior agreement used the occasion to renew the peace process. (This was repeated at the inaugurals of Latin American presidents during the entire period of Contadora/Arias/Esquipulas.) The foreign ministers called for a new Verification Commission and a UN peacekeeping presence, as requested by the Honduran foreign minister at the UN General Assembly. The UN peacekeeping presence should have "sufficient power and authority to request the intervention of whatever corresponding UN agencies . . . it may deem necessary in order to persuade the irregular forces of insurrectional movements to adhere to these commitments."[6] The multinational force, they suggested, might be used to relocate the Contras back to Nicaragua and prevent both the Contras and the Salvadoran guerrillas from engaging in cross-border actions. At the inauguration, Ortega called Esquipulas a synthesis of Contadora and Arias's ideas (among others).[7] He noted the void created by the "death sentence" meted out to the CIVS in January, and said that this had deprived the Central American nations of an effective verification instrument and made them more susceptible to U.S. influence; thus, the need for a strong UN peacekeeping presence.

Bilateral confidence building was also strengthened in late 1988 when the joint Nicaraguan–Costa Rican border patrols began. There were reports that the Reagan administration was privately annoyed at the Costa Ricans for allowing these patrols, which were seen as denying the Contras the possibility of operating across the border from Costa Rica.[8] The patrols were also potentially another precedent for the establishment of a peacekeeping force along the far more critical Honduran-Nicaraguan border, which would mean the end of the Contra sanctuaries in Honduras.

UN PEACEKEEPING PLANS
AND PROPOSALS, JANUARY–JULY 1989

UN Secretary-General Pérez de Cuéllar responded to the Central American presidents' Mexico City request for peacekeeping with a strong letter regarding the problems involved in UN peacekeeping. (The *Washington Post* described the letter as "sternly worded.") The Secretary-General told the Central Americans that they had to "finalize the criteria and come to a clear agreement on the mandate" before any UN peacekeeping force could be sent. He also said that any irregular forces in the area would have to agree to the UN presence; this would include both the Contras and the Salvadoran FMLN. The UN Secretary-General's letter, and its rejection of their first verification proposal as too vague, was something of a shock to the Central American presidents.

It was later revealed that Pérez de Cuéllar had felt embarrassed in 1987 when the Central Americans requested that the UN prepare plans for a peacekeeping operation that got bogged down in regional politics and never came to fruition, and he was determined to be sure they were serious about meeting basic UN requirements before committing his people to another planning effort.[9] The Secretary-General's frustrations also reflected the fact that many nations, including the superpowers, were asking the UN to do more and more peacekeeping without providing the resources. Speaking in Oslo in early January, Pérez de Cuéllar appealed for a special fund to support UN peacekeeping, saying the UN needed additional budgetary support to fund the 10,000 troops involved in peacekeeping throughout the world.

The five Central American foreign ministers met in New York in early February 1989 to discuss a United Nations role in Central American peacekeeping. In talks with the Secretary-General, a 50-person mobile observer force to monitor the Contras was discussed; the contingent would come from Spain, Germany, and Canada. It should also have Latin American participation and the involvement of the OAS Secretary-General. In part because of Pérez de Cuéllar's strong letter in January, the Central American nations now had a much more realistic vision of what UN peacekeeping would involve. The talks also managed to bridge the gap between Honduras, which wanted a large and strong UN force, and El Salvador, which opposed any foreign military observers. The Guatemalan government, previously very negative on the idea of UN peacekeepers, was also beginning to accept it.[10]

As usual, the Canadians played a low-key but essential role. Their reluctance to support a Central American peacekeeping operation unless basic preconditions were met dampened Spanish and German enthusiasm for agreeing to the Central American request, and permitted the Secretary-General to be firm, even stern, in giving the Central American leaders a dose of realism on the peacekeeping issue. In effect, quiet Canadian diplomacy had assured that ONUCA would have a clear and attainable mandate.[11] On his April 1989 trip to Ottawa to thank the Canadians, Arias said:

> When nobody believed in the Central America peace process, Canada became our first ally. When the time came to take on the risk of participating in the verification process of the peace effort, Canada made the first offer. . . . When we had to disagree with countries (like the United States) with whom we enjoyed a deep and strong friendship, it was from Canadians that we first received understanding and encouragement, and the strength to be patient.[12]

The early February UN talks set the stage for the crucial El Salvador summit the following week on 12–14 February 1989. Meeting in Costa del Sol (Tesoro Beach), the presidents of the five Central American nations discussed implementation of the 1987 Esquipulas II agreement, including UN observers to verify the removal of Contras (estimated at 11,000 in Honduras) from the Honduran-Nicaraguan border and the dismantling of their bases. In exchange, the Sandinista government agreed to implement full political reforms, including elections in February 1990 verified by the UN and the OAS. Mobile UN observer teams of 10–15 personnel would be based in each Central American country, although the main focus would be Nicaragua-Honduras with El Salvador–Honduras as the second priority.[13] On the peacekeeping issue, the Costa del Sol Summit showed how the Esquipulas process differed from Contadora in one crucial aspect: whereas Contadora attempted to lay out enormously detailed provisions for verification, Esquipulas left these details to the professional peacekeepers of the UN, led by Canada. As Guatemalan Foreign Minister Alfonso Cabrera put it as he left the summit: "If we had tried to work out the details, we wouldn't have succeeded and the Summit would have broken down."[14]

The Costa del Sol Summit achieved what Arias had been seeking for the previous six months: it breathed new life into the Esquipulas process and gave the UN peacekeeping element its basic working document. It also moved the Contras one more step down the road to their eventual repatriation from Honduras and demobilization. In describing why Nicaragua supported the idea of UN peacekeeping, Vice Minister of Foreign Affairs Tinoco was later to explain that they perceived that UN involvement was the only way to get the United States and Honduras to accept Contra demobilization.[15] Honduras, he felt, was finally realizing the danger the Contras posed while on their territory, and the United States, he speculated, might be interested in UN peacekeeping as a way of cutting the alleged Nicaraguan support to the FMLN in El Salvador (support Nicaragua denied).

With the approval in principle granted by the Costa del Sol Summit, United Nations officials drafted plans for a 160-person Central American peace-observing unit (the eventual ONUCA) to monitor the proposed halt in aid to rebels. As decided previously, the contingent would come from Spain, Germany, and Canada and would consist of about 100 unarmed military personnel and 60 support staff and civilians; a six-month renewable UN mandate would be their authority. They would be stationed as teams in all five nations, but would concentrate their efforts on the Nicaraguan-Honduran and Salvadoran-Honduran borders. On 15 March the Central American representatives tentatively approved the plan. Although the UN teams would be unarmed, they could request armed escorts from the host countries if needed. Radio Managua observed that

> the work to be done by the observers will depend greatly on the attitude assumed by the rebel groups. These rebel groups must refrain from the use of force against the observers. . . . The UN Secretary-General has warned that the goal of the UN peacekeeping force will not be to disarm the rebel groups in the area; instead, it is hoped that its presence in areas of conflict will help curb the activities of those groups.[16]

There was concern over the possibility of the UN being caught in the middle between the Central American presidents, who wanted a UN presence for Contra demobilization, and the United States, which was apparently interested in keeping the Contras as pressure against the Sandinistas until after the February 1990 elections.[17]

UN officials were stunned at how readily the Central American presidents accepted their requirements for a UN peacekeeping presence, including provisions that the force be unarmed and be given a mandate approved by the UN Security Council. Disagreement over details of such a force had stalled UN verification proposals in the past, and apparently there was a feeling that the same thing would happen again. UN officials were also concerned about involvement in the February 1990 elections in Nicaragua because they might have to referee U.S.-Nicaraguan disputes over the election's legitimacy as well as the status of human rights.

Another major breakthrough was achieved in early May when the five Central American foreign ministers, meeting in Guatemala, agreed to a plan that would give the UN (along with the OAS) total responsibility for dismantling the Contras, receiving their arms, and helping them find third-party countries that would accept them. In the interim they would be relocated to temporary camps in Nicaragua. Details of the plan included the establishment of an International Commission of Support and Verification (Comisión Internacional de Apoyo y Verificación—CIAV), which would be created with representatives of the UN and the OAS. They would work with the governments concerned and specialized international organizations to facilitate demobilization and resettlement, setting up temporary camps as needed. Border posts would be set up, and documentation would be provided to those being demobilized. The resettlement would begin five days after the date decided by the presidents, and a week later CIAV officials would go to the camps to assist the repatriates. Forty-five days after their settlement, all Contra weapons and other military equipment would be turned in to CIAV officials for disposition.

The preliminary work of establishing the foundations for ONUCA was completed when the Secretary-General submitted his report to the Security Council, which in turn approved Resolution 637 commending all concerned for their work in establishing mechanisms for verification of the Esquipulas II agreements, approving the efforts of the Secretary-General, and calling on all interested states to support the peace process.

THE UNITED STATES, THE SOVIET UNION, AND CENTRAL AMERICAN PEACE, 1989

In January 1989 a much more pragmatic Bush administration replaced the ideologically inclined Reaganites. The flavor of the old regime's thinking on Central America was nicely caught in remarks made by Assistant Secretary of State Elliott Abrams as he vacated his post: he argued that President Reagan should have launched an invasion of Nicaragua, using the Monroe Doctrine as justification, immediately after the assault on Grenada.

There was paralysis in the Central American peace process until the Bush administration made its policies known. A Central American summit scheduled for January was canceled, and President Arias argued that the Central American nations needed to know what new policies the Bush administration would set for the area. There was some pessimism that the Arias plan was finished, and that the initiative was in U.S. hands. The touchstone issue was, as always, U.S. Contra aid. The new administration initially sought to continue Contra aid as a way of keeping the pressure on the Sandinistas, and in March the Bush administration attempted to get $40–50 million in humanitarian aid for the Contras for the 10-month period from 31 March (when the current aid would run out) until the Nicaraguan elections. Secretary of State James Baker indicated that he did not expect the

Contras to mount military actions during the period in which the Bush administration would continue temporary humanitarian aid. At the same time, he said the presence of the Contras would be an incentive for the Sandinistas to fulfill their promises of political reforms and elections in February 1990. He added that the United States supported the notion of an international peacekeeping force in Central America because it "was not inconsistent with the U.S. policy."[18]

In late March the administration and the Congress struck an extraordinary deal based on a bipartisan Central American policy. The terms of the agreement called for humanitarian funding of $4.5 million per month for the Contras (for the 10 months until the Nicaraguan elections) and strong U.S. support for the Central American peace process. Four congressional committees would have oversight on the agreement and the flow of funds. The funding could also be used to assist the Contras in relocating within the region. The bipartisan agreement reached fruition in April, when in a lopsided vote the Congress approved Bush's plan to provide nonlethal Contra aid through the February 1990 elections. The package included $49.8 million of direct aid to the Contras, as well as provisions for transportation and administration (through USAID) and help for civilian victims of the war. Conservative Republican legislators felt it was a betrayal of the Contras, and called it a "modern-day Bay of Pigs."[19]

U.S.-Soviet understandings on Central American issues in 1989 were also important. In early March Soviet Ambassador Yuri Dubinin indicated a willingness to discuss Central America as part of the U.S.-Soviet regional agenda in connection with the 7 March Vienna meeting of Secretary of State James Baker and Soviet Foreign Minister Eduard Shevardnadze. Later that month, President Bush sent Soviet President Mikhail Gorbachev (who was about to leave for Cuba) a letter urging him to use his influence to bring peace to Central America by reducing Soviet support to the Nicaraguan government.

In Havana, Gorbachev hardly sounded conciliatory. He denounced U.S. policies in Central America, stating that the Soviet Union would end its military assistance to Nicaragua if the United States would stop aid to its Central American allies. He also called for zones of peace and cooperation in Latin America, and said his government would support an international conference to help create them. Gorbachev made specific reference to the fact that "mutual restraint and confidence-building among countries of the region is taking on paramount importance now."[20] Gorbachev also said the "USSR favors enhancing the nuclear-free status of Latin America on the basis of the Treaty of Tlatelolco and supports the creation of a zone of peace and cooperation in the southern Atlantic and of similar zones in Central America, the Caribbean, and the waters of the Pacific off South America." In response to Gorbachev's speech, a U.S. spokesperson denounced continuing Soviet aid for Nicaragua and denied any equivalence or linkage between U.S. and Soviet interests in Central America.

Despite Gorbachev's tough rhetoric in Cuba, which could have been the result of a need to appear supportive of Castro and the Sandinistas, the Soviets continued to send quiet messages that their desire for better relations with the United States was more important than Nicaragua. In May there were reports that the Soviets gave Secretary of State Baker strong indications that they would soon undertake a major shift in their Central American role, stressing negotiated settlements and de-emphasizing military support for Nicaragua and its allies in the hope that this could lead to closer U.S.-Soviet relations.

In an October 1989 visit to Nicaragua and Cuba, Soviet Foreign Minister Shevardnadze called for stability and peace in Central America. His reception in Managua was subdued, and the Nicaraguans were nervous that his remarks signaled a cutback in Soviet aid. Shevardnadze also suggested that the Soviet Union and the United States jointly guarantee peace and security in Central America and establish a permanent mechanism to cut armed forces and arms supplies in the region to the minimum required for legitimate self-defense. He suggested that the two superpowers could guarantee an agreement on the equilibrium of forces. These suggestions were interpreted in some circles as a bid for a greater Soviet role in Central America, which had been historically an area of U.S. predominance.

The year ended with a new form of U.S.-Soviet cooperation: at the UN, the United States and the Soviet Union announced their first joint resolution, calling for all nations to strengthen the UN and defend peace and human rights. Both sides said this marked the end of Cold War rhetoric at the UN and the beginning of a new era. The Soviets called for "the creation of special peace-keeping forces to be ready for instant action, and the strengthening of the UN Military Staff Committee to deal with incipient crises."[21]

THE TELA SUMMIT, 5–7 AUGUST

The five Central American presidents met again for three days in August 1989 in the Honduran town of Tela at a key turning point in the peace process. The Tela meeting cleared the way for the creation of ONUCA and CIAV and moved the process one step closer to the elimination of the problem of the Contras and the Nicaraguan civil war.[22] The overall tone of the meeting was shaped by a dramatic breakthrough that occurred the day before it started: the Nicaraguan government and opposition groups reached a broad agreement on conditions governing the February 1990 elections. This was seen as seriously undercutting the U.S. argument that the Contras must be kept in place as a guarantee through the elections, and it provided Ortega with a strong bargaining tool for dismantling the Contras.

The Tela agreement signed on 7 August 1989 had three major elements:

1. The voluntary demobilization, repatriation, or relocation of the Contras by the end of 1989. At the same time, Nicaragua would move toward free and open elections in February 1990. These provisions were to be jointly monitored by the UN and the OAS, for which purpose three organizations would be established: the International Commission for Support and Verification (CIAV), the UN Observer Group in Central America (ONUCA), and the UN Observer Group for the Verification of Elections in Nicaragua (ONUVEN).

2. A call for constructive dialogue between the FMLN guerrillas and the government of El Salvador.

3. A separate agreement by which Nicaragua withdrew its International Court of Justice suit claiming war damages against Honduras.

Among the major issues discussed at Tela was the so-called symmetry between the Contras in Nicaragua and the FMLN in El Salvador. This had been pushed previously by the United States, and by Salvadoran President Alfredo Cristiani at Tela, but it was strongly attacked by Nicaragua's Ortega, who argued that the Contras were supported by an outside power—the United States—and were operating from a third country—Honduras. In contrast, he said the FMLN was operating as a true guerrilla force within its own country with little outside support. Ortega added that "the Contras can be demobilized by Honduras and a UN force because they are an international problem, but the UN cannot demobilize a guerrilla force [the FMLN] within its own country."[23]

The El Salvador/FMLN issue at Tela involved another in the long series of offers by both sides to dialogue. In the past these offers had rarely borne much fruit because of the different criteria both sides applied to the dispute. But Tela was different. The FMLN had sent a letter to the five Central American presidents at Tela expressing its willingness to participate in a direct and constructive dialogue for peace with the Salvadoran government. At Tela, Cristiani called for the symmetrical disbanding of the Contras and FMLN, but the final accord separated the two issues and called for a dialogue in El Salvador to get the process moving. The section dealing with the FMLN called for dialogue and a cessation of hostilities that would lead to the guerrillas' voluntary demobilization and participation in institutional and democratic life. On his return to San Salvador, Cristiani hailed the accords, noting that Tela was the first time the five presidents had addressed the internal situation in El Salvador head on.

The issue of the Guatemalan insurgency was kept to a low profile. The right wing in Guatemala had pressured President Vinicio Cerezo not to enter into any symmetry arrangement, and the Tela accords did not mention any

Guatemalan guerrilla group by name. The only reference was to "armed groups," which were called upon to end "all actions contravening the spirit of the peace accords."

Honduran President Azcona was concerned over the 10,000–12,000 Contras in his country (plus perhaps 40,000 family members) who might be abandoned by the United States. Thus, at Tela, Honduras called for UN help to supervise the repatriation, using force if necessary, a possibility that would cause problems for the United Nations. Shortly after Tela, Honduran troops began to seal off the Contra camps, and Azcona took an increasingly hard-line position, saying that if the Contras were not disbanded in the 120-day deadline set by Tela, then UN forces should use "coercive methods."[24] Finally, the five Central American presidents agreed on a plan to disband the Contras voluntarily by 5 December.

To accomplish all this, the Tela accords called for the creation of a CIAV, which had been included in prior draft proposals prepared by Central American technical groups (foreign ministers and their deputies), and which would involve both the UN and the OAS. The schedule for the CIAV was for it to be operational by 8 September. In the following three months, the Contras would be demobilized, and the CIAV would report to the five presidents in Managua 10 days after the demobilization was completed. There was some criticism that one weakness of Tela was that it relied on the UN and the OAS "to do what amounts to the summitteers' dirty work";[25] but as was evident in the Contadora process, the demobilization problem exceeded the political and technical capacity of the Central American nations, and they were correct in seeking outside help from international organizations.

Tela can be seen as a significant victory for the Sandinistas because it guaranteed the dismantling of the Contras. On his return to Managua, Daniel Ortega spoke of "*humo blanco en la región*" ("white smoke in the region")—a reference to the election of a pope or other momentous event.[26] Several participants and observers noted that Tela meant the end of the Contras as a military and political problem for Nicaragua; now they were simply a refugee problem. Tela could also be seen as a further step in the erosion of U.S. influence in Central America, in a process that began with the 7 August 1987 peace accord. Ever since that date, the Central American presidents had become more assertive in each of the five summit meetings and less responsive to U.S. demands.

One important difference between Tela and the Contadora approach was that Contadora had become so immersed in the details of solving the security and military problems of the area that it seemed to have lost sight of the real socioeconomic and political roots of the Central American crisis. Tela, on the other hand, exemplified the Esquipulas approach of emphasizing democratization and the root causes of Central American conflicts, while leaving the resolution of the military aspects (for example, Contra demobilization) to the outside helpful fixers of the UN and the OAS.

In their first response to the Tela accords, on 7 August the Contras, through Nicaraguan Resistance leaders Israel Galeano and Boanerges Mathus, defied the Tela agreement by saying that they would not give up their weapons and would continue fighting in the mountains inside Nicaragua if necessary. Contra leader Enrique Bermúdez added that any Contra demobilization would have to be preceded by a dialogue with the Managua government.[27]

At the UN, Honduras withdrew its opposition to ONUCA, which had been based on its request that Nicaragua withdraw its case against Honduras at the International Court of Justice; at the same time, as agreed at Tela, Nicaragua asked the ICJ to defer judgment on its suit.[28] A few days later (16 August), Honduras formally requested the UN Security Council to send ONUCA, to be made up of troops from Spain, Canada, and Germany, to its borders with Nicaragua and El Salvador.

Despite threats by the Contra leadership that they would ignore Tela, in late August the first direct peaceful contact between the Sandinista Army and Contra units occurred. They met accidentally while patrolling in northern Nicaragua, and initially both sides drew their weapons. Unit commanders on both sides called out not to fire, eventually talked, and, after cautious feelers, exchanged cigarettes. According to an Associated Press stringer who was present: "The decisive point in lowering the tension was when the Sandinista soldiers started offering cigarettes to the Contras. From there on, both sides sort of mingled—still being careful, though—and started talking to each other in small groups."[29] Interestingly, the Sandinista lieutenant had copies of the 7 August Tela agreement, which he gave to the Contras. The encounter stands as a fitting monument to the Tela accords, and evokes Alford's image (described in Chapter 1) of the two swordsmen who distrust each other but wish to avoid combat and, eventually, through confidence-building measures, convince each other of their peaceful intentions.

THE PEACE PROCESS IN EL SALVADOR, 1989

The 1989 Salvadoran election campaign was historic in that the Left participated by presenting candidates for the first time in the 10 years of civil war. The participation was controversial and divisive within the FDR/FMLN—for example, one of the Democratic Convergence (FDR) leaders, Rubén Zamora, criticized the FMLN's tactics of assassinating pro-government mayors as being contrary to the Geneva Convention. He was concerned that this would have a negative impact on the candidacy of the FDR's Guillermo Ungo and others in the 19 March elections.

In late January 1989 five comandantes of the FMLN (using Archbishop

Arturo Rivera y Damas as an intermediary) offered to participate in the presidential elections if they were postponed six months, and if negotiations to end the conflict were initiated. Their proposal included the comment that "the current trend in the international field is that most wars are being solved through negotiations."[30] This major shift in the FMLN's traditional position of avoiding or blocking elections was apparently taken after diplomatic demarches in Europe, in which they found little support for continuing their insurrection. Further, the Kremlin had apparently told them that in the unlikely event of a Sandinista-style FMLN victory, the Soviet Union would not have the resources to support them, and thus they should make serious efforts at a negotiated solution.

Talks between representatives of the FDR/FMLN and the major Salvadoran political parties began in Mexico in February 1989. But senior members of the army and Duarte's Christian Democratic Party rejected the FMLN plan to stop fighting in return for reducing the size of El Salvador's military and postponing the elections. In response, the FMLN refused to recognize the legitimacy of the March elections and began a campaign to disrupt them. The elections were held on schedule 19 March 1989, although the FMLN anti-election campaign was undoubtedly a factor in keeping the participation rate down to about 50 percent. ARENA (Alianza Republicana Nacionalista) candidate Alfredo Cristiani won the presidential race with a surprising 53 percent of the vote over Christian Democrat Fidel Chávez Mena with 36 percent and five other candidates (including one from the Democratic Convergence, associated with the FMLN). After the elections there was a lull of six months in the nascent Salvadoran peace process, although some low-level preliminary contacts were made between the FMLN and the UN. In one of these meetings, the FMLN assured the UN that they would respect the presence of any UN observers in El Salvador to verify security matters, but that this presence "should be the result of an overall negotiation process, including not only military aspects but also conditions for democratization."[31]

Renewed talks between the two sides took place again in Mexico City in September and October 1989. The FMLN opened with a peace proposal that would integrate the guerrillas into the country's legal political processes after a cease-fire that would start before 15 November 1989. Although the FMLN proposal spoke of entering the political system as a party, it made no mention of surrendering its weapons, which had been a basic government demand. The two parties agreed to continue the talks on a regular basis with the presence of international observers from the UN and the OAS (the government had previously opposed this), as well as mediation by the Catholic Church. The basic FMLN proposal, considered to be the most flexible yet, would recognize the legitimacy of the Cristiani government, but the administration would be required to make basic reforms in the constitution and electoral laws, as well as reduce the size of the armed forces. Observers noted that both sides were under pressure from many factions in war-weary El Salvador, as well as internationally, to find a peaceful solution to the 10-year-old civil war. The Mexico City talks included suggestions (which were discussed without controversy) that regional and international observer teams monitor human rights and cease-fire agreements, and this discussion was the genesis of the UN human rights observer and verification team, ONUSAL, that eventually was set up in mid-1991.

The second series of talks, held in San José, yielded no concrete results other than an agreement to meet again in Caracas in a month. The talks were suspended, however, when the FMLN launched a major offensive in November 1989, which was seen as a major gamble to the point that some called it the FMLN's "Tet offensive." The Vietnam Tet analogy suggested that the guerrillas might lose militarily, but achieve political objectives and shift U.S. public support, which might lead to their ultimate victory.

During the FMLN offensive, the Conference of American Armies was holding its biannual meeting in Guatemala and issued a communiqué in support of the El Salvador government. One observer called this "one small token of the internationalization of the nine-year Salvadoran civil war,"[32] and went on to note border violations, including Honduran crossings into El Salvador, and a charge that 126 elite Guatemalan troops (*Kaibiles*) had intervened in the Salvadoran conflict. The specter of a CONDECA-type intervention was thus raised in the Salvadoran context, a fact that was reflected in the FMLN's demand that the Salvadoran government should withdraw from both CONDECA and the Rio Treaty.

The international aspects of the FMLN offensive included accusations from the United States that the Soviets were still supporting the guerrillas with weapons, and that AK-47 rifles captured from the FMLN were previously used by Cuban troops in Angola. On 25 November a small unmarked Cessna aircraft carrying 24 Soviet-bloc SA-7 antiaircraft missiles and other weapons crashed in eastern El Salvador. Salvadoran government officials said the weapons, which could represent a major escalation of the war, were coming from Nicaragua and were intended for the FMLN. A second aircraft also carrying weapons was reported to have landed, unloaded, and been burned. The FMLN confirmed that it had surface-to-air missiles, but said it would refrain from using them in the current offensive if the Salvadoran Air Force stopped its bombing. Nicaraguan Colonel Ricardo Wheelock, the Sandinista intelligence chief, denied that the missiles came through Nicaragua with the Nicaraguan government's knowledge, "because that would be a violation of the Central American peace accord."[33] He accused the United States of creating a dangerous situation with regard to missiles by giving the Contras 300 Red Eye antiaircraft missiles. As a result of these incidents, El Salvador formally cut its diplomatic ties with Nicaragua, and President

Cristiani said he would not attend a regional summit scheduled for early December in Managua.

The FMLN offensive and the Salvadoran government's reaction to it were beginning to threaten the Central American peace process. Compounding the situation were the strong indications of stepped-up Sandinista support for the FMLN guerrillas, which, if proved, would in all likelihood lead to a collapse of the Esquipulas accords. In Washington there was anger that the cutoff of aid to the Contras had seemingly led the Sandinistas to increase their support of revolution in Central America. In New York UN officials were expressing second thoughts about the wisdom of launching a peacekeeping mission and questioned the purpose and security of such an operation. As a Costa Rican official put it: "The whole peace plan is on the threshold of being blown to pieces."[34]

MONITORING THE FEBRUARY 1990
NICARAGUAN ELECTIONS

The request that an international organization monitor the February 1990 Nicaraguan election was made in mid-March 1989 when Foreign Minister Miguel d'Escoto asked the United Nations to provide observers.[35] The decision to create ONUVEN followed a study by a joint UN-OAS commission that concluded that Nicaragua's plans for the elections were basically democratic and within acceptable norms.

The 4 August agreement between the Sandinistas and the opposition coalition provided the ground rules for the election. Coming as it did just before the Tela meeting, the agreement helped pave the way for Tela's equally sweeping provisions for the dismantling of the Contras. The election monitors started their "invasion" of Nicaragua in early October. This was the first time the UN had ever supervised elections in this manner; prior requests for UN election monitoring had all been in partitioned territories or were in countries becoming independent, such as Zimbabwe. There was another unique feature: the head of the UN election monitoring mission, Elliott Richardson, was from the United States. A senior UN official noted: "We've done something that is almost unheard of, which is to appoint an American to oversee elections in a country with which the United States is virtually at war."[36]

ONUCA AND CIAV PRELIMINARIES, LATE 1989

Despite misgivings stemming from the FMLN offensive in El Salvador, the pre-ONUCA reconnaissance team was sent to Central America from 3 to 23 September, headed by Brigadier General Péricles Ferreira Gomes of Brazil, Chief Military Observer of the UN Angola Verification Mission

(UNAVEM). The full ONUCA reconnaissance team was 18 members strong and included members from Spain, Germany, Canada, Fiji, Venezuela, Peru, and Sweden. The key member of the team was Canadian Colonel Don Ethell, who had been involved in the planning for ONUCA (and Canadian participation in it) from the beginning.

The ONUCA advance team encountered some problems in getting helicopter support in Honduras and was not able to do a full air reconnaissance of the Honduran-Salvadoran border, although a partial land reconnaissance was accomplished. Shortly before leaving Honduras for Nicaragua, three members of the ONUCA team expressed surprise at how little cooperation they had received in Guatemala and Honduras.[37]

The information accumulated by the reconnaissance team formed the basis for the UN Secretary-General's reports to the General Assembly on 9 October 1989 and to the Security Council on 11 October. This latter extensive document contains the detailed operational concept of ONUCA described in the next chapter. It incorporated the recommendations of General Ferreira Gomes to the effect that ONUCA should include 260 military observers; aircrew support personnel (about 150); naval support (about 50 personnel); about 104 UN staff; 14 medical personnel; and about 82 locally recruited civilians. The operation was estimated to cost about $41 million for the first six months.

Meanwhile, the UN and CIAV-OAS personnel were having their first contacts with the Contras in Honduras, with some unpleasant results. The Contras were not at all willing to accept directions that they disband, and instead stressed that the Tela agreements spoke of voluntary demobilization. In any case, many of them argued, they had never signed the Tela agreements and did not feel bound by them. The CIAV personnel in Central America had a different perspective, arguing that if the Contras did not want to demobilize voluntarily they would be demobilized by force.[38] CIAV also delivered several documents from the Sandinistas to the Contras outlining the plan to receive them back into Nicaragua and promising that the ex-Contras would be free from repression and could be politically active. The plan involved setting up reception centers, supervised by UN and OAS officials of CIAV, to process the Contras and provide them with documentation, including passports.

In October UN representative Francesc Vendrell traveled to the main Contra base in Yamales, Honduras, and in a blunt meeting told the Contras that they should disband because they were objects of "an anachronistic policy that has been abandoned by the country that helped you" (the United States). He also told Contra leaders, including Bermúdez, and reporters that the Contras would not be reactivated, and that the Contra presence in Honduras had ceased to have any raison d'être. The Contras were reported to be stunned by his remarks. News of Vendrell's undiplomatic approach quickly made the U.S. newspapers and reached the policymakers in Washington, where the Bush administration feared that it would lead to a firestorm of protest from conservative Republicans, who had argued all along that the UN was out to destroy the Contras. In a few days, strong U.S. pressure persuaded the UN Secretary-General to repudiate Vendrell's remarks, and Pérez de Cuéllar said that Vendrell's words were part of an impromptu statement that did not reflect his own views. A UN spokesperson said that "the comments have given rise to misunderstandings concerning the rigorously impartial position of the United Nations. This, the Secretary-General regrets."[39]

Despite these strains, the stage was now set for the creation and deployment of ONUCA and CIAV; peace verification had indeed finally come to Arias/Esquipulas.

NOTES

1. Paris, AFP, 3 September 1988, in Foreign Broadcast Information Service (FBIS), 6 September 1988, 15.
2. *Diario las Américas,* Miami, 10 September 1988; Panama, ACAN, 8 October 1988, in FBIS, 12 October 1988, 1; interview with Contra leader Enrique Bermúdez, Miami, January 1989.
3. *New York Times,* 5 October 1988, A-8; Tegucigalpa, Televisora Hondureña, 8 October 1988, in FBIS, 11 October 1988, 20.
4. *Tiempo,* San Pedro Sula, 14 October 1988, in FBIS, 18 October 1988, 16.
5. UN General Assembly Resolution A/RES/43/24, 12 January 1989. See also *UN Chronicle,* March 1989, 65.
6. *Times of the Americas,* 14 December 1988, 4; Rojas Aravena, *Política Exterior,* 176.
7. *El Día,* Mexico, 30 November 1988, in FBIS, 7 December 1988.
8. *Washington Times,* 9 December 1988, 7.
9. "Central America: Send in the UN?" *The Interdependent,* Spring 1989, 2.
10. Panama ACAN, 14 January 1989, in FBIS, 17 January 1989; Managua, Radio Sandino, 9 February 1989, in FBIS, 10 February 1989.
11. *Toronto Globe and Mail,* 16 February 1989; communications with a member of the IPA involved in the February UN discussions, 10 February 1989; discussions with Canadian Ambassador Richard Gorham and Member of Parliament John Bosley, Ottawa, May 1989. For an extensive Canadian analysis of this process, see North, *Between Peace and War,* especially 164–165, 190–192, 228.
12. *Toronto Globe and Mail,* 10 April 1980, A2.
13. For text of the agreement, see *New York Times,* 16 February 1989, A-6. See also *Central America Report,* 17 February 1989, 49–51; and Herrera Cáceres, *Democracia,* 39–45.
14. *West Watch,* February/March 1989, 2.
15. Tinoco, *Conflicto y Paz,* 73–76.
16. Managua, Radio Sandino, 11 March 1989, in FBIS, 13 March 1989.
17. *Washington Post,* 18 March 1989, A24.

18. *Washington Post*, 15 March 1989, A26.

19. *Washington Post*, 14 April 1989, A1, A20.

20. *Times of the Americas*, 19 April 1989, 10.

21. *Washington Post*, 4 November 1989, A1.

22. For texts and analysis of Tela, see *Barricada Internacional*, 19 August 1989, 11–17; *Central American Report*, 11 August 1989, 241–242; Rojas Aravena, *El Proceso de Esquipulas*, especially 218–231; Flores Pinel, "De Esquipulas a Tela," 809–832; and Tinoco, *Conflicto y Paz*, 83–91, 104–106.

23. *El Espectador*, Bogotá, 7 August 1989, 9A.

24. *Barricada Internacional*, 2 September 1989, 7; Council on Hemispheric Affairs (COHA), *Washington Report*, 13 September 1989.

25. *Washington Post*, 9 August 1989, 1.

26. *El Tiempo*, Bogotá, 8 August 1989, 10A.

27. *El Tiempo*, Bogotá, 8 and 9 August 1989.

28. FBIS, 14 August 1989, 1; 18 August 1989, 8–9.

29. *New York Times*, 27 August 1989, 15.

30. *Washington Post*, 24 January 1989, A15. For text of the FMLN offer, see *Times of the Americas*, 8 February 1989.

31. Managua AFP, 11 May 1989, in FBIS, 12 May 1989, 17.

32. COHA, *Washington Report*, 20 December 1989.

33. *Washington Post*, 1 December 1989, A45.

34. *Barricada Internacional*, 9 December 1989, 3; *Central America Report*, 1 December 1989, 373–376; *Los Angeles Times*, 27 November 1989, 1; *New York Times*, 3 December 1989.

35. Although the monitoring of elections is not one of the major topics of this book, it will be dealt with here to provide the context for the actions of ONUCA and CIAV in this same period of late 1989 and early 1990. There are several accounts of the 1990 election, such as the Latin American Studies Association's, *Electoral Democracy under International Pressure (the 1990 Nicaraguan Election)* (Pittsburgh: LASA, 1990). The UN has also published an extensive report (Document A/44/642, 17 October 1989).

36. *New York Times*, 2 October 1989, 8.

37. Panama ACAN, 13 September 1989, in FBIS, 18 September 1989, 17–18.

38. Interview with Francesc Vendrell, 6 May 1989; *Heraldo*, Tegucigalpa, 14 October 1989; *Barricada Internacional*, 28 October 1989, 3; *Excelsior*, Mexico, 17 September 1989, 2A.

39. *Washington Post*, 14 October 1989, A1; 17 October 1989, A7.

PART 4
IMPLEMENTING THE PEACE PLAN, 1989–1991

6

ONUCA AND CIAV IN THE EARLY IMPLEMENTATION PHASE, 1989–1990

THE CREATION OF ONUCA, 7 NOVEMBER 1989

The United Nations Security Council formally created ONUCA when it approved Resolution 644 on 7 November 1989 with a composition and mission as described by the Secretary-General in his 11 October report.[1] The fielding of ONUCA ("D-Day") was to occur one month later on 7 December. The 625-person group, located in 33 regional bases, would be responsible for halting cross-border infiltration and cutting support for rebels in the region. It would consist of 260 unarmed military observers along with 365 technicians (115 aircrew and support; 50 naval crew and support; 14 medical staff; 104 UN international staff; and 82 locally hired civilians). The cost was placed at $41 million for the first six months, of which $18.2 million was start-up costs.

ONUCA's original mandate (which was later to be expanded twice, in December 1989 and March 1990) was in two parts: (1) Verify the cessation of aid to irregular forces and insurrectional movements; (2) Verify the nonutilization of any state's territory to commit aggression against another state.

In his 11 October report, Pérez de Cuéllar outlined the operational concept and identified some of the problems faced by ONUCA, relying heavily on the work of his preliminary reconnaissance team. He noted the special political and topographic features of the Central American conflict situation that would limit the effectiveness of static observation posts, such as were commonly used by the UN in Middle East peacekeeping. In contrast, ONUCA would have mobile teams of at least seven members each; they would have home bases but would accomplish their missions through frequent patrols by four-wheel-drive vehicles, helicopters (a total of 12 was mentioned), and fast patrol boats (in the Gulf of Fonseca and a few other coastal and riverine areas). In addition to the helicopters, there would be light aircraft for administrative transport of the Chief Military Observer (CMO) and team members between their headquarters in Tegucigalpa and the other principal cities of Central America.

The mobile teams would have full freedom of movement and access, and would be able to make spot checks on their own and respond to specific complaints or reports of violations. As with standard UN peacekeeping operations, the chain of command flowed from the Security Council (which established the operation by its mandate), through the Secretary-General, to the Chief Military Observer in the field. On 21 November the Security Council approved the naming of Spanish paratrooper Major General Agustín Quesada Gómez as CMO. The members of the ONUCA team would come from a variety of nations that were being contacted by the Secretary-General even as the mandate was approved; two weeks later UN officials were holding meetings with representatives from the contingents in order to launch Phase I, the initial deployment on 7 December.

ONUCA's initial mandate, composition, and operational concept reflected UN reluctance to get involved in internal conflicts.[2] It was to be a verification and peace-observing mission, not a full-scale peacekeeping interposition mission, and certainly not a peace-enforcement mission, although as events unfolded there were brief periods when Contra reluctance to disband threatened to convert ONUCA's role to one of enforcement. The scope of the operation was briefly moved up the conflict resolution spectrum (see Figure 1.1) for the period of Contra demobilization, but the UN consistently defined ONUCA's mission as one of verification. This definition of ONUCA was also a reflection of the Latin American resistance to peacekeeping noted in Chapter 1 and the preference for smaller observation missions with the lowest possible military profile. The Canadians, who were used to larger peacekeeping missions, frequently called ONUCA a minimalist operation, noting that it would have difficulty verifying Esquipulas in the large geographic area assigned to it.[3]

THE CORONADO SUMMIT
AND THE EXPANDED ONUCA MANDATE

In December 1989 the five Central American presidents met at San Isidro de Coronado, Costa Rica, for an intense and confrontational encounter, with Azcona of Honduras walking out at one point because of basic disagreements with Ortega of Nicaragua. The Costa Rican government had not given visas to the FMLN representatives, so their position was presented by Ortega, and this tended to isolate him from his four colleagues. The Coronado Declaration was an important document. It asked that ONUCA's mandate be expanded to include supervising the demobilization of irregular forces. One source remarked that "the measures could also set the stage for the forcible disarming and relocation of the Contra fighters by the United Nations."[4] This meeting gave ONUCA considerably more responsibility while reaffirming the humanitarian and aid distribution role of CIAV. ONUCA's role, in effect, was broadened from peace observing with unarmed observers to peacekeeping, demobilization verification, and conceivably peace enforcement if the Contras resisted. Considering the numbers of Contras, and the length of the Honduran-Nicaraguan border (420 miles), this had the potential of becoming a major operation for the UN.

Coronado established strong parallels between the Contras in Nicaragua and the FMLN in El Salvador, which had not been the case at previous Central American summits. As a result, one important aspect of the declaration was the hard line taken on the FMLN, which was agreed to by Ortega when he signed the declaration. In effect, the five Central American presidents called on the FMLN to halt their offensive and join the Salvadoran government in talks aimed at achieving their demobilization as a fighting force. The FMLN reacted angrily to this suggestion, since it had never accepted the idea of symmetry between its insurrection and that of the Contras.[5] The instruments suggested for demobilizing the FMLN would include the CIAV and ONUCA, which was asked to accelerate its activities to prevent arms deliveries to both the Contras and the FMLN.

The UN could anticipate severe problems in carrying out this expanded mission, especially because both the Contras and the FMLN guerrillas could be expected to oppose it. Thus, instead of the original authorization of 625 personnel for ONUCA, it might be necessary to have as many as 2,000 with a correspondingly higher budget. It might also be difficult to find countries willing to participate in such a risky UN undertaking.

Coronado also reflected the reality that the UN, and the five Central American presidents, represented nation-states, not insurgencies. Thus, they had a vested interest in stability, and in limiting the strength of non-national entities such as the Contras and the FMLN. To this extent symmetry between the two armed guerrilla movements *was* valid, and the fears of both the Contras and the FMLN that UN peacekeeping was a threat were indeed justified.

THE INITIAL DEPLOYMENT
OF ONUCA, DECEMBER 1989

ONUCA's deployment began with the December arrival of the advance party in Tegucigalpa and the setting up of a provisional ONUCA headquarters, under very crowded conditions, in the offices of the United Nations Development Program (UNDP) in Honduras.[6] The first ONUCA troops arrived in Tegucigalpa a few days later, including officers from Spain,

Venezuela, Ireland, and Canada, and were headed by General Agustín Quesada Gómez of Spain, the CMO. Liaison offices were established in Nicaragua, Guatemala, Costa Rica, and Honduras, and the advance team visited El Salvador while the CMO paid courtesy calls on key military and civilian authorities. The vehicles began to arrive, as did Germany's nonmilitary contribution of a civilian medical team and a Dornier 228-200 light aircraft.

For different reasons, ONUCA's operations in El Salvador, Guatemala, and Costa Rica were slower to start up and were of a lesser magnitude than those in Nicaragua and Honduras, where the Contra demobilization operation would take place. During the key phases of demobilization (called Operation Home Run by ONUCA), there was a pattern of stripping the ONUCA groups in El Salvador, Costa Rica, and Guatemala of their personnel and moving them to where they were critically needed in Honduras and Nicaragua. The ONUCA observer group in El Salvador (OGELS—Observer Group in El Salvador) was severely restricted as to what its members could do and where they could go, for political and security reasons. The government was reluctant to have them go into combat areas or regions controlled by the FMLN, while the FMLN itself was still unenthusiastic about ONUCA, despite a meeting between General Quesada and senior FMLN representatives in Mexico in late January 1990.

In Costa Rica ONUCA's presence was mainly symbolic, except for some involvement in Contra demobilization along the Costa Rican–Nicaraguan border. According to ONUCA's unofficial history, the *ONUCA Observer,* they were well received in Costa Rica, even though there were some problems adapting to conditions in the countryside. The *ONUCA Observer* also noted some language problems, including one instance in which a Costa Rican *Tico* had problems understanding the Castilian of one of the Spanish Military Observers (UNMOs) and asked a non-Spanish UNMO to "translate what the Spanish gringo was saying."[7]

Despite problems, ONUCA's Phase II began on schedule with the establishment of all the national capital Verification Centers (VCs), except in El Salvador, and the arrival of contingents from Colombia, Venezuela, India, and Spain. By early January ONUCA had opened Verification Centers at Esquipulas, Managua, Nacaome-Choluteca, and Estelí (all in Nicaragua), and ONUCA officers had made their first inspection of the Nicaraguan–Costa Rican border. ONUCA's official 31 December 1989 monthly personnel status report showed 77 UNMOs, 3 medical team members, 3 Dornier pilots, 46 UN international staff, and 25 local employees. Despite the fact that it was the Secretary-General's stated policy to involve more women in peacekeeping and political missions,[8] the only women who appear in the *ONUCA Observer's* plentiful photographs were secretaries, medical personnel, and administrators. There were no women among the UNMOs, and the senior female UN staffer was the press officer.

The complexity of peacekeeping, and the thorough planning required for it, can be seen in the preparations by the Canadians for Operation Sultan, which was the code name for their national participation in ONUCA.[9] The Canadian commitment to ONUCA was for one year (six months for the helicopters) and consisted of 146 military personnel, including 36 observers, an aviation unit with eight CH-139 Jet Ranger light observation helicopters (84 aircrew, ground crew, and support staff), several ONUCA headquarters staff officers, and assorted communications and support elements. The helicopters were to be configured per the standard Canadian Forces checklist with some exceptions: UN aircraft markings, jungle survival kits, special communications equipment, distance measuring equipment, and infrared suppression kits. The latter were a wise precaution because they provided some protection against the heat-seeking surface-to-air missiles that the FMLN guerrillas and the Contras were believed to have. Medical precautions were presented in great detail, including an impressive number of shots and warnings about sexually transmitted diseases (with suggestions for safe sex), drug abuse, and alcohol consumption (which was "medically discouraged").

CIAV, ONUCA, AND THE
INITIAL REPATRIATION OF CONTRAS

CIAV was created as a joint approach to repatriating the Contras by the Secretaries-General of the UN and the OAS on 25 August 1989 in support of the Esquipulas II peace plan. It was, in effect, the replacement for the old CIVS, although its tasks were much broader. Its mandate was to assist in the voluntary demobilization, repatriation, or resettlement in Nicaragua and third countries of the Nicaraguan Resistance (the Contras), as well as to assist in the voluntary demobilization of all persons involved in armed actions in all countries of the region. UN involvement in CIAV was relatively short (from late 1989 through mid-1990), while the OAS participated in CIAV from the beginning and was still deeply involved as of late 1991. In part, this situation was due to the UN's emphasis on ONUCA, but it also reflected a geographic division of labor. The UN was assigned repatriation responsibilities in Honduras (where it was active only in late 1989 and early 1990), Costa Rica (where there were few Contras), and El Salvador (where there were practically none, and where the FMLN was having no part in any voluntary repatriation). CIAV-OAS, on the other hand, was assigned geographic responsibilities for Nicaragua, which meant that it was responsible for every Contra and Contra family member when they crossed the border into Nicaragua, and continued to be responsible for the support of most of them through 1991.

Initially, the UN and OAS components of CIAV worked closely together. But they soon found that they had different procedures, approaches, and accounting systems and began to operate independently,[10] although there was always contact between them, especially in the capital cities. In 1991, as CIAV-OAS began to get more deeply involved in internal Nicaraguan political matters, the UN half of CIAV in effect disappeared (its residual responsibilities were turned over to the UN High Commissioner for Refugees—UNHCR), and CIAV became wholly identified with the OAS.

One of the unintended and unfortunate aspects of CIAV-OAS in Nicaragua stemmed from the high Argentine profile of its staff: the head of CIAV was an Argentine OAS official, and many of the personnel CIAV hired for key positions in Nicaragua were also Argentine.[11] The high Argentine profile was unfortunate because it was Argentine military and intelligence officers who had first trained the Contras in 1980 and 1981, and memories of this remained fresh among many Sandinistas. As one put it: "Alpha and omega and thanatos [Greek letters symbolizing the beginning, the end, and death]: it is appropriate that it be Argentines who are handling the end and the death of the Contras in 1991, because it was Argentines who helped create them at the beginning in 1981."[12] The comment was basically an unfair one because the Argentines involved in 1981 (military and intelligence officials with experience fighting their country's "dirty war") were very different from the civilian international functionaries and short-term hired professionals (mainly academics and bureaucrats) involved in CIAV-OAS in 1990–1991. Nevertheless, the psychological connection was made and the perception created.

Another unfortunate negative feature of CIAV, at least in the minds of Sandinistas in Nicaragua, was that it was to some extent an instrument of the U.S. government. As one Sandinista jokingly put it: "the CIAV should simply drop the last letter [v] in their name and then we would know who they really are."[13] This perception was based on the reality that CIAV's funds for repatriating the Contras, and for providing them with humanitarian assistance, were U.S. public monies flowing through the U.S. Agency for International Development. From the beginning, the source and amount of these funds were surrounded by controversy. On 5 January 1990 the Bush administration offered $3 million to the CIAV to help relocate the Contras with the stipulation that the relocation must be voluntary and carried out under safe and democratic conditions. The offer appeared to be a significant gesture to the Central American presidents, but it fell far short of their call (at Coronado) that all the $67 million earmarked for Contra aid be turned over to CIAV and the joint UN-OAS repatriation operation. A few days later President Daniel Ortega said the U.S. offer of $3 million for CIAV was insufficient and violated the Central American peace accords signed by the five presidents.[14] The United States eventually increased the offer substantially, but CIAV funding remained an area of some friction between the United States, the OAS, and Nicaragua. The Contras, meanwhile, were not happy over comments from U.S. officials that aid to them would end after the February 1990 elections.

The first repatriations started in early January 1990 when Luis Fley González (Comandante Johnson) and nine other Contras were repatriated through CIAV. However, since CIAV and ONUCA were not yet fully organized, the repatriation was handled with the help of officials from UNHRC and the OAS who were permanently stationed in Central America. Honduran President Azcona emphasized that his government had no responsibility for demobilizing the Contras, and his Army commander, General Humberto Regalado Hernández, commented that Honduran troops would not get involved in the demobilization. The number of Contras involved was embarrassingly small, prompting Honduran Foreign Minister Carlos López Contreras to note that if all countries involved did not support the repatriation process, the prestige of the international organizations involved could be damaged.[15]

The issue of repatriation was creating a crisis within Contra ranks. In late January Contra leader Enrique Bermúdez was ousted as the titular head of the Nicaraguan Resistance after a meeting of Contra commanders at their camp in Yamales, Honduras. He was replaced as the Contra field commander by Israel Galeano (Comandante Franklin), who had been in day-to-day control of the estimated 12,000 Contras for more than a year while Bermúdez operated out of Miami and Tegucigalpa. Galeano represented a different kind of leader, much more representative of the campesinos who made up the bulk of the Contra's ranks and less responsive to the wishes of U.S. policymakers in Washington.

EL SALVADOR: PEACE TALKS, EARLY AND MID-1990

In January 1990 the FMLN agreed to mediation by the UN in its talks with the Salvadoran government. UN involvement was seen as a possibly key breakthrough in the inconclusive talks, begun in 1984, in which each side had presented inflexible positions. The optimism was supported by a new FMLN position statement that there could be peace in El Salvador if the United States stopped its aid to the Cristiani government. President Cristiani traveled to the United States in February, and while there he visited the UN to discuss the UN-mediated talks. This too was something of a breakthrough because the Salvadoran government in the past had resisted the idea of UN involvement inasmuch as this would internationalize the conflict.

In March UN special envoy Alvaro de Soto met with Salvadoran President Cristiani in San Salvador and indicated that the UN role in the coming FMLN-government dialogue would not be mediation but rather the more limited function of lending its good offices. He also discussed the need to increase the size of ONUCA in order to handle the demobilization of irregular troops, and the need for patrol craft to cover the Gulf of Fonseca. President Cristiani also requested the establishment of UN posts along the "pockets" of the still undefined border between El Salvador and Honduras, which was an irritating remnant of the 1969 war between the two countries.[16] This was an indication that the Salvadorans were now looking to the UN more and more for solutions that in the past would have come from the OAS as the regional international organization. It seemed as though the presence of ONUCA's OGELS was leading the government, and perhaps Salvadorans in general, to consider the possibility of an increasing role for the UN in solving regional problems.

THE NICARAGUAN ELECTIONS AND THE TRANSITION

The February 1990 Nicaraguan elections were without a doubt the most closely observed in Latin America's history. There were over 2,000 election observers, including Baena Soares of the OAS with 430 personnel, Elliot Richardson of ONUVEN with 240 observers, and numerous other private groups, such as those led by former President Jimmy Carter and the Latin American Studies Association. The election results were a surprise to many when Violeta Chamorro of the National Opposition Union (UNO) coalition defeated President Daniel Ortega of the incumbent Sandinista government by a margin of 55.2 percent to 40.8 percent.

The Contras were jubilant over the results, which they attributed to their armed struggle against the Sandinistas, and said that the need for conflict no longer existed. However, some of their leaders stated that they would not be disbanding until they received assurances that the Sandinistas were giving up control of the military and security apparatus. The U.S. Contra aid authorization ($50 million in nonlethal supplies and services) ran out with the elections on 25 February, but the U.S. Agency for International Development received last-minute authorization to continue aid through April, which would continue to be channeled through international organizations (mainly the OAS).[17] In her first postelection national radio address, Violeta Chamorro called for the Contras to disband, reflecting an earlier comment by Daniel Ortega that such a demobilization would be a necessary condition for the peaceful transition to the new government. Ortega appealed to Bush to "cut off the Contras' oxygen" and transfer any remaining Contra funds to CIAV for demobilization, adding that the day would come when the Sandinistas would return to power; "in the meantime, we will continue governing from below."[18]

As they were recovering from the shock of their defeat, the Sandinistas received a second surprise when they realized that there had been large numbers of desertions from the Ejército Popular Sandinista (EPS) and other branches of the military during the election. Many of the draftees who went home to vote never returned, frequently with the approval of their commanders. An estimated 40,000 of the military's 70,000 troops were draftees with a questionable commitment to the Sandinista political cause. The Sandinistas were also dismayed at their poor electoral showing in garrisons and military towns. In early March it appeared that Violeta Chamorro was backing away from her original plan to abolish the army, and would instead seek to gradually reduce its size from the estimated 65,000 active-duty troops to more traditional Central American levels. The focus would also be on the political independence of the restructured force. Agustín Joaquín Anaya, a senior member of Chamorro's UNO party, said that the object would be the depoliticization of the military and the demilitarization of politics. Responding, President Ortega warned of national war if the Chamorro government tried to replace the leadership of the Sandinista Army with members of the Resistance or former members of the Somoza National Guard.[19]

A third shock came to the Sandinistas when it appeared that Cuban-Soviet assistance, including substantial amounts of military equipment and advisors, would be cut off soon. In April, making virtue out of necessity, Defense Minister General Humberto Ortega referred to the demilitarization provisions of Contadora and said that "if peace is achieved in Nicaragua, we could immediately begin reducing the number of forces that have been mobilized to defend our sovereignty—several tens of thousands of forces."[20] Events were setting the stage for Chamorro's proposals for broad Central American demilitarization and the creation of a zone of peace.

DEMOBILIZATION AND
NEW EXPANSION OF ONUCA'S MANDATE

In the weeks after the 25 February election, an armed standoff developed between the Sandinistas, weakened by their electoral loss and the numerous desertions from the EPS, and the Contras in Honduras and Nicaragua, who were weakened by the diminishing support from the United States and pressure from just about everybody to demobilize and return to peaceful pursuits in Nicaragua. One source described the situation as resembling two tired boxers who were each wary of dropping their guard lest the other attack.[21] There was a surface resemblance between this description and Alford's confidence-building metaphor of the two swordsmen, but the key difference was the questionable sincerity of their peaceful motives as they each faced the endgame of the long Contra war.

There was also the specter of renewed civil war. In early March there were disturbing reports that Sandinista militants, embittered over the electoral loss, were distributing arms to supporters in preparation for resisting any drastic measures taken by the new Chamorro administration. Among their slogans were: "The FSLN [Frente Sandinista de Liberación Nacional] will govern from below," and "Violeta can keep the throne, the Front will keep the lead." On the Contra side there was confusion, and mixed messages. Under intense U.S. pressure, many of the Contra leaders in Honduras had agreed to lay down their weapons and return to Nicaragua in return for economic and security guarantees. But there were contradictions, including the call by a Contra leader to prepare for civil war. One explanation was that the change in Contra leadership caused the confusion. Most of the older, educated, English-speaking leaders of the Contras, such as Enrique Bermúdez, who were in close touch with the CIA had left for Miami or Nicaragua, and the field leadership of the Contras was now in the hands of poorly educated and traditionally antigovernment peasants. One of these newly emerging leaders, Comandante Franklin, said that he was thankful for past U.S. aid, but was deeply hurt by pressure to demobilize before Chamorro's inauguration.

The Contras had good reason to suspect abandonment by the United States. The Chamorro electoral victory and the presence of UN and OAS peacekeepers were allowing the United States to back away from earlier commitments to the cause of the Nicaraguan Resistance. Three days after the election, in testimony before a Senate committee, Secretary of State Baker said that the Contra war was over and they would soon be laying down their arms. This was the first time a Bush administration official had publicly said that the United States expected the Contras to disarm. He also warned that a standoff over whether the Contras or the Sandinistas should step aside first could undermine the peaceful transfer of power to Chamorro. He added that with the support and goodwill of the international community, the OAS, and the UN, the problem could be resolved. A few days later, U.S. Special Envoy Harry Shlaudeman and U.S. Ambassador to Honduras Cresencio Arcos traveled to the Contra base at Yamales to meet with Contra leaders to give them the same message. This was repeated two weeks later in what was in effect an ultimatum to the Contras that they must lay down their weapons and demobilize before they would receive any U.S. funding or assistance for their transition to civilian life. The administration was becoming increasingly concerned over the stalemate and the delays in the demobilization process.

Adding to the concern were indications that Contras were slipping back across the border into Nicaragua on their own, with weapons, to avoid being trapped in their bases in Honduras. The number of returning Contras was estimated at between 3,500 and 5,000 in mid-March 1990.[22] Some Contra leaders were now saying that their troops in Nicaraguan enclaves would remain armed for months after Chamorro's inauguration, and that only the troops staying in Honduras (a small number) would turn in weapons. Most of the Contras who remained in the Honduran "ghost town" camps were the sick and wounded. In late March armed clashes were reported between Sandinista forces and groups of Contras returning from Honduras.

The OAS's response was to request more funds from the United States, specifically the sum of $139 million for Contra resettlement of 8,000 guerrillas and 12,000 dependents. These funds would be used by the OAS to carry out its responsibilities for transporting the Contras from Honduras, resettling them, and providing them with educational and employment training programs. The UN representatives, for their part, were taking a tougher line even as they offered assurances to the Contras. ONUCA head General Quesada warned the Contras "that they will be harmed if they insist on rejecting their repatriation."[23] Quesada was reacting to Contra leaders' statements that they would not demobilize until the size of the Sandinista Army was reduced and control was established by the Chamorro government. Quesada also said that the Contras should accept demobilization because if they did so CIAV would assist them with international support for repatriation, relocation, and demobilization within the peaceful conditions that they wanted. In March ONUCA began setting up observation posts near the Contra zones in Honduras and established an operations center in Danli, the town closest to the large Contra camp at Yamales.

The hard line being taken on the Contras was undermined by the reality that 260 unarmed UN observers were not going to force the Contras to do anything. Thus, setting aside their historical aversion to peace enforcement, the UN Security Council decided to expand ONUCA's mandate and temporarily give it some combat power: a battalion of paratroopers with their basic weapons. On 15 March the UN Secretary-General asked the Security Council, on an urgent basis, to expand ONUCA from its 260 observers and add 116 more for observation plus an armed infantry battalion of at least four rifle companies (about 800 troops) for Contra demobilization supervision. Venezuela, which already was providing observers to ONUCA, had agreed to provide this battalion. The cost for a limited period of two months would be about $7 to $9 million, not including helicopter support. Although the Secretary-General's report did not say that the demobilization would be forced, there was a clear implication that adding armed paratroopers to the unarmed UN military observers would be a powerful message to the reluctant Contras.

Venezuela's willingness to supply the infantry battalion stemmed from President Carlos Andrés Pérez's eagerness to play a major role in Central American pacification. Interviewed during his May trip to Honduras, Pérez praised the Central American peace process and noted that it was the Central Americans themselves who were doing it. Ignoring the fact that the Central Americans were getting considerable outside help and unsolicited advice, including Venezuelan, Pérez said: "We are definitely laying aside the absorbing paternalism that for so many years divided Latin American forces."[24] In late March the foreign minister announced that the Venezuelan peacekeeping contingent would consist of about 700 paratroopers from the Antonio Nicolás Briceño Battalion, stationed in Maracay, which had previously served with a UN peacekeeping mission in Namibia. There was some suggestion that paratroopers were chosen because of their reputation for physical and mental toughness, but the overriding reason appears to have been their recent UN peacekeeping experience.[25]

THE MONTELIMAR "FAREWELL" SUMMIT, APRIL 1990

The framework for concluding Contra demobilization under the expanded ONUCA mandate was established at the Montelimar "Farewell" Summit, so called because it was the last one for two key figures in the Esquipulas peace process: Presidents Ortega and Arias. (After Montelimar Guatemalan President Cerezo was the only remaining original member of the Central American peace process.) The main agreement at Montelimar was to set a 25 April 1990 deadline for Contra demobilization, and to ask the United States to channel all aid through CIAV and ONUCA. Contras already in Nicaragua would turn their weapons in to UN peacekeeping troops inside security zones, and the weapons would be destroyed on the spot. However, the UN troops were not in Nicaragua in the required numbers because the Venezuelan infantry battalion had not yet arrived, and the zones themselves had not been defined. Like many other deadlines for demobilizing the Contras, this 25 April one was not met either. The agreement also called on the parties in the Salvadoran and Guatemalan internal conflicts to speed up their peace talks and invited Panama to join the Central American peace process.

Article 9 of the Montelimar agreement called for a reactivation of the Esquipulas II Security Commission (see Figure 4.2), which would move forward on matters dealing with security, verification, control, and limitation of weapons.[26] This commission, made up of civilian and military personnel from the five nations, would meet in May to discuss arms reductions, force levels, and the international military presence in the region. As demonstrated in the following chapters, it laid important foundations for confidence-building measures and a possible zone of peace in Central America.

NOTES

1. For details of ONUCA, see the report of the Secretary-General, UN Document S/20895, 11 October 1989; and United Nations, *Blue Helmets*, 393–396.

2. Discussions with Francesc Vendrell, UN special assistant to the Secretary-General, Ottawa, May 1989.

3. North, *Between Peace and War in Central America*, 190; Joly, "ONUCA," 12–19.

4. *New York Times,* 13 December 1989, 1.

5. Discussion with Mario López, FMLN representative, Ottawa, May 1989.

6. For the detailed history of ONUCA's deployment, see United Nations, *Blue Helmets*; and *ONUCA Observer.*

7. *ONUCA Observer,* 16-19.

8. *ONUCA Observer,* 9-10.

9. Canadian Department of National Defence messages: DCDS 128, 13 December 1989, Subject: Operations Order—Operation Sultan (ONUCA); DGMPO 544, 6 December 1989; DCDS 134, 14 December 1989, Subject: Operations Order—Sultan Administrative Order. These documents were kindly provided by a Canadian colleague, who obtained them through Canadian Freedom of Information provisions.

10. Interview with Santiago Murray, chief of the CIAV-OAS, Managua, June 1991.

11. Personal observation, CIAV-OAS in Managua and other Nicaraguan cities, June 1991. See also the detailed list of CIAV officials and their nationalities in Dallanegra Pedraza, *Proceso de Desmovilización,* 5. Dallanegra Pedraza, who was one of the Argentines involved in the CIAV demobilization effort, also acknowledges the role of Argentine military officers in training the Contras (8).

12. Remark made during discussions with Sandinista officials in Estelí, Nicaragua, June 1991. For information on Argentina's role in the creation of the Contras, see Dickey, *With the Contras,* especially 89–91, 114–117, 123–124, 144–147; and "Sharing Know-how with the Contras," *NACLA Hemisphere Report,* July–August 1987, 25-26.

13. Remark made during discussions with Sandinista officials in Estelí, Nicaragua, June 1991.

14. Panama, ACAN, 8 January 1990, in Foreign Broadcast Information Service (FBIS), 9 January 1990, 32.

15. Tegucigalpa, Televisora Hondureña, 9 January 1990, in FBIS, 11 January 1990, 13.

16. *El Mundo,* San Salvador, 7 March 1990, in FBIS, 13 March 1990, 15.

17. *Washington Post,* 27 February 1990, 16, 17.

18. "A Gobernar Desde Abajo," *Barricada Internacional,* 10 March 1990, 3–4.

19. *New York Times,* 5 March 1990, 1.

20. FBIS, 4 April 1990, 17; Paris, AFP, 7 March 1990, in FBIS, 7 March 1990, 23.

21. *Washington Post,* 3 March 1990.

22. *Washington Post,* 17 March 1990, A30.

23. Tegucigalpa AFP, 28 February 1990, in FBIS, 28 February 1990, 17; and *ONUCA Observer,* 34–39.

24. Tegucigalpa, Televisora Hondureña, 12 May 1990, in FBIS, 1 June 1990.

25. Interview with ONUCA and CIAV personnel, Nicaragua, June 1991; *ONUCA Observer,* 64–68; Caracas, DPA, 23 March 1990, 55.

26. *Barricada Internacional,* 21 April 1990, 11.

7

CONTRA DEMOBILIZATION AND RESETTLEMENT, 1990

ONUCA'S VENEZUELAN BATTALION AND CONTRA DEMOBILIZATION

The first contingent of 170 armed Venezuelan soldiers arrived in Tegucigalpa, Honduras, on 11 April 1990 to begin disarming the Contras in what was designated Operation Home Run. In greeting the troops, General Quesada said: "Your mission is exclusively military. You will be in charge of verifying, providing protection for, and supervising the demobilization. . . . Nothing will happen with the combatant who does not want to demobilize. That will be his problem and that of his country, not of ONUCA or the Venezuelan battalion." The Venezuelans set up their headquarters at Los Trojes, a border village, and from there they moved to the Contra camp at Yamales, Honduras, to begin the demobilization process. They arrived wearing olive-green uniforms and brown paratrooper berets, which they replaced with blue UN berets; they carried Belgian-made FAL rifles, described as defensive weapons. The battalion's mission was called "critical because the ONUCA contingent in both countries so far has only performed administrative duties."[1]

But before the Venezuelans could start demobilizing Contras, the matter of the security zones inside Nicaragua for the Contras under ONUCA protection had to be agreed on by all concerned. The Contras had legitimate doubts about their safety inside Nicaragua, and there were differences of opinion as to what these zones meant, and if the Contras would be allowed to retain any weapons for their protection. The basic proposal involved five sites of between 500–600 square kilometers each. The Sandinista security forces would withdraw from the zones, which would each have an assembly area with an ONUCA headquarters where the Contras would gather. Contras were to surrender their weapons to ONUCA troops as they entered the area, so disarmament was to be automatic. Contras who turned in weapons and supplies would get a demobilization certificate from ONUCA. In describing the security zones, Sandinista Army Chief of Staff Major General Joaquín Cuadra said that the zones were strictly temporary and would last only as long as demobilization took place: "The Contras will enter these zones to be demobilized, not to set up camp."[2] However, some Contras (and their supporters in the United States) argued that these security zones should be converted into permanent settlement areas for the Contras with ONUCA security guarantees. This notion of permanent settlement areas was the basis for the Contra "poles of development" described later in the chapter.

A formal agreement between the Sandinista government, the Contras (represented by Oscar Sovalbarro—Comandante Rubén), and the incoming Chamorro administration was reached on 19 April. Under its provisions the Contras would start turning in their weapons on 25 April and finish by 10 June. The significance of this agreement was that this was the first time the Contras had committed themselves to a firm timetable, even though there were doubts and internal differences on its meaning. The agreement specified that the Sandinistas would withdraw 20 kilometers from the perimeters of the five security zones (two additional zones on the Atlantic coast were added later), that these zones would be under the control of ONUCA, and that there would be no military forces or weapons (except for those of ONUCA's Venezuelan battalion) inside them. Any Nicaraguan police inside the zones would be unarmed, and CIAV would be responsible for the distribution of humanitarian aid to the Contras and their families inside the zones.

The carefully prepared plans for demobilization were threatened by squabbling in Washington over funding. The OAS's Chief Administrative Officer Robert Sayre urgently requested the funds from USAID in early April, but a senior administration official said the funds were being held up due to sloppy planning and lack of coordination between the OAS and the UN, which were fighting over turf and over who should handle the moneys.[3] Some of the things the $138.8 million was to be spent on (for as many as 28,000 Contras and their families) included: 300 schools, 3,520 hammers and saws, 64,000 corrugated roofing panels, vaccinations for 15,000 children, and training for 300 technical instructors.[4]

But despite the delays, demobilization was acquiring a momentum of its own, stimulated by U.S., UN, international, and local pressures on the Contras, with the not-so-subtle reminder that the ONUCA presence was now backed up with combat power. For a few weeks in April, what had started out as UN peace observing, and had then become peacekeeping, was showing a disturbing potential for becoming peace enforcement.

The first Contras began demobilization on 16 April at Sirsitara, Honduras. About 260 Atlantic Coast Miskito Indians surrendered their weapons (169 rifles and 26 support weapons such as machine guns and

CONTRA DEMOBILIZATION & RESETTLEMENT

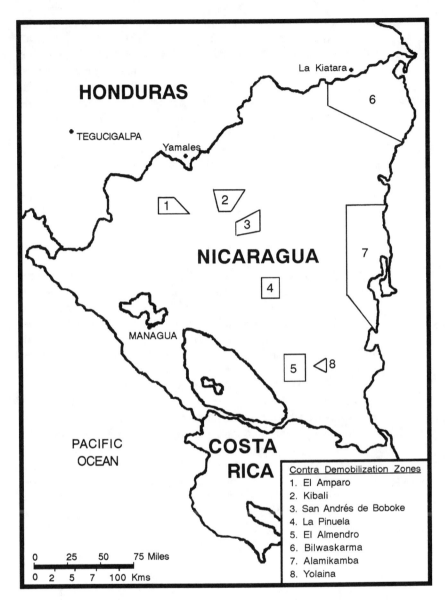

Map 7.1   Contra Demobilization Security Zones

mortars) to Venezuelan peacekeeping troops, who promptly cut them up with blowtorches or if ammunition blew it up. The first to turn in his AK-47 assault rifle was the leader of the Yatama Contra group, Serefino Bencie, who gave it to General Quesada, along with his web belt and compass. He then put his thumbprint on an ONUCA form and received the certificate that recognized his status as a demobilized rebel (see Figure 7.1). After noting the rifle's serial number, Venezuelan paratroopers cut it up into three pieces and threw them onto a quickly growing pile of scrap metal.

About 500 more Contras were demobilized by ONUCA on 18 April at the main Yamales camp in Honduras. These Contras were different from the Miskitos; they were mainly sick, wounded, and old, and the weapons they turned in were rusty and poorly maintained.[5] An amazing total of 365 different types of weapons and weapons parts were turned in, including pieces of rifle barrels and empty surface-to-air missile launch tubes. Three tubes were kept as "historic pieces" because they had tags on them explaining that they had shot down Sandinista helicopters.

Most of the able-bodied Contras from this main camp had apparently returned to Nicaragua. Ironically, this ceremony, which was supposed to highlight the end of the Contra war, only emphasized the problem of continuing conflict within Nicaragua if the main body of the Contras did not demobilize. When asked about this, ONUCA spokesperson Angelica Hunt said: "We're here to assist the process of demobilization. If they want to demobilize, we're here. We can't force a demobilization, because the operational word is 'voluntary.' We're not here to control, we are here to verify." A Tegucigalpa paper provided additional details, including the fact that most of the weapons were rusty junk, except for some heavy, Soviet-made machine guns, some mortars captured from the EPS, and 16 SA-7 surface-to-air missiles (SAMs). When General Quesada was asked if these obviously old and battered weapons were the kinds he had expected to find at Yamales, he replied: "One needs to be optimistic."[6]

In late April the UN Secretary-General wrote a frank report to the Security Council in which he detailed the scope and slow progress of the demobilization operation, as well as ONUCA's investigation of complaints by the governments of Nicaragua and El Salvador that violations of the peace treaty and subsequent agreements had occurred.[7] The Secretary-General also candidly revealed that while ONUCA was established with a limited mandate of verifying only one aspect of the Central America peace process (nonsupport of guerrillas in another country), he had always hoped that the mandate would be increased to cover additional peacekeeping functions. He noted that this had indeed happened with the two enlargements of the mandate, and expressed his expectation that he could soon come to the Security Council with a request to permit ONUCA to monitor peace in El Salvador. Pérez de Cuéllar concluded his report with a request that ONUCA's

Figure 7.1   ONUCA Contra Demobilization Certificate

UNITED NATIONS   NACIONES UNIDAS

Grupo de Observadores de las Naciones Unidas en Centroamérica
United Nations Observer Group in Central America

ONUCA

El General Jefe del Grupo de Observadores Militares
de las Naciones Unidas en Centroamérica,
Sr. D. Agustín Quesada Gómez,
en virtud del Plan Conjunto de Desmovilización,
Repatriación o Reubicación Voluntaria
de los Miembros de la Resistencia Nicaragüense,
acordado y firmado en Tela por los Presidentes
de Costa Rica, El Salvador, Guatemala, Honduras y Nicaragua
el 7 de agosto de 1989
y reafirmado por los cinco Presidentes
en la Declaración suscrita en San Isidro de Coronado
el 12 de diciembre de 1989,
y de conformidad con la resolución 650 (1990)
del Consejo de Seguridad de las Naciones Unidas,

CERTIFICA

Que el miembro de la resistencia nicaragüense

D._____,

el día _____ *en* _____,
se ha presentado ante el ONUCA para proceder a su desmovilización voluntaria,
y, con ese propósito, ha entregado el siguiente material:

1._____

2._____

3._____

De lo que doy fe en _____, *a* _____ *de 1990.*

_____
Agustín Quesada Gómez
General Jefe del ONUCA

Source: ONUCA Observer, 53.

six-month mandate be extended by six months. The Security Council concurred.

CONTRA DEMOBILIZATION
AFTER THE CHAMORRO INAUGURATION

President Violeta Chamorro was inaugurated on 25 April 1990. Among her first actions were proclaiming a sweeping amnesty, declaring herself defense minister (and pledging civilian control over the armed forces), ending the unpopular military draft, and ordering the army to establish a plan to cut back in size. In a controversial move that cost her support in the UNO coalition, she retained General Humberto Ortega as armed forces chief of staff. A number of Contras still in the mountains had said they would not disband if Ortega remained in the military, but this might have been the price Chamorro had to pay for Sandinista cooperation. The day after the inauguration, General Ortega announced plans to cut the army in half (from its 70,000 maximum) over the next 18 months. He also resigned from the Sandinista National Directorate and indicated that he would accept the new civilian government's authority. In practice, despite Chamorro's titular role as defense minister, it was General Ortega who ran the army, with little outside interference from the president, her cabinet, or the UNO-dominated legislature.

The Contras were still cautious after the inauguration, especially with General Ortega remaining at the head of the military. Demobilization, for this obvious reason, lagged. In some cases the Contras simply took over sections of the Nicaraguan countryside as if they were an occupying army and refused to surrender their weapons to ONUCA. An example of this was in the village of Las Colinas within one of the Contra security zones. The regular Sandinista military pulled out, and the local Sandinista militia reluctantly turned their remaining weapons over to an Irish ONUCA officer (Colonel Kenneth Kelly) as required under the agreement setting up the security zones. Shortly afterward, a 15-man Contra patrol walked into the village and took it over, ignoring the ONUCA military observer. The Contras were under the nominal control of Comandante Franklin, who claimed that he had 3,000 armed men in the area. ONUCA officials refused to intercede on the grounds that their only mission was to be there and observe, and nothing more. Colonel Kelly said: "We don't enforce the agreement, we don't separate the forces. We only receive arms."[8] In practice, all ONUCA could do outside of the areas controlled by the Venezuelan paratroopers was peace observing and treaty verification.

In an attitude that was typical, Contra Comandante Wilmer (Max Rodríguez) said that his men were not turning in their weapons and would not until they could negotiate with President Chamorro. He said that he could not force his men to turn in their weapons if they did not want to, and at present they would not because there was no confidence in the government or the Sandinista Army.[9] The government was concerned. On 27 April Managua Radio broadcast an interview with former Deputy Foreign Minister Tinoco in which he explained that ONUCA and CIAV had warned that if the demobilization was not completed by the 10 June deadline, they would depart the country and leave the problem in the hands of Nicaraguans, even if that meant civil war.[10] On 3 May the UN Secretary-General criticized the Contras for not honoring agreements to disarm; he added that ONUCA was not in the business of helping them set up permanent armed camps. A few days later, the Security Council met to discuss this "grave situation" and expressed its concern.

Faced with these pressures, and keenly aware of the strong carrot and stick offered by the various forces arrayed against the Contras, Comandante Franklin traveled to Managua on 3 May, escorted by a Spanish ONUCA officer, to negotiate with the Chamorro government on demobilization. An agreement was signed a few days later that did not differ much from prior ones except for the important fact that it was signed by Franklin, and presumably committed the men under his command to comply (although there was always doubt about this). The Contras were given until 10 June to turn in their weapons, and they agreed to demobilize at a rate of 200 per day. In return, the Chamorro government repeated its guarantee of protection and promised that after the 10 June deadline was met, it would reduce the size of the military. Franklin backed off from his earlier demand that General Ortega be removed, saying the problem was the institution as a whole, not an individual.[11]

Although the agreement was a positive step, it highlighted the fact that very few Contras had turned in weapons so far. In fact, the original 25 April deadline passed without a single weapon surrendered on Nicaraguan soil. One report noted that a mocking Contra turned in a plastic toy machine gun painted red and black (the FSLN colors). One problem was that Contra leaders seemed to have little real control over the demobilization process, which ultimately was an individual and voluntary decision. Spanish ONUCA Colonel Manuel Maldonado was quoted as saying, "we know the leaders have signed the disarmament agreement, but we do not know what the combatants will do."[12]

The demobilization of some 80–90 Contras at El Almendro, Nicaragua, on 8 May was a turning point. This was the first time Contras surrendered weapons to the UN authorities inside Nicaragua, even though there were doubts about the kinds of weapons and Contras involved. Many of the weapons were old and rusty, and many of the Contras were adolescent boys in ill-fitting uniforms. One Contra was a teenage girl in a pink satin dress (she carried no weapons). There were several timid boys between the ages of 11 and 14; one, nicknamed *"Pulga"* ("Flea"), was 8 years old. Most of the men were able-bodied, but were too young to be battle-hardened Contras. Radio Sandino described the weapons as museum pieces and characterized the demobilization as "another mockery of the disarmament agreement," just as in Yamales.[13] The Contras turned in their AK-47 assault rifles, stripped off their camouflage uniforms, and were issued civilian clothes, food, and ONUCA demobilization certificates. Radio Sandino noted there were indications that the rebel leadership regarded this group as guinea pigs whose demobilization was a sort of security test: if they were left in peace, the pace of demobilization would pick up; if they were harassed or harmed, the Contras were ready to launch reprisals.

Comandante Franklin said later that the weapons turned in at El Almendro were only a fraction of the total, and that the remainder were being kept in hiding for future use. *Barricada* called the surrender of weapons at El Almendro "the May 8 show," and claimed (supporting Comandante Franklin's statement) that the really significant weapons were being stashed away for later use.[14] Some of the Contras who demobilized admitted they were selected as test "volunteers" only 48 hours before the event. Moreover, the 500-square-kilometer site was only partially under ONUCA control because only the main road entrance was guarded, and the mountainous back areas familiar to the Contras were not. Thus, the Contras could leave and re-enter the camp without going through the UN checkpoint, and the concept of tight ONUCA control of the demobilization was seriously undermined.

The crucial U.S. funds to support the demobilization were again caught up in bureaucratic squabbles. On 11 May CIAV-OAS officials said they were running out of supplies for the Contras and had food for only another 8 to 10 days. Part of the problem was that the funding was held up in Congress because it formed part of a larger bill for aid to Nicaragua and Panama. The OAS had also underestimated the number of Contras it was being asked to help, and even more were on the way. OAS Administrator Sayre stated that "the whole Central American peace process is riding on this," because the administration's credibility with the Contras was at stake.[15] To compound the problem, the Contra leadership was pressing for direct control of U.S. funds allocated for their demobilization instead of having them come through CIAV-OAS channels.[16]

Reflecting their suspicion and distrust not only of the Sandinistas, but also of the Chamorro government and the United States, the Contras suspended the demobilization on 18 May, with only about 700 Contras having turned in their weapons. Comandante Franklin said they were suspending demobilization because they believed President Chamorro's government was not living up to its end of the Tocontín agreements, and that in any case she was not really in control of Nicaragua and its security forces. Contra spokespersons also said they were unhappy with the way the demobilization was proceeding, and specifically with CIAV's inadequate funds. Typically, there was confusion among the ranks of the Contras because some of the leaders were in favor of suspending demobilization and others were not.

The Contras' suspension of demobilization did not last long. Repeating the familiar cycle, pressures mounted until the fragmented Contra leadership went to Managua to negotiate the best deal they could get. Negotiations were briefly suspended when the Contras accused the Sandinista security forces of massacring 14 demobilized Contras in Zinca (Jinotega). An investigation commission from ONUCA and CIAV, named to verify the facts, reported that there was no evidence of a massacre. With that problem disposed of (amidst Sandinista accusations that the whole thing was a Contra-U.S. attempt to stall demobilization), on 30 May the Contras and the Chamorro government signed the Protocol on Disarmament, witnessed by Cardinal Obando y Bravo. It confirmed the 10 June date for final disarmament and repeated the usual government guarantees for security. It also called for an extension of the ONUCA mandate as an additional confidence-building measure for the Contras. The government made a major concession to the Contras by committing itself to creating 23 self-governing development zones (for a total of 25,000 square kilometers, or almost 20 percent of the country) in which the former Contras could settle with government help. These areas were to be protected by a new rural police made up predominantly of Contra forces. The Sandinistas objected to these provisions, arguing that Chamorro had given in to Contra pressures and created "a state within a state."[17]

Despite the Sandinista bitterness over these very favorable concessions to the Contras (which were to lead to major problems in 1991), they did achieve their goal of accelerating the demobilization process. The day after the agreement was signed a record number of Contras (498) disarmed in the security zones. Before the agreement an average of 90 had demobilized per day since the process started on 8 May. The increased rate of demobilization was to continue until the last Contras were processed in early July.

Sandinista anger at the Chamorro concessions also was aimed at the international organizations. In late May *Barricada* carried a long and critical article on ONUCA and CIAV, claiming they were biased against the Sandinistas.[18] It also suggested that the real reason for OAS participation in CIAV was to gain experience and, more importantly, to increase its prestige. Working closely with ONUCA and CIAV were PAHO (Pan American Health Organization) officials, who supervised health care; most of the medical workers (90 percent) were local, and because they were very well paid, they tended to drain off professional health care personnel who would otherwise be working in Sandinista-run clinics. ONUCA's Venezuelan battalion was described thus: "The infantry—slim, young Mestizo soldiers trained not to

talk to the press—belong to the elite battalion of the Venezuelan army."
Under the sidebar, "Taking the credit," *Barricada* editorialized: "The unusual
and painful situation Nicaragua is experiencing has provided ONUCA and
CIAV with the opportunity to strengthen the images of two international
organizations which have intervened in this country. The verification
commission's general coordinator, Santiago Murray, has called the experience
gained by its staff 'extremely important for the OAS' prestige.'"

The next issue of *Barricada Internacional* continued the attack, reporting
that ONUCA officers had come under fire from Managua media because of
their interfering attitude and their bias toward the Contras.[19] The article noted
that Comandante Franklin was allowed to use ONUCA headquarters in
Managua for a press conference; and ONUCA officers referred to him as
"Comandante," while calling senior EPS officials "Señor" (a breach of
military etiquette). According to the Sandinista newspaper, high-ranking
foreign officers from ONUCA could be seen driving their vehicles at high
speed through the streets of Managua and changing their dollars on the black
market. There were also tensions reported between some of the European
military officers of ONUCA, who had been acting with arrogance and disdain,
and civilian officials of international organizations.

THE CONCLUSION OF DEMOBILIZATION, JUNE 1990

With Contra reluctance to demobilize crumbling, the major obstacles to
completing the process before the 10 June deadline became logistical. On 5
June a record number of 832 Contras (for a total so far of almost 5,000)
turned their weapons in, and the capacity of ONUCA, CIAV, and the
Venezuelan battalion to process Contras was being reached. On 9 June there
was a major demobilization ceremony at the El Almendro security zone
attended by President Chamorro. She recognized the important contributions
made by ONUCA and CIAV, and spoke of the need to build trust, especially
in her government. She also announced that she would soon reveal her
government's plan to reduce the Nicaraguan armed forces, which was the
other half of the demobilization deal according to the Contras. She noted the
example set by former President José Figueres of Costa Rica (who had died
the day before) in demilitarizing his own nation. At a symbolic moment in
the ceremony, President Chamorro kissed Contra Comandante Wilmer on the
cheek just below a bullet wound he had received fighting the Sandinistas.
Many of the ex-Contras at the ceremony said that not enough was being done
for them because all they got when they demobilized was a certificate, a blue
and white striped shirt, a pair of jeans, a pair of rubber boots, and a few
pounds of beans and rice. Many complained this was a poor reward for years
of fighting.[20]

Despite the favorable publicity and positive feelings about the demobilization, concerns remained that the Contras were not finished as a fighting force because many of the arms being turned in were suspiciously old, suggesting that the better Contra weapons were being held back for future use. There were also indications that not all of those who turned themselves in were Contras: some were opportunists who simply wanted the benefits and supplies being handed out, and some were reportedly Sandinista intelligence agents attempting to infiltrate the Contras to make sure they were not planning any further operations.[21]

Almost lost in the drama of the final stages of the Contra demobilization was the arrival of four Argentine Navy "fast boats" to patrol the Gulf of Fonseca. These small patrol boats had come by Argentine naval transport from their base in Ushuaia, where they were presumably not needed because of the settlement of the Beagle Channel border dispute between Argentina and Chile. ONUCA's interest in patrolling the Gulf of Fonseca stemmed from the old concern that it was a major conduit of weapons from the Sandinistas to the FMLN in El Salvador. It was not clear, however, how much good the Argentine patrol boats could do, since Honduran and U.S. vessels, equipped with highly sophisticated radar, had been unable to intercept any significant shipment of weapons despite many years of trying. Even before their arrival, the Argentine boats had gotten caught up in old disputes between El Salvador and Honduras, which had flared up in 1990; it was reported that the arrival of the boats had been delayed to avoid placing them in a potential confrontation between the naval and air forces of those two countries. In Argentina the sending of the boats (followed by the deployment of two larger ships to the Persian Gulf as part of the UN blockade against Iraq) was a politically touchy issue for President Carlos Menem. It was also a sensitive topic in the always delicate relationship between the Argentine Navy, which was very proud of its involvement in UN peacekeeping, and the army, which was not happy to see the navy in the spotlight.[22]

Pressures to complete the demobilization were building as the 10 June deadline approached. ONUCA and CIAV personnel worked frantically to demobilize the Contras, and it went remarkably smoothly, considering the numbers and logistical difficulties involved. In reports dated 5 and 8 June, the UN Secretary-General notified the Security Council of the progress being made and the likelihood that the 10 June deadline would not be met, and recommended pressuring the Contras to make sure they really were complying. He also expressed concern over the fact that substantial numbers of Contras were retaining their weapons and could be a threat to security.[23] In his second report, he acknowledged that the deadline could not be met and reluctantly requested an extension of ONUCA's demobilization mandate (including the use of the Venezuelan battalion) for another 19 days, to 29 June, which the Security Council granted. Two days later a new record number of 1,886 Contras were processed.[24]

By the end of June, almost all the Contras had been demobilized. On 27 June an exhilarated Violeta Chamorro declared "today the war ends" as she and ONUCA representatives accepted the demobilization of one of the last groups of Contras, led by Israel Galeano, at San Pedro de Lovago. The weapons turned in included over 60 Red Eye missiles. On 29 June the Secretary-General presented Document S/21397 (the "Final ONUCA Demobilization Report") to the Security Council and stated that 19,369 Contras had been disarmed and demobilized. The five security zones had been closed, and it was expected that the Venezuelan battalion would be going home soon. The weapons that had been turned in included 120 surface-to-air missiles, of which 70 were Red Eyes. There was speculation that a significant number of surface-to-air missiles might still be hidden because the United States had provided some 200 of these (30 were fired in combat and 120 had been destroyed by ONUCA).

It was also possible that small armed groups of former Contras could turn up. For this reason ONUCA would maintain demobilization posts for renegades as well as observation posts in areas where there was danger of hostility between the Contras and the population. Marrack Goulding, UN sub-secretary for special political affairs (in charge of peacekeeping), said that ONUCA's presence in Nicaragua would not be permanent, and that it was seeking to create trust in the process of reintegrating the Contras into civilian life at the request of the Nicaraguan government; this confidence-building function was similar to the process the UN carried out with ONUVEN during the February 1990 elections. ONUCA's mission in Central America was to end on 7 November, but it could be extended at the request of the countries involved. He added that the mandate to supervise demobilization of guerrillas might be extended to El Salvador and Guatemala.[25]

The demobilization process did not officially end until 5 July when the last elements of the Venezuelan battalion returned home. Exact figures on the number demobilized were somewhat questionable, but there were approximately 23,000 Contras processed and close to 17,000 weapons recovered and destroyed. In a symbolic final act, General Quesada turned over a large container of scrap metal that had once been Contra weapons to the World Rehabilitation Fund to be converted into crutches, wheelchairs, and prosthetic devices for the handicapped and wounded.[26]

THE POLES OF DEVELOPMENT
AND UNREST IN MID-1990

The "poles of development" were an important inducement offered by the Chamorro government to the Contras to persuade them to demobilize. In theory these would be remote and undeveloped lands that would be given to the Contras to farm and develop, with government assistance for infrastructure projects and start-up costs. They were significant in the peace process for two principal reasons: because of the role they had played in getting the Contras to disband, and then later, when the project failed, in contributing to the unrest that came to haunt the new government in its first two years. The poles were controversial from the start. For many Sandinistas it seemed as though giving land and assistance to the Contras was an excessively (and suspiciously) generous act on the part of the Chamorro administration.[27] For many Contras the poles looked like traps, or at least an attempt to isolate them by sending them far away from the centers of power in Nicaragua. They could also conceivably become "concentration camps" in which they would be held and harassed by the strong and still very Sandinista-oriented security apparatus.

A Managua newspaper caught some of the prevailing currents of opinion in early June. In a lengthy article, the paper commented on the proposal to create poles of development for former Contras, including a large area at Río San Juan (16,000 square kilometers), which it called "a dangerous project" because of ecological damage and the fact that it would be an autonomous zone under Contra control by means of a "rural police force."[28] Former Contra Comandante Franklin said the rural police in the development poles would be formed exclusively by Contras, and that there would be no Sandinista forces or national police in the area. He added that there were 500 Contras who would not turn in their weapons because they felt they needed protection. Some of these Contras would be involved with a new ecological protection battalion in the Río San Juan development pole, which would be supported by the UN.

From their inception the poles had a lot more to do with security and pacification than agriculture and development. In an attempt to calm Sandinista concerns that the poles would be "trophies of war" or armed Contra fortresses, the government announced that the police assigned to the development poles would be trained by Spain. In late June the director of the Institute of Agricultural Reform, Gustavo Tablada, dismissed the possibility that the poles would permit the future grouping of the Contras as a fighting force. He said that there was no attempt to set up autonomous sectors, but rather that they would be a factor for reintegration into society. Sandinista newspapers noted the opposition of many of the inhabitants of the areas, and quoted one of them as saying that the Contras wanted to be close to the Costa Rican border, as well as the hills and jungles, which would offer them the conditions they needed for smuggling and drug trafficking. They might also want to be near the possible site of an interoceanic canal or a U.S. base along the Costa Rican–Nicaraguan border.[29]

Within a couple of months, it became clear that the poles were not going to be either the fortresses the Sandinistas feared or the "golden parachutes" the Contras had hoped for.[30] Aid and development assistance was slow in reaching the poles, and there was little or no potable water or electricity available on most of the sites. As a result of the deteriorating conditions, many of the former Contras started drifting away and returning to their homes. In the large El Almendro pole, there were only about 3,000 Contras in July, about half the number expected, with the number declining fast.

Some observers felt that the melting away of the Contra strength from the development poles reduced their cohesion and political leverage and led the emboldened Sandinistas to launch violent and crippling strikes in July 1990. In any case, the remaining Contras and their leaders were increasingly embittered. In late July the principal Contra leader, Israel Galeano (Comandante Franklin), called on the government to fulfill its promises to upgrade and pay adequate attention to the development poles or pay the price with unspecified consequences.

One set of consequences came from the Sandinista side in the form of a series of crippling and bloody strikes in July as they set out to prove that they could indeed govern from below, or at least make it impossible for President Chamorro and the UNO coalition to govern from above. On 9 July the week-old general strike turned violent when four people were killed and many injured in a series of clashes, and both Sandinistas and Chamorro supporters were seen with AK-47 assault rifles. The Central American presidents released a statement of support for the Chamorro government, citing the Esquipulas II peace procedure as justification for what might be seen as interference in the internal affairs of another state. Two of the principal outside supporters of the peace process potentially became involved when former President Daniel Ortega asked Venezuelan President Carlos Andrés Pérez to mediate the strike, and other Sandinista leaders suggested that Spanish Prime Minister Felipe González might be asked to try to use his good offices. There were also reports that some UNO government supporters felt the only solution was armed intervention by the United States or the UN (that is, peace enforcement).[31]

ONUCA personnel became involved in the strike and associated violence when 12 of their members negotiated the withdrawal of some 15–20 armed Contras, led by Comandante Rubén, who had occupied the Managua Central Bus Station and the Radio Corporación broadcasting studios. CIAV representatives were accused by the Sandinista press of helping Contras during the strike, specifically that their vehicles transported Comandante Rubén. The Sandinistas also claimed that both ONUCA and CIAV hid Contras in their installations during the strikes, and despite denials by the international organizations, there was a popular perception that the two organizations had lost some of their impartiality.[32]

By 12 July the Sandinista unions agreed to end their violent strike in return for a broad package of wage and economic concessions. The strike was the gravest crisis in Chamorro's early tenure and reached a delicate point when she ordered Sandinista Army troops to reimpose order. After some hesitation, they did so, although they avoided direct assaults on the Sandinista strikers. General Ortega said that the army would obey orders, and would never launch a coup against the government, but it would also never fire on civilians. Nicaragua's politics, always polarized, were becoming more so, and were pulling the heretofore neutral international organizations into the domestic battle.

HONDURAN–SALVADORAN STRAINS

Although the peace process in Nicaragua was the major focus of attention in the first half of 1990, there were reminders of enduring regional tensions, including the old Salvadoran-Honduran strains that predated the Central American crisis of the 1980s. In late June there was an incident in the Gulf of Fonseca in which Honduran and Salvadoran boats exchanged fire. The Hondurans requested air support, but the Salvadoran boats withdrew before the F-5 jet fighters arrived (four were reportedly sent). In a tribute to the value of confidence-building measures, direct contacts between the chiefs of staff of the two countries prevented "a regrettable incident."[33]

The area involved was near the Meanguera and Meanguerita islands, which had been in dispute between the two countries for many years. ONUCA could potentially have become involved in such incidents because its four Argentine patrol boats had been searching the area for illegal weapons transfers from Nicaragua into El Salvador. Later in the year, Nicaragua became more involved in the bilateral Salvadoran-Honduran dispute when the International Court of Justice in The Hague agreed to allow Nicaragua to participate in the pending case of the Salvadoran-Honduran border dispute in the Gulf of Fonseca. Nicaragua would not be a litigant, but wanted to be present at the ICJ proceedings to protect its interests in the maritime spaces of the gulf.

There were also frequent incidents in the old *"bolsones"* ("pockets") of disputed territory along the Salvadoran-Honduran border. Some contacts were probably accidental, such as detachments of both armies inadvertently crossing the unmarked frontier while patrolling or looking for guerrillas, cattle rustlers, or smugglers. But other incidents were something more. On 21 July a Salvadoran community development organization reported constant incursions by Honduran troops into Salvadoran territory, while Honduran civilians claimed incursions by Salvadoran troops in the bolsones.[34] As in the Gulf of Fonseca, there was potential for ONUCA involvement because of its basic mandate to verify that the nations of the region were not supporting guerrilla movements in another state. In addition, the governments of both El Salvador and Honduras requested ONUCA assistance to reinforce surveillance along the border in order to control the smuggling of weapons into their countries.

DISARMAMENT AND THE
ESQUIPULAS SECURITY COMMISSION

The end of the Contras as an organized military force through their demobilization did not solve the problem of the large number of arms floating around Nicaragua and Central America, nor the problem of the bloated military institutions in all five countries. This even included Costa Rica, which, although it had no army, had seen the size of its police and border security apparatus increase dramatically in the 1980s. By history and tradition the military in Central America (with the exception of Costa Rica) always exercised considerable political power, and the conflicts of the 1980s greatly increased that power as the military establishments grew in size, troop strength, weapons, and budgets. With the formal end of the Nicaraguan civil war, and the glimmer of peace in El Salvador and possibly even Guatemala, it appeared logical to begin to look at how these establishments could be reduced. The militaries of the Central American countries became very sensitive to this issue in 1990 as they heard the message from many national and international sources, including the United States, which was anxious to lower its military profile and assistance in the region.

Part of the legacy of 10 years of fighting in Nicaragua (and to a lesser extent Honduras and Costa Rica) was the development of a gun culture closely linked to machismo and the easy availability of weapons, including automatic ones such as the ubiquitous AK-47. The cliché that "Central America is awash in arms" was indeed true. One source of weapons was the Sandinista government, which had distributed some 50,000 AK-47s to its militia during the Contra war and another 20,000 to civilian backers between the election in February 1990 and the Chamorro inauguration two months later. The Contras were estimated to have received at least 31,000 weapons from the United States and other sources, but they turned in only about 17,000 to ONUCA. Many of the remaining weapons were buried by the Contras in Honduras before returning to Nicaragua, or in northern Nicaragua after they crossed the border. Witnesses also told of Contras in Honduras receiving two weapons each: an old one to turn in to ONUCA and a new one to hide. A former intelligence agent put it more bluntly: "Let me tell you how it is. In any of these guerrilla organizations, when they turn in weapons you can bet they will be rusty old pieces of crap."[35]

The Esquipulas II agreement provided for a Central American Security Commission, and at the Antigua Summit in June 1990, the presidents called for it to meet in San José, Costa Rica, in late July. The commission was to be made up of the deputy ministers of foreign affairs and their advisors, who were expected to represent their defense and military establishments. This was a crucial point because any discussion of disarmament that did not include the military was not going to achieve very much. The purpose of the Security Commission, as stated at the Antigua Summit, was to "urgently press forward with negotiations in the areas of security, verification, control and limitation of armaments in line with the Esquipulas II agreements, so as to make the most of resources by redirecting them towards the development of our countries."

The July 1990 meeting of the Security Commission was held as scheduled in Costa Rica with the attendance of the deputy foreign ministers and deputy defense ministers of the Central American nations plus observers from the UN and OAS (who were there to advise the commission). The meeting produced general agreement at the diplomatic level, but there was much doubt about what they could actually accomplish in terms of real reductions. The group spent much of its time working on procedures, and agreed to meet about once every 60 days. The next formal step was to make assessments of each nation's military strength, and then establish ceilings with an eye toward regional parity. After the Antigua Summit, Honduras became the principal advocate of parity, which was understandable inasmuch as Honduras had the smallest military and thus would be favored by parity. El Salvador and Guatemala argued that they could not reduce their military as long as they were fighting insurgencies.

The Nicaraguan proposal at Costa Rica made specific suggestions on limiting, controlling, and reducing the following categories of weapons: all kinds of military planes and helicopters, tanks, mortars larger than 120 mm, self-propelled antiaircraft weapons, multiple rocket launchers larger than 122 mm, heavy artillery larger than 160 mm, self-propelled artillery, rocket launchers installed on ships, and military vessels larger than 100 metric tons. There was also a call for suspension of the purchase of any kind of military materiel except ammunition and spare parts. A ban on military maneuvers involving foreign powers was also part of the Nicaraguan proposal. To verify the demilitarization plan, Nicaragua suggested that the Secretaries-General of the UN and OAS head a control commission, which would also provide advisory assistance. The participants at the meeting spoke of "the need to define a new model in security relations among the Central American countries," and the desire "to bolster communications and cooperation."[36] If carried out, the suggestions made at this meeting would take Central America significantly closer to a confidence-building regime and a zone of peace as they went through the process of reducing weapons and military establishments.

The commission's November 1990 meeting introduced a greater measure of realism with more limited goals. A Honduran representative said that it was a mistake to think that they were seeking to demilitarize the region because that would only bring instability and the possibility of other conflicts. The commission did agree to create a verification mission for weapons inventories that included the participation of OAS and UN personnel (there were OAS and UN observers present at the meeting). The commission reflected the tendency to rely on international organizations for help (and yet also showed little reluctance to criticize them) when it called for an increase in the numbers of ONUCA troops, "so that its verification activities can be more effective," and for Pérez de Cuéllar to become personally involved in the FMLN–El Salvador negotiations. The concluding document pointedly suggested that "ONUCA should improve its communications with the armed forces and foreign ministers of Central America, improve or acquire the necessary communications systems to carry out its work, and install radar equipment for air, ground and maritime surveillance."[37] The document also proposed that ONUCA strengthen its presence and verification activities at border and customs checkpoints.

With the exception of Nicaragua, which had its own special circumstances, none of the Central American nations was really doing very much to reduce arms and soldiers. Reporting on the November meeting of the commission, a Mexican newspaper said that three nations, Guatemala, El Salvador, and Honduras, had rejected demilitarization proposals.[38] Two of these, Guatemala and El Salvador, argued that insurgencies in their countries did not permit reductions. Guatemala actually called for an increase in its army, while Honduras suggested a reduction to 30,000 troops in each country. Nicaragua and Costa Rica were arguing for total demilitarization, which most outside observers deemed unrealistic, at least in the short and medium term.

The Nicaraguan disarmament situation was special because of the way it was driven by economic necessity, the end of the Contra war, internal political pressures, and Violeta Chamorro's strong personal commitment to disarm. In an emotional speech at the 12 June 1990 funeral of former President José Figueres of Costa Rica, Chamorro said that her goal was to disarm Nicaragua, and indeed the whole region. Her first problem was to try to recover some of the thousands of weapons in the hands of Nicaraguans of all political stripes. In early July the government launched a campaign to do this; but the results were limited, and because it was being handled by the Sandinista-controlled security forces, there were suspicions that more weapons were being squeezed out of former Contras and UNO supporters than out of the Sandinistas.[39]

Even though the Nicaraguan military had a slice of the budget guaranteed by the Chamorro administration, they were beginning to feel the pinch, to the point that they attempted to sell their Soviet tanks and helicopters on the international arms market to raise cash to pay for an unemployment program for laid-off soldiers. (The Kremlin had turned down an offer to buy back the weapons.[40]) Despite opposition charges of exaggeration, the cuts being made in the EPS (Sandinista People's Army) were real. In early November General Ortega met with about 2,000 Sandinista officers to explain the procedure for the coming reductions in the military. The emphasis in the new EPS, he said, would be on quality, not quantity. From the more than 90,000 troops in January 1990, there would soon be reductions to 33,000, and finally to 28,000. Officers who were discharged would have 6 to 12 months back pay and access to medical and other benefits, as well as parcels of land.

Demilitarization was always a sensitive issue in the delicate balance of power between the Sandinistas and the Chamorro government. The legislature, however, was more independent and did not necessarily feel bound by commitments made by the Chamorro administration to the Sandinistas. In December 1990 this caused a crisis when the National Assembly rejected a carefully negotiated reduction in the armed forces budget (worked out between General Ortega and President Chamorro's advisors) and instead called for greater cuts that would lower defense spending from U.S. $166 million in 1990 to $58.8 million in 1991. Chamorro, who had proposed $78.6 million, said she would veto the bill. The army warned that it would not permit further reduction in troop strength (under the assembly budget, almost all the officers would have to be discharged because salaries made up 60 percent of the budget). The assembly action showed the depth of the revolt against President Chamorro in her UNO coalition, even though she was later able to sustain a veto against the assembly budget. General Ortega accused the United States of pressuring assembly deputies to vote against the proposed Chamorro budget.[41]

CONFIDENCE-BUILDING MEASURES

In parallel with the disarmament work of the Security Commission, some progress was being made in developing confidence-building measures, including greater contacts between neighboring militaries. In August 1990 General Ortega and Honduran Armed Forces Commander General Arnulfo Cantarero met in Managua as part of a rapprochement between the two military institutions. They discussed support for the plan for proportional reduction and balance in the Central American armies, as well as security issues such as disputes over the Gulf of Fonseca and fishing activities. Ortega said: "We are also going to try to strengthen our military institutions by exchanging experiences to further modernize operations and military science. This will benefit the eminently defensive doctrines and strategies of the two military institutions." This was followed by a November agreement to conduct joint operations to fight arms trafficking, contraband, and other criminal activity along the border. The two countries also exchanged information on troop deployments to avert accidents.[42]

Another confidence-building measure that was gathering momentum in this period was the idea of Central American "peace parks," which would straddle borders and have ecological, economic, and security functions. The first peace park was on the border between Costa Rica and Panama, and others were planned for Belize-Guatemala, Mexico-Guatemala, and Costa Rica–Nicaragua. These parks were supported by Conservation International (a U.S. organization) and the OAS. The parks tended to be located on international rivers, which was a logical choice because what happened to a river in one country could be vitally important to the other. Many of these international rivers, such as the San Juan along the Costa Rican–Nicaraguan border, had also been traditional routes for smuggling, drug and arms trafficking, and guerrilla operations.

Confidence-building measures tended to be heavy on symbolism, such as the use of scrap metal from Contra weapons to make prosthetic devices. In late November former President Oscar Arias of Costa Rica attended a ceremony in Managua in which 10,000 rifles surrendered by the Contras were buried in cement to form the base of a monument. President Chamorro was present and announced the creation of a National Disarmament Commission with Arias as honorary president. The commission was to include EPS, government, Contra, church, and political party representatives with OAS and UN observers.[43]

NOTES

1. Panama, ACAN, 11 April 1990, in Foreign Broadcast Information Service (FBIS), 11 April 1990, 14; and *ONUCA Observer*, 34–44, 59–62.

2. *Barricada*, 5 April 1990, 1.

3. *Washington Post*, 9 April 1990, A1.

4. *Washington Times*, 11 April 1990, 3.

5. Dallanegra Pedraza, *Proceso de Desmovilización*. The descriptions of the demobilizing process were also based on interviews with demobilized Contras in Managua, Estelí, and Yalí, Nicaragua, June 1991.

6. *La Tribuna*, Tegucigalpa, 19 April 1990, in FBIS, 23 April 1990, 33–34; and *Washington Post*, 19 April 1990, A47.

7. Secretary-General's report on ONUCA, UN Document S/21274, 27 April 1990.

8. *Los Angeles Times*, 27 April 1990, 1; and FBIS, 30 April 1990.

9. *Barricada*, 29 April 1990, in FBIS, 2 May 1990, 21–22.

10. Managua, Radio Sandino, 30 April 1990, in FBIS, 30 April 1990, 32–33.

11. For text of the "Managua Declaration," see FBIS, 7 May 1990, based on Radio Sandino, 5 May 1990.

12. Panama ACAN, 7 May 1990, in FBIS, 8 May 1990.

13. Managua, Radio Sandino, 9 May 1990, in FBIS, 10 May 1990, 30–31.

14. *Barricada*, 19 May 1990, 1.

15. *Washington Post*, 11 May 1990, A14.

16. Panama ACAN, 22 May 1990, in FBIS, 22 May 1990, 19–20; and interviews with UN Development Program personnel, Managua, June 1991.

17. Managua, Radio Católica, 30 May 1990, in FBIS, 31 May 1990.

18. *Barricada Internacional,* 19 May 1990, 11–13.

19. *Barricada Internacional,* 2 June 1990, 6–7.

20. Managua Domestic Service, 9 June 1990, in FBIS, 11 June 1990, 28–33.

21. Interviews with ONUCA and CIAV personnel, Managua and Estelí, June 1991.

22. Discussions with Argentine naval officers, Newport, R.I., and Washington, D.C., 1991.

23. UN Documents S/21341, 4 June 1990; and S/21349, 8 June 1990.

24. United Nations, *Blue Helmets,* 399–400.

25. *Barricada Internacional,* 14 July 1990, 3–4.

26. *ONUCA Observer,* 63.

27. Interview with representatives of UNAG (Unión Nicaragüense de Agricultores y Ganaderos), León, June 1991.

28. *Barricada Internacional,* 2 June 1990, 5; 16 June 1990, 3.

29. *Barricada Internacional,* 30 June 1990, 5.

30. *Washington Post,* 15 July 1990, A23.

31. Panama ACAN, 10 July 1990, in FBIS, 11 July 1990; *Washington Post,* 10 July 1990, A1.

32. Managua, Radio Sandino, 11 July 1990, in FBIS, 12 July 1990, 36; Managua, AFP, 11 July 1990, in FBIS, 12 July 1990, 24–25; Panama ACAN, 14 July 1990, in FBIS, 16 July 1990, 45–46; *Barricada Internacional,* 28 July 1990, 10–11.

33. *Heraldo,* Tegucigalpa, 28 June 1990, 29.

34. San Salvador Cadena, YSKL, 21 July 1990, in FBIS, 23 July 1990, 28.

35. *Miami Herald,* 25 December 1990, 1A.

36. See FBIS, 2 August 1990, 1–2.

37. Panama ACAN, 23 November 1990, in FBIS, 27 November 1990, 2–3.

38. *Excelsior,* Mexico, 24 November 1990, 1.

39. Managua Domestic Service, 5 July 1990, in FBIS, 6 July 1990, 27.

40. *Washington Times,* 24 September 1990, 1.

41. Managua, Reuters, 20 December 1990, in DoD News Summary, 21 December 1990, 16.

42. Managua Domestic Service, 29 August 1990, in FBIS, 30 August 1990, 23–24; Panama ACAN, 9 November 1990, in FBIS, 14 November 1990, 31.

43. Managua Domestic Service, 27 and 28 November 1990, in FBIS, 29 November 1990, 15–16, 27–28.

8

THE AFTERMATH IN NICARAGUA
AND THE PEACE PROCESS ELSEWHERE

ONUCA AND CIAV AFTER DEMOBILIZATION, LATE 1990

With the demobilization of the Contras completed in early July 1990, both ONUCA and CIAV substantially changed their roles, budgets, and significance. The Venezuelan battalion went home and the ONUCA mandate reverted to the original rather limited one of concentrating on the borders and watching for violations of the Esquipulas II prohibition on cross-border support of irregular forces. CIAV, on the other hand, assumed full responsibility for supporting the former Contras in Nicaragua, as well as those who remained in Honduras (mainly dependents and the sick and wounded). Under the geographic division of responsibility, the Honduran operation of CIAV belonged to the UN side, while that in Nicaragua was under the OAS. CIAV-UN in practice was handled by an existing UN organization, the UN High Commissioner for Refugees (UNHCR), and concentrated on repatriating the Nicaraguans out of Honduras, much to the relief of the Hondurans.

As the number of Nicaraguans in Honduras decreased, so did the problems and activities of CIAV-UN/UNHCR. At the same time, the activities, problems, and financial requirements of CIAV-OAS in Nicaragua increased. Because CIAV's mandate was to help former Contras and their families, practically anything they did inevitably got them involved in postelection Nicaraguan politics. CIAV-OAS soon found itself in a politically very difficult situation: if it did its job poorly and failed to support the former Contras, it would be criticized by the Contras, by its OAS superiors in Washington, and by the U.S. government, which was financing the entire Contra support operation. On the other hand, if it did its job well and effectively helped the Contras, it would be criticized by the Sandinistas for going too far in keeping the Contras together, and possibly even for stimulating them to take up their arms again. While ONUCA's profile was being lowered and its personnel focused on the border areas, ONUCA could bask in the general goodwill stemming from the demobilization process that was now over. But at the same time, fairly or unfairly, CIAV-OAS was being blamed for contributing to the unrest that characterized Nicaraguan politics from mid-1990 through the end of 1991.[1]

During this period, no violations of the Esquipulas II agreement were discovered by ONUCA military observers, although there were investigations of several complaints of Esquipulas violations lodged with ONUCA by the Nicaraguan and Honduran governments. One Nicaraguan complaint concerned a Salvadoran allegation of a secret FMLN transmitter in Managua. ONUCA personnel accompanied Nicaraguan security personnel on an inspection of the alleged site where, to no one's surprise, no transmitter was found, and the Nicaraguans could state that this proved they had not violated Esquipulas II. Another situation involved a Honduran seizure of weapons coming across the border illegally from Nicaragua, and ONUCA's role was simply to verify that the Hondurans had indeed found the weapons they said they had.

In November 1990 the Security Council accepted the Secretary-General's recommendation that because of its reduced mission, the size of ONUCA could be cut back somewhat. The smaller size also meant that a brigadier general would be a more appropriate chief of ONUCA, and thus Spanish Major General Quesada was replaced by Canadian Brigadier General Lewis McKenzie, and later by Spanish Brigadier General Victor Suanzes Pardo. The council also extended the mandate for six months (twice, to November 1991) and agreed that its main focus would be to maintain a UN presence in the region as a confidence-building measure and to deter cross-border support for insurgencies. In effect, ONUCA was now becoming a token and "flag-showing" presence waiting for a possible expanded mandate if the situation in El Salvador should lead to an agreement requiring UN verification. There was no longer even the pretense that ONUCA could seal any Central American borders or provide effective surveillance of the long and topographically difficult frontiers of the region.[2]

The increased activity of CIAV-OAS in Nicaragua stemmed from its mandate, which also charged it with verification and investigation of human rights violations and the application of justice. This task was to bring it frequently into confrontations with both the Chamorro government and the Sandinista-dominated security and juridical apparatus, and inevitably made it a significant actor in the Nicaraguan political game.[3] The best source of information on the first year of CIAV-OAS activities (through April 1991) is the report of the OAS Secretary-General submitted to the OAS General Assembly in Santiago, Chile, in April 1991. It contains detailed statistical and anecdotal information on the scope of CIAV-OAS activities and makes clear that the organization could not avoid getting involved in internal Nicaraguan affairs.

The OAS had never tackled a refugee or resettlement problem of this nature before. In early 1991 it was providing protection and assistance of various kinds to 94,953 people in Nicaragua: 22,413 former Contras, 13,819 repatriates, and 58,721 immediate family members. Among other things, CIAV was providing basic foodstuffs, grains, roofing materials, tools, and a range of technical and professional services. Compounding the political sensitivity of this part of its program was the reality that these activities were frequently interpreted by the Sandinistas as excessive and partisan, and by the Contras as inadequate. The investigation of reported violations of the human rights of the former Contras, and misapplication of the justice system, also fueled the friction between CIAV-OAS and the government and Sandinistas. In its report to the OAS General Assembly, a total of 563 violations reported by former Contras were documented, including illegal deprivation of freedom, threats and harassment, assault with firearms, assault and battery, homicides (35), theft/larceny, illegally owned firearms, deportations, abuses of authority, and disappearances.

The unhappiness of the former Contras found outlets in late 1990 in proposals (at times consummated) that they should retrieve their hidden weapons, get whatever support they could from political parties, and reconstitute themselves as an armed resistance. At times these were simply individual decisions by different comandantes of the resistance who would take their old followers with them into the hills. Other cases, however, involved political links between former Contras and factions within the UNO coalition (including that of Vice President Virgilio Godoy), which had the potential of making the re-armed Contras the fighting arm of a political group pitted against both the Chamorro government and the Sandinista-controlled security forces. A third kind of Contra activity occurred when groups of disgruntled former combatants took land by force, or stole cattle and belongings from farmers. Sandinista cooperatives were a favorite target, and in October 1990 there were a series of violent confrontations between former Contras and members of Sandinista cooperatives. In Waswala, 250 miles north of Managua, some 2,000 former Contras, desperate because of their economic conditions, invaded farm cooperatives. Both sides blamed the government for the situation and the lack of land given to the former Contras. At the same time, some 2,000 former Contras in southeast Nicaragua threatened to march on Managua and install Vice President Virgilio Godoy as president.[4]

A month later the challenge to Chamorro from the Right grew when former Contras and supporters of Godoy blocked several main highways and seized more farmland from Sandinista cooperatives. Reportedly, these actions involved thousands of former Contras and were supported by 35 of the country's 147 mayors.[5] On 15 November national police, representatives from Cardinal Obando y Bravo, and other officials (including observers from CIAV) tried to convince some 300 blockaders to open the road and clear a bridge near Matagalpa, without success. Finally, police used tear gas, and gunfire was exchanged, resulting in two dead and several wounded. Later incidents, including the taking of hostages and several town halls, raised the death toll to 24 before calm was restored in December. The links between the protesters and anti-Chamorro groups within the UNO coalitions, especially the so-called Godoy faction, were evident. One source reported that the former Contras manning the highway blockades would harass journalists armed with official government passes, but allowed any journalist with a pass from the Godoy camp to go through unmolested.[6]

THE RECONTRAS AND CIAV, 1991

The birth of the "Recontras" in Nicaragua represented a turning point for the two international organizations involved in Central American, and specifically Nicaraguan, peacekeeping and peace observing. The UN, either out of prescience or luck, was able to remain aloof from the problem of the Recontras, arguing that this was an internal matter and that their mandate required them only to concentrate on the borders and ensure that there was no cross-border support of insurgents. CIAV was not so lucky. Its mandate specifically required it to support the former Contras inside Nicaragua and administer USAID funds for their support and reintegration into Nicaraguan society. This inevitably meant close links between CIAV-OAS and the former Contras, a link that was viewed with much suspicion by the Sandinistas.

Even during the heady days of Contra demobilization in mid-1990, there had always been some discontent among the Contras, and many had kept some, at times their best, weapons hidden as insurance against the day they might have to fight again. It did not take long for discontent to increase in the face of the Chamorro government's inability to meet the sometimes unreasonable demands of the former Contras for land, protection, security, seed, food, and the infrastructure required to make a new start in a country in which they still had many enemies.

The first Recontra actions in early 1991 seemed more like publicity ploys to get the government's attention than anything else. On 2 January, for example, some 40 demobilized Contras and their relatives seized a church in Managua to pressure the government into giving them aid, annuities, housing, and jobs. A more serious situation was developing in the northern part of the country, which traditionally had always been a pro-Contra area. In January Comandante Franklin (Israel Galeano) said that in desperation, and in response to the government's failure to provide them the land they had been promised, members of former Contra groups might have gone into the jungle near Wiwili with arms they had cached during the demobilization process.[7]

The Chamorro administration attempted to squelch this dangerous development by signing an agreement with the Nicaraguan Resistance reiterating the commitment it had made to the Contras when they demobilized. Among other things, the former Contras would be given an office in the government's Repatriation Institute (to be headed by Galeano) and would work with CIAV-OAS to "coordinate their actions in finding the best way to provide food rations and medical assistance to the demobilized Contras."[8] This was no small task: in early 1991 CIAV had on its rolls about 22,400 former Contras, who, with their dependents, accounted for about 95,000 people CIAV had to feed and provide medical assistance. This link between CIAV and the former Contras was fraught with dangers. Everyone involved knew that CIAV's funds were from the United States, and there was the frequent suspicion that in dealing with U.S. officials and the U.S. Embassy, CIAV was also providing information to political and intelligence offices in the embassy.[9] There was also recurring resentment at the high profile of Argentines in CIAV and the fact that international civil servants could live very well on their dollar salaries and allowances in Nicaragua. Although this latter factor was also true for ONUCA and the other international organizations in Nicaragua, they managed to escape the criticism to a large degree because they had few contacts with the former Contras and kept a lower profile than CIAV personnel.[10]

CIAV officials defended themselves as best they could, arguing (quite correctly) that they had no choice but to work closely with the former Contras because that was their mandate. Some even tried to calm criticism by helping people, including Sandinistas, who were not former Contras, which in fact violated their mandate and could have led to a cutoff of funds from the United States if publicized. CIAV's delicate role (and the relatively large amount of money it had available) could be observed in mid-1991 in Nicaragua by comparing the operations and physical installations of the two OAS offices in Managua. The permanent OAS office in Managua was a modest coordinating bureau that handled routine business such as documents, magazine subscriptions, scholarships, and long-range technical assistance missions with few people involved. In contrast, CIAV-OAS was a bustling place with many more vehicles and a considerably higher profile. Large trucks carrying CIAV supplies to former Contras in the countryside were a common sight on the streets around CIAV headquarters and on the roads leading to the major Contra resettlement areas.[11]

In February 1991 the Recontras were angered by the news that Enrique Bermúdez, former Contra leader and ex-colonel in Somoza's army, had been killed by a lone sniper in the parking lot of the Hotel Intercontinental in Managua. Nicaraguan officials promised an exhaustive investigation, which predictably did not produce results because the police and investigative organs were in the hands of Sandinistas. A rightist radio station blamed the assassination on Sandinista sympathizers, and hard-line Vice President Virgilio Godoy warned that unless justice was done quickly, the assassination could bring a new round of civil war. Ironically, by early 1991 Bermúdez no longer exercised much influence among the Contras because he had been formally removed from the leadership before demobilization. However, he was the best known of the Contra leaders and an important symbol. The *Miami Herald* noted that even though Bermúdez had little charisma and was under CIA control, he had led the largest peasant army in Latin America since the Mexican Revolution. When he was killed, many former Contras felt their own safety was now in jeopardy.

Bermúdez had supporters in Washington, including retired General Gordon Sumner, with whom he had served on the Inter-American Defense Board as Nicaraguan delegate in the late Somoza years.[12] On 14 March the *Washington Times,* with good ties to the U.S. intelligence community and conservative sources, published a story alleging that U.S. intelligence agencies had circumstantial evidence linking General Ortega to the assassination of Bermúdez. Two weeks later it published an indignant letter from General Humberto Ortega denying the allegation.

After Bermúdez's assassination the Recontras gathered strength in the face of the slow investigation of the murder and the continuing inability of the Chamorro government to satisfy their material demands. It was hard to get reliable information on numbers, but there were reports in April of groups of perhaps up to 200 who had taken up arms, and there were shooting incidents with isolated EPS units in May. One group called itself "Reunification of Nicaragua Resistance 3-80" in honor of the radio call sign "3-80" that had been used by Bermúdez. A settlement of former Contras in Managua also took the name of Bermúdez and his identification number.[13] General Ortega blamed the rearming of the Contras on the hard-line UNO mayor of Managua, Arnaldo Alemán, and on sympathizers of Vice President Godoy. He called them "vigilante minorities that want war again, though the people do not wish that." Godoy replied in kind, calling Ortega a liar who "misrepresents history," and later said *"ese generalito es el que quiere encender la llama de la violencia"* ("that little general is the one who wants to light the flame of violence").[14]

The partisan press in Managua played up the Recontra story, especially alleged Recontra links to CIAV and hard-line UNO politicians such as Alemán and Godoy. Sandinista newspapers, *Barricada* and *Nuevo Diario* for example, were able to find disgruntled former Contras who told of CIAV payoffs to Recontras and secret meetings between CIAV and Recontras.[15] There were, of course, contacts between CIAV and former Contras that provided much room for misinterpretation. Not only was CIAV working with former Contras in fulfillment of its humanitarian and rehabilitation mission, but it also was attempting to keep lines of communication open between the Chamorro government and the Recontras. CIAV chief Santiago Murray made numerous denials and explanations to the effect that the purpose of these contacts was to persuade the Recontras to lay down their weapons,[16] but in politically polarized Nicaragua, readers tended to believe what they wanted to believe.

By June 1991 the estimated number of Recontras was put at between 300 and 1,100, located mainly in the northwest, although there were reports of groups on the Costa Rican border. Violent encounters were becoming more numerous, and in one publicized incident in June, a group of former Contras killed the chief of police of Yalí and his secretary on a highway near Jinotega.[17] *Barricada* noted that CIAV chief Murray had been in the area just before the assassination and reported that Contra representatives would soon be presenting the OAS's Inter-American Human Rights Commission with a detailed report of alleged violations of formers Contras' human rights by the Sandinistas.[18] *Barricada* also attacked CIAV-OAS for turning over to the police a list of addresses of individuals (many of them Sandinistas) who were believed to hold weapons, and for assisting the authorities when they searched their houses. The newspaper said this showed how CIAV exceeded its mandate through involvement in internal Nicaragua affairs, even though a CIAV official, Dr. Roberto Menéndez, argued that the Tela mandate required it to receive this kind of "denuncia" (accusation) and then turn it over to the local authorities for action.

In June it was the Sandinistas' turn to vent their frustrations through violence; they took over a number of radio stations, mayors' offices, and other public buildings. The spark that set the Sandinistas off was a set of proposed laws in the UNO-controlled legislature that would overturn the so-called piñata[19] of land, houses, and privileges the Sandinista leadership had awarded themselves and their followers just before turning power over to President Chamorro and her UNO coalition. The Sandinista deputies withdrew from the legislature and attempted to mount a series of strikes and public demonstrations, but without much impact. A few small bombs were exploded (without casualties), and the takeovers of the mayors' offices were done with little violence or damage. Sandinista police held back and allowed the takeovers to run their course and be settled though nonviolent negotiation. The process was accompanied by sensationalistic press reporting, much of it exaggerated.[20]

CIAV officials interviewed in mid-1991 reported on cases (later included in CIAV's formal submission to the OAS General Assembly) in which the Sandinista militants, apparently with the support of police and military, interfered with CIAV attempts to mediate situations in which hostages were taken and buildings occupied by former Contras. In some of these situations, the CIAV officials felt that the Sandinistas had murdered former Contras in cold blood after surrendering.[21]

Tensions did not abate in Nicaragua during 1991, even though the Chamorro government took some steps to try to lower strains. These steps included the removal of Sandinista military personnel who were acting as police officers in key areas and a series of talks between the Nicaraguan Resistance and the Sandinistas and between the government and the Recontras. Although the military had drawn down sharply, most of the reductions were in the southeast region, where tensions had been minimal. There were few reductions of the military in the northern areas with the greatest problems. In commenting on the situation at midyear, CIAV chief Murray warned that if there were an armed clash the whole conflict could break out all over again. He added that "if the government doesn't begin to address some of these issues, you'll see more and more former Contras become Recontras."[22]

Visits to resettlement areas in which former Contras lived in mid-1991 revealed their frustrations and their lack of confidence in both the Chamorro government and the CIAV-OAS efforts to help them. In a typical rural settlement area near Yalí in northern Nicaragua, a group of about 25 Contra *desalzados* (former combatants) were building permanent housing with materials supplied by CIAV-OAS, which daily sent a representative to check on their well-being. But they complained of harassment by the Sandinista police and problems in getting medical care. They expressed little hope for a better life in the future, and there appeared to be little work to sustain them. In a parallel visit to an urban resettlement area (named "3-80" after Enrique Bermúdez; see Figure 8.1), things were also bleak, with complaints that they got little help from either the government or CIAV-OAS. At the Managua 3-80 site, the leaders complained that it seemed as though CIAV was conspiring with the Chamorro government to force them away from their settlement and into the countryside where they would be a less visible problem. They spoke of a violent option available to them, but said they were reluctant to go that route.[23]

A new word was added to the Nicaraguan political dictionary in late August 1991: "*Recompas*."[24] The word was coined to identify Sandinistas who had taken up arms to confront the Recontras. Since the Sandinistas had often called each other "*Compas*" (short for "*compañeros*") during the period of fighting against Somoza in 1977–1979, the term "Recompa" seemed an appropriate label, in that it stressed the parallel with the "Recontras." By and large, the Recompas were former members of the Sandinista military or security apparatus who had seen combat against the Contras, and who had access to weapons and ammunition. This latter point was frequently cited by the Recontras as proof that the Recompas continued to have ties to the Sandinista leadership.

**Figure 8.1   Rubber Stamp of the "Comandante 3-80"
Barrio Enrique Bermúdez Communal
Committee on the Outskirts of Managua**

Note: Obtained by Jack Child on LASA research seminar, June 1991.

Both Recontras and Recompas were active in the northwestern part of Nicaragua in late 1991. Although actual combat between the two groups was rare, it was not uncommon for patrols from one side to enter small towns and villages only a few days after the other group had passed through. Since their logistical structures were quite primitive, both groups relied on support volunteered, or extracted by threat, from campesinos and villagers. Anarchy and violence were beginning to take over large sections of northwest Nicaragua, prompting some deputies in the Congress to call for the insertion of a peace-enforcing multinational body large and powerful enough to disarm both groups and restore order.[25]

Violeta Chamorro's response was to create a National Security Commission to try and persuade all armed civilians, both Recontras and Recompas, to put down their weapons. The commission included the key ministries, the Sandinista People's Army (EPS), both major political groupings (FSLN and UNO), and representatives from the Catholic Church and CIAV-OAS. ONUCA, because of its mandate and reluctance to get involved in internal matters, was not a member of this commission. One innovative idea was to create a bipartisan National Disarming Brigade that would be charged with negotiating with both groups and persuading them to turn in weapons. Another approach was to invite Recompas into the ranks of the rural police as a way of assuring their safety.[26]

CIAV-OAS was very active in these negotiations, and Santiago Murray did not hesitate to criticize many of the participants, including those in the Chamorro administration, for mistakes.[27] In turn, they frequently criticized CIAV-OAS for going beyond its mandate and becoming too deeply involved in internal Nicaraguan matters. The Sandinistas continued to feel that CIAV-OAS favored the Recontras over the Recompas; in an interview in October, former President Daniel Ortega said that "the work the CIAV is doing at the government's request does not contribute to strengthening the CIAV's role but rather tends to weaken it. The CIAV favors only one group, not all the citizens involved in the recontra problem."[28] In response, Santiago Murray issued a lengthy press release defending CIAV's neutrality, explaining that CIAV had been contacted by the Recontras as a channel to the government, and suggesting that it might leave Nicaragua if these unfair attacks on it continued.[29]

In agreements signed with the Chamorro administration in October and November 1991, both the Recontras and Recompas committed themselves to seeking a peaceful solution to their differences, but as 1991 came to an end, the groups remained armed, the situation tense, and the potential for more violence high. CIAV's role was positive in that it was mediating, but it continued to pay a price for involvement in Nicaraguan politics.

Even though CIAV-OAS had a mandate to operate in Nicaragua through 1992, there were doubts in Nicaragua and Washington that this would be wise or even possible due to the polarization of Nicaraguan politics and the way in which CIAV was being caught up in the political battles. CIAV personnel in Nicaragua were concerned about their own physical safety when, in some of their mediating tasks, they had to literally step between warring and heavily armed factions. At OAS headquarters in Washington, and in U.S. government policy circles, there was concern over the declining effectiveness of CIAV in this environment, and a nagging worry that a politically committed CIAV (or even the perception of one) could have a negative impact on the OAS as a whole.[30]

ONUCA IN 1991

ONUCA's role in 1991 was reduced to a token one in Nicaragua, and it played a waiting game to see if an expanded mandate in El Salvador would give it another significant peacekeeping or peace-observing role such as it had with the demobilization of the Nicaraguan Contras. Thus, in strong contrast with CIAV, ONUCA was able to keep a low profile and avoid getting bogged down in internal politics. The Secretary-General's report to the Security Council on ONUCA in late April 1991 makes clear the extent of the reductions and changes in the organization after Contra demobilization, and after the implementation of the changes in ONUCA recommended by the Secretary-General in his October 1990 report to the Security Council.[31] In April 1991 ONUCA's strength was down to 158 military observers and 29 Argentine naval crew on the Gulf of Fonseca patrol boats, plus civilian support personnel. There were further temporary reductions in ONUCA in late 1990 and early 1991 to support the UN Election Verification Mission in Haiti (ONUVEH).

The retrenchment in ONUCA was not due just to the end of the Contra war; there were other major UN peacekeeping commitments in this period that demanded many of the UN's peacekeeping management resources, to say nothing of troop contributions. In April the Security Council authorized the creation of a peacekeeping mission on the Iraq-Kuwait border. The total personnel commitment was 1,440, with 300 observers and 680 infantry (five companies) for security. With these commitments the UN's worldwide peacekeeping operations now involved some 11,000 observers and peacekeepers from more than 40 countries in nine active operations. Meanwhile, UN members were $1.5 billion behind in dues, and this new operation was predicted to cost $123 million for the first six months. Two months later the UN mounted a Joint Verification and Monitoring Commission to supervise and verify the cease-fire in the Angolan civil war. The Angolan commitment was 440 monitors to enforce the truce and demobilization and 90 observers to monitor the national police. UN costs were estimated at $132 million.

With its reduced strength and limited helicopter assets, ONUCA was only able to conduct patrolling and verification in a few small areas, although the Secretary-General maintained that it continued to serve as a deterrent to illegal support of insurgents across borders and was always available to investigate specific complaints. As in the past, ONUCA did not directly observe any violations of the Esquipulas agreements, leading the Secretary-General to delicately raise the issue of ONUCA's cost-effectiveness in his April report to the Security Council. Pérez de Cuéllar was also diplomatically critical of the various nations of Central America, which, he felt, should be doing more on their own to control their borders:

> It was noted, however, that the presence of national army and security personnel in some sensitive border areas did not always appear to be sufficient to enable Governments concerned to comply with those (security) undertakings. Indeed, during the past six months, ONUCA observers have discerned a tendency to reduce the presence of national army and security forces in certain areas where violations of the undertakings might have occurred in the past and might still be taking place.[32]

It seemed as though the countries involved, mainly Nicaragua, Honduras, and El Salvador, wanted to turn the whole problem of border surveillance over to ONUCA, leading the Secretary-General to further observe "that ONUCA is not mandated, staffed or equipped to detect clandestine activities or to take physical action to prevent them. Those functions properly belong to the five Governments, which agreed at Esquipulas to cease aid to irregular forces and insurrectionist movements and to prevent the use of one State's territory for attacks on others."

Although ONUCA did not directly detect any Esquipulas violations, it was called on a few times in this period by the Central American governments to investigate alleged violations of the Esquipulas agreements. One important issue was the source of surface-to-air missiles in the hands of the FMLN. The Nicaraguan government (and especially the EPS) was anxious to prove that they were not the source of the missiles, other than the 28 that had been "illegally" transferred from EPS stocks in October 1990. (Seventeen of these were subsequently returned, and the FMLN claimed it had fired the remaining 11.) Thus, about once a month the Managua office of ONUCA was requested by the EPS to verify and report its missile stocks as an indication that they were not supplying them to the FMLN.

ONUCA was also involved in investigating several incidents in which Salvadoran soldiers had crossed the border into Honduras during firefights with the FMLN. The Hondurans were very sensitive to this type of incursion given their history of conflict with El Salvador, and specifically the 1969 war. ONUCA served a useful, if limited, role in assuring the Hondurans that these incidents were related to the Salvadoran civil war and did not represent any attempt to restart the 1969 conflict. ONUCA also collaborated in a limited way with the Central America Security Commission, sending observers to its various meetings to provide advice and comment on the commission's work, especially as it related to ONUCA.

Finances continued to be a problem. Even at its reduced level, ONUCA was costing close to $3 million a month, and the ONUCA special account was constantly in arrears. Furthermore, the commitments of the five Central American nations to provide rent-free office space was honored by only one country. The Central American nations, nevertheless, continued to press ONUCA to increase its activities to include clearing minefields, verifying arms inventories, disarming civilians, and installing surveillance radars on their borders. UN officials on the ground and in New York resisted these appeals on the grounds that they exceeded ONUCA's mandate, and that staffing was not available.[33]

In contrast to CIAV, ONUCA was held in almost universally high regard by the Central Americans who knew of it or worked with it, an indication of its success in staying above partisan politics. Extensive discussions with a broad range of Nicaraguans in mid-1991 confirmed this high regard for ONUCA, with no significant criticisms except for minor complaints by some former Contras, who felt ONUCA could do more for them, as CIAV was attempting, and by a few frustrated CIAV officials, who felt they were being blamed unfairly for some of ONUCA's problems. One notable exception to this high regard for ONUCA was the Salvadoran extreme Right, which felt that any UN involvement in the Salvadoran peace process would be a sellout to the FMLN.

Some of the minor criticisms leveled at ONUCA inside Nicaragua were the usual ones heard in poor developing nations that resent international civil servants accustomed to a standard of living well above the norm in the receptor nation. In a land where most people traveled by jam-packed buses or trucks, and horses or mules in the countryside, the sight of clean new white UN jeeps and pickup trucks was bound to have an impact. In fairness to the UN personnel, many of them cheerfully accepted conditions that were somewhat of a hardship and certainly not what they were accustomed to. The professionalism of ONUCA was immediately and continually recognized. Political partisans knew and respected their impartiality, and realized that the blue berets were not about to be pulled into supporting one side or another. There were misunderstandings, language problems (including some difficulty in understanding Spanish speakers from Spain), and many frustrations, but on the whole ONUCA left a very positive impression, especially in Nicaragua.

There were some strains between ONUCA and CIAV-OAS. The constant, and frequently unfair, attacks on CIAV-OAS by the Sandinista press was a source of deep frustration for CIAV personnel; denials and clarifications were ignored or distorted. One incident in June 1991 illustrates the problem. On 7 June near Sébaco, a Nicaraguan by the name of Hildebrando Dávila was struck and killed by an ONUCA vehicle. *Barricada* claimed it was a CIAV-OAS vehicle, but also noted that the driver was Irish and that he was accompanied by an interpreter (this would make it highly unlikely that they were from the OAS). In fairness to the Sandinista newspaper, the inaccurate story could have been based on confusion caused by the fact that a CIAV vehicle, which looked very similar to the UN jeep, arrived shortly after the accident. However, even after it was made clear that ONUCA, and not CIAV, was at fault, there was no retraction or correction to the story. In fact, *Barricada* continued to harp on the recklessness of CIAV personnel and their cruelty in refusing to compensate the family. CIAV personnel were annoyed that ONUCA had not done more to take public blame for the accident, especially since they felt that the mob of relatives and friends had been about to lynch the ONUCA driver, who was saved only by the fortuitous arrival of the CIAV vehicle.[34]

Strains of a different sort for ONUCA became apparent in late June 1991 when a rocket-propelled grenade (RPG-7) hit its headquarters in Tegucigalpa, with no casualties but some damage to the building. The Honduran guerrilla organization Frente Patriótico Morazonista (FPM) claimed credit, saying in a communiqué that it was "a protest against the UN's submissive attitude toward U.S. imperialistic diplomacy" and "the way in which the UN was being used by the CIA to permit foreign intervention in the Third World. . . . The original objectives which the UN had in its foundation have been denatured, and with this the UN's reason for being has ended."[35] Observers and UN personnel discounted the FPM's claim, believing that the attack was probably related to the violent anti-UN views expressed by right-wing extremists in El Salvador. In November ONUCA's offices in Managua were hit by two small bombs that did little damage; no one claimed credit for the attack.

THE SALVADORAN PEACE
PROCESS IN 1990–1991: ONUSAL

The situation in El Salvador in these two years was characterized by a continuing civil war and hopes for peace that culminated in intense UN-sponsored talks. A cease-fire agreement was reached in a dramatic New Year's Eve Act of New York that set up a major new UN verification and observation mission. Contra demobilization in Nicaragua provided a useful precedent for El Salvador, although other events in Nicaragua continued to affect the search for peace in El Salvador and the region as a whole.

Even while the Sandinista military continued to deny they were involved in supplying the FMLN in El Salvador with weapons or other support, incidents occurred that made these denials suspect, and that threatened not only stability in Nicaragua, but also any progress in the Salvadoran peace process. In July two FMLN members were caught transporting weapons (grenades and rocket-launchers) close to Managua, and the Chamorro government informed ONUCA of the arrests. The *Washington Post* reported that the U.S. government had information that the Sandinistas were still supplying the FMLN, but "very carefully."[36] It was also possible that the arms were being transported from one FMLN site within Nicaragua to another to avoid detection. The *Post* quoted a European military attaché as saying that even though ONUCA was watching the borders, they were very porous, which offered tempting opportunities for the Sandinistas to help their ideological counterparts in El Salvador. Other factors facilitated the possible transfers of weapons: the Chamorro government had allowed insurgent groups such as the FMLN to keep offices in Nicaragua, and one of the Sandinista government's final acts was to grant Nicaraguan citizenship to some 300 Salvadorans living in Nicaragua, many of them with FMLN ties.

In an attempt to control the flow of weapons, the Salvadoran foreign minister asked ONUCA to increase its border surveillance, and ONUCA responded by requesting that its Argentine naval patrol craft watch for arms trafficking from Nicaragua. However, no interceptions were made. FMLN spokespersons denied that they were getting arms from Sandinistas, and said that former Contras were the biggest source of their weapons, including the antiaircraft missiles the guerrillas had been using in recent fighting against the Salvadoran government. They added that the weapons turned in to ONUCA by the Contras were only the "arms that didn't work. They hid the rest to sell and make money."[37] This had been going on for about two years but increased after the Contras demobilized. Another source of weapons, according to the FMLN, was corrupt officers of the Guatemalan, Salvadoran, and Honduran militaries.

The latter part of 1990 saw more talks between the FMLN and the government of El Salvador. From the earliest stage of talks, both sides expressed an interest in having the UN (but not the OAS) involved in verifying any agreements reached. The Nicaraguan experience with ONUCA was seen as positive by almost all parties, although the FMLN was more enthusiastic about the possibility than the government and the far Right remained firmly opposed to UN involvement. In an interview after his October 1990 UN trip, President Cristiani stressed the importance of his meeting with the Secretary-General to discuss the peace process under his sponsorship, adding that there was agreement to extend ONUCA's mandate beyond 6 November so that it could "make even greater efforts to address the Salvadoran problem and the continuous flow of weapons to the FMLN."[38]

In late 1990 there were several incidents involving ONUCA that raised questions about whether either side really wanted an effective UN presence and that pointed out the difficulties the UN would have in setting up a peace-observing or peacekeeping mission in El Salvador. In one incident, on the Honduran-Salvadoran border near Perquín, the FMLN claimed to have detained members of ONUCA who were trying to pass through areas under FMLN control to visit Sabanetas (Morazán Department). The FMLN accused the government of risking the lives of the foreigners, stressing that this was an irresponsible provocation. The FMLN communiqué noted that the observers did not follow the procedures agreed on with the UN under which any ONUCA visit to FMLN areas had to be previously coordinated with them. The ONUCA delegation was quoted (in an FMLN "Press Bulletin") as saying that the Salvadoran government did not recognize the existence of any areas controlled by the FMLN and therefore had authorized ONUCA's travel.[39]

In late December the Secretary-General announced that the Security Council had authorized the creation of the UN Observer Group in El Salvador (ONUSAL), whose mission would be to supervise the accords signed by the FMLN and Salvadoran government. ONUSAL's first task would be limited to verifying respect for human rights, but this would not happen until it became clear to what extent the group could function in El Salvador, especially since a cease-fire had not been agreed on. The deployment of ONUSAL was delayed until mid-1991, but in the meantime preparations were being made. ONUCA personnel were alerted that they might be detached and become the advance party of ONUSAL, as was the custom in creating new UN peacekeeping and peace-observing missions. The basic plan was to follow the successful Nicaraguan experience and first send a small peace-observing group with a limited mandate (observing human rights and elections) that could be expanded later if warranted. Some of the ONUCA personnel were more than a little concerned over the security situation in El Salvador, given the level of violence that country had experienced for so long, and especially in the face of threats against the UN by different factions involved in the civil war, particularly the far Right.[40]

Events in early and mid-1991 were leading both the FMLN and the Salvadoran Army to the realization that neither could achieve a decisive military victory. Two significant events were the "missile crisis" (the transfer of surface-to-air missiles to the FMLN) and the January 1991 shooting down of a U.S. helicopter, and subsequent killing of two surviving crewmen on the ground, by the FMLN. The Bush administration reacted by saying that because of the killing of the helicopter crew, they would now push to restore military aid to El Salvador, which the Congress had frozen because of human rights abuses. This tended to bolster the army, while possession of the missiles strengthened the FMLN. Thus, both felt they could negotiate from a position of some strength, but since this strength might not last very long, there were important time pressures to make concessions.

UN-mediated talks opened in Mexico in January 1991 with the presence of Pérez de Cuéllar's right-hand man, Alvaro de Soto. Little initial progress was made, and the question of the structure and role of the armed forces was the principal area of disagreement. There was pressure for a cease-fire to end the 12 years of bloodshed, but de Soto said that the negotiating agenda ruled out an immediate cease-fire. A cease-fire, monitored by UN peacekeeping personnel, could be put in place only after political agreements had been reached. He added: "As in many or most attempts at conflict settlement, we are stuck with wartime negotiations, and the FMLN considers military pressure essential to push those negotiations forward."[41]

By mid-February the shape of some of the proposals, including UN involvement in peacekeeping and peace observing, was becoming clearer. An early proposal for the FMLN to withdraw to "peace pockets" was rejected by them as unconditional surrender. The FMLN proposal for the creation of zones based on territorial control was not acceptable to the Salvadoran government and the military because it would force them to acknowledge that the FMLN controlled territory. A third proposal, put forward by the UN, called for the creation of a zone of three concentric circles, similar to the security zones used in Nicaragua. The Salvadoran government security forces would be on the outside, a UN peacekeeping force in the middle, and the FMLN in the innermost circle. The FMLN continued to demand a purge of the armed forces and major changes in the security and political structure, however, and the talks ended with no agreement.[42]

Reflecting its increasing prestige and success in Nicaragua, the UN was playing a critical role in the Salvadoran search for peace. In his October speech in the UN General Assembly, President Cristiani said that he "highly valued the verification of the UN peace process," and that "the model of verification that we have proposed and agreed upon to definitely end the conflict is unprecedented." He mentioned two guarantees of peace in El Salvador. The first was "the will of the people to sustain it. . . . The other guarantee is international verification."[43]

A UN proposal, leaked to the press in mid-February, would have divided El Salvador into two sets of zones under either government or FMLN control after a cease-fire. The draft proposal was seen as favoring the FMLN in that it set them up as a parallel force to the government and because the zones assigned to them would be under their complete political and economic control. The government interpreted these FMLN zones as simply being areas—similar to the security zones in Nicaragua—in which the rebels might disarm and then disband to form a political party, a notion the FMLN rejected. According to FMLN sources, the proposed scheme to set up separate areas would last for an open-ended transition period that would begin with a cease-fire and last until the peace talks led to the final disbanding of the FMLN. In the meantime, up to 8,000 UN peacekeeping troops would be deployed to patrol the zones. Although the location of the zones was not specified, a senior military official from the UN's peacekeeping planning staff had reportedly drawn up a detailed map that recognized the areas in which the guerrillas had traditionally exercised control. In any case, the proposal became moot when Salvadoran government representatives in Mexico refused to accept it.[44]

In March the Secretary-General dispatched another of his high-ranking assistants with Latin American experience to Central America. Pakistani diplomat and international civil servant Iqbal Riza went to El Salvador ostensibly to verify compliance with the UN-mediated agreement on human rights, but mainly to prepare the way for further UN involvement.[45] If the Mexico talks being mediated by de Soto progressed, the human rights portion of the UN activity would be enhanced and the mandate extended to include supervision of a cease-fire. During the visit, UN representatives for the first time visited areas of El Salvador held by the FMLN, who received them warmly.[46]

A new extended round of talks took place in April and May in Mexico. But things were now different: in March El Salvador's governing ARENA (Alianza Republicana Nacionalista) party won the legislative elections, but lost its majority with 44.3 percent of the vote. These were the first elections not sabotaged by the FMLN since the war began. The Christian Democrats (the party of the late President Duarte) came in second, and there was a strong show of support for the leftist Democratic Convergence led by Rubén Zamora (12 percent, up from 3.8 percent in the 1989 presidential elections). The elections were monitored by over 200 international observers, including 160 from the OAS. The presence of rebel-backed leftist deputies in the legislature was seen as boosting the chances for a peace agreement by getting them involved in the open political process. There were indications that both sides now seemed to think the time was right for peace talks.[47] The Left believed the government realized that it could not win militarily, that U.S. aid was not likely to continue indefinitely, and that business interests wanted peace. The Right felt that the FMLN had lost international and domestic support with the end of the Cold War and the defeat of the Sandinistas, and also realized that it could not win on the battlefield. Nevertheless, there was concern that hard-liners on both sides would not accept the peace process.

The Salvadoran military's unhappiness with the peace process was showing up in various ways. On 12 April a key FMLN commander (and nephew of President Chamorro), Antonio Cardenal, was killed in an army ambush along with 13 other guerrillas. There was speculation that the army targeted him to provoke the FMLN and derail the peace talks.[48] When de Soto's plan for restructuring the army, under UN supervision, and geographic separation of the two sides became known, it caused a strong negative reaction within the army senior command, who tried to discredit it by insinuating that de Soto had been co-opted by the FMLN. But the Salvadoran Army leadership was stunned when told that the UN plan had been cleared with U.S. UN Ambassador Thomas Pickering, who had been ambassador to El Salvador from 1982 to 1985. The army made a counterproposal for military reform under presidential control that was much more modest and totally excluded UN participation. The army's strong feelings on this issue were to be a constant stumbling block in the peace process because the Salvadoran military was deeply suspicious of the UN's motives and felt that going along with this plan would lead to its destruction as an institution.[49]

Despite these problems, in late April 1991 the Salvadoran government and FMLN representatives reached a general agreement in Mexico on government and military reforms, although there were no concrete measures for a cease-fire. These were the first substantive agreements in years of talks, and led FMLN representative Joaquín Villalobos to say that the negotiating process was irreversible. There was to be a UN-appointed commission to investigate human rights abuses and a Truth Commission to investigate the more serious crimes in the 11 years of war. The three members would be appointed by the Secretary-General, and the commission would make a report to him in six months, and then disband. Both sides still had to address the thorny issues of purging the military and determining the size and location of rebel and army zones under their control. The government recognized the need to turn the army into a less repressive and authoritarian force, but categorically rejected the long-term FMLN goal of eliminating the army entirely, arguing that a government had a right to have a military. An FMLN leader noted, in response to a comment about changes in the Soviet Union and its satellites, that "the Berlin Wall was in Europe. In El Salvador, the Berlin Wall is the armed forces. That's what people here have to bring down."[50]

Encouraged by the progress in the talks, the UN Security Council authorized the formal creation of ONUSAL in late May 1991 with the initially limited mandate of only investigating human rights violations. The original group would include 70 observers, 28 police, and 15 military officials, and would have offices in San Salvador and the departments of San Miguel, San Vicente, Morazán, and Chalatenango. The Security Council also authorized U.S. $32 million to finance it for one year. If a cease-fire was signed, ONUSAL would assist in supervising the agreement through peace observing and would receive additional personnel. Most of the Salvadoran political spectrum welcomed ONUSAL. Radio Farabundo Martí praised the Security Council decision to establish ONUSAL, calling it "an indisputable victory for the negotiations and the civil rights to which all Salvadorans are legitimately entitled."[51] It also applauded the United States for supporting the international verification of human rights in El Salvador.

But the extreme Right bitterly opposed ONUSAL. Fliers distributed to restaurants and stores in San Salvador demanded that they refuse to serve foreigners or Salvadorans working for the United Nations, the International Red Cross, or other relief organizations. *El Diario de Hoy* harshly attacked the peace process, calling the UN mediators Communist bureaucrats, and labeling the accords a sellout to Communists. The Crusade for Peace and Labor argued that ONUSAL was unconstitutional and violated El Salvador's sovereignty. And the Salvadoran Anti-communist Front issued a communiqué threatening to wage "a real and bloody war if there is an attempt to impose the will of internationalists." It further said that if the government signed an agreement with the FMLN, "Salvadorans will never accept impositions from ONUSAL, the CIA, and the FMLN, even if agreements are signed abroad."[52] UN personnel were understandably nervous about serving in ONUSAL under these threats, which, in the context of the history of the violent Right in El Salvador, were quite credible.

ONUSAL was formally opened in San Salvador on 26 July 1991 when Iqbal Riza signed the implementing protocol with the Salvadoran foreign minister. Riza pointed out that ONUSAL's work would be in two stages. In the first two months, the observer team would study El Salvador's judicial and administrative system and meet representatives from all the parties involved in the conflict. After this preliminary process, the second stage would begin, when ONUSAL would receive accusations of human rights violation and investigate them. Riza noted that ONUSAL was unprecedented for the UN because it had never before authorized such a mission prior to the signing of a cease-fire.[53]

The unprecedented arrangement was a calculated gamble by the UN, and especially the Secretary-General. It was an open secret that Pérez de Cuéllar badly wanted a signed agreement and a cease-fire between the FMLN and the Cristiani government before he stepped down as UN Secretary-General at the end of 1991.

With increasing pressure from the UN, a new round of talks in September 1991 produced the New York agreement, which established the general framework for conditions and guarantees under which the guerrillas would lay down their weapons and become integrated into the political and economic life of a post–civil war El Salvador; it also laid out the general steps for the purging, reorganization, and reduction of the armed forces.[54] The agreement would be administered by a new National Commission for the Consolidation of Peace (COPAZ), which would have the support of outside parties, to include the UN and ONUSAL. The key outside parties were the so-called friends of El Salvador: Mexico, Colombia, Venezuela, and Spain, which represented the original Contadora countries, less Panama and with the addition of Spain. The UN senior official charged with peacekeeping matters, Marrack Goulding, reportedly had his staff prepare a plan for separating the Salvadoran military and the FMLN by confining them to secure areas, which would be observed by ONUSAL, backed up by peacekeeping troops.[55] This arrangement, similar to the use of the Venezuelan infantry battalion in Nicaraguan Contra demobilization, placed the UN's role somewhere between peacekeeping and peace enforcement, at least during the critical stages of reorganizing the military and demobilizing the FMLN guerrillas.

However, the agreement did not include the crucial cease-fire, which was hopefully to be negotiated in December.[56] This left both sides with the incentive to improve their tactical situation on the ground as quickly as possible, and in effect led to more intensified fighting as the year drew to a close.

Reaction to the New York agreement ranged from positive (especially the FMLN), to cautious (the Salvadoran military), to hostile opposition (the Salvadoran right-wing). The strongest criticism came from the more conservative elements of the ARENA party, who went so far as to accuse President Cristiani of making a deal with the FMLN to sell out the country to the guerrillas.[57] ONUSAL was the target of much of this hostility, such as when Armando Calderón Sol, head of ARENA, denounced it as ineffective and harmful to Salvadoran sovereignty: "The ONUSAL people were not sent to the country to enjoy our beaches or to intervene politically in the domestic life of the country."[58] He added that the Salvadoran armed forces must be the only body in the country authorized to carry out an armed pacification process that would end the war and violence. ONUSAL representatives felt obligated to defend themselves from accusations that they had been accomplishing little while waiting for the results of the New York talks and the possibility of a cease-fire. The cease-fire came with the 31 December 1991 Act of New York, signed by the Salvadoran government and the FMLN in the final hours of Pérez de Cuéllar's tenure; the gamble had paid off and ONUSAL's time had come.

THE GUATEMALAN PEACE PROCESS, 1990–1991

The peace process in Guatemala was from the beginning much more difficult than in Nicaragua or even El Salvador because of the very inflexible positions of the major players. On the government side, the civilian presidents exercised limited power, and only to the extent that the military permitted. On matters of security, including any hint of negotiations with the guerrillas, the army had veto power over any decisions, and no negotiations could be considered realistic unless the military was involved. Because of human rights violations, U.S. military assistance had been cut off, and the Guatemalan military, after an initial period of some difficulty, adjusted to the cutoff and in effect welcomed it because it meant they could to a large extent ignore U.S. pressures. The guerrillas in Guatemala were equally intractable. They had been fighting in the hills since the early days of the Cuban-inspired *foco* guerrillas in the early 1960s; they held substantial portions of Guatemala's remote mountain areas; and they could count on the loyalty of many Indians who were alienated by the army's violent and frequently abusive counterinsurgency campaign. It is against this setting that a series of meetings in 1990 and 1991 must be seen as representing limited, but significant progress toward a Guatemalan peace agreement with international verification and observation perhaps similar to that undertaken in Nicaragua.

The first of these meetings took place in March 1990 in Oslo, Norway, and concluded with little more than an agreement to continue the process. The agreement made reference to the reconciliation called for in Esquipulas II, and called on the UN Secretary-General to observe the process and serve as guarantor of the agreements and commitments undertaken.[59] It is important to note that one of the National Reconciliation Commission (NRC) delegates to the Oslo talks was Jorge Serrano, who was to replace Cerezo as the next elected civilian president in 1991. The Oslo meeting was followed by others in El Escorial, Spain, and Metpec, Mexico, with little substantive progress, although each meeting mentioned the need for verification by the United Nations.

In early 1991 there was an important change in the Guatemalan situation when President Serrano assumed office. Outgoing President Cerezo had lost much of his credibility with the various factions in the Guatemalan conflict by the middle of his term in office and barely lasted to the end of his term. President Serrano was a conservative representing the Solidarity Action Movement, a coalition of center-Right groups, and had some support in the army. In early April 1991 he announced an "Initiative for Total Peace in the Nation." It was based on the Esquipulas agreement, called for a cease-fire, and asked for continued church and UN good offices, noting the involvement of the UN Secretary General's representative Francesc Vendrell in previous talks with the guerrillas. As was the case in El Salvador, the demobilization issues were the first big problem, with the army arguing that there could be no movement until the Unidad Revolucionaria Nacional Guatemalteca (URNG) laid down its arms, which they, not surprisingly, interpreted as surrender.[60] Serrano's initiative came at a time when the URNG was beginning to feel the same kinds of pressures to negotiate that were convincing the FMLN in El Salvador that the time for peace might be at hand. The Cold War was seemingly over, the peace process in Central America was gathering momentum, they had little to show for almost 30 years of fighting, and the army seemed as strong as ever. The older leaders of the insurgency seemed tired and lacked new initiatives, and the younger ones were more flexible.[61]

Several rounds of talks between the government and the URNG took place in Mexico in early and mid-1991. In April Guatemalan armed forces representatives and guerrilla representatives sat down at the same table for the first time ever. It was described as a feeling-out process, and an army spokesperson indicated no change in their basic position that the guerrillas must first put down their weapons before any meaningful dialogue could take place. Despite this comment, the head of ONUCA, Canadian Brigadier General Lewis Mackenzie, was optimistic that the two sides would eventually be able to negotiate a settlement, and UN representative Francesc Vendrell, who was an observer at the talks, also expressed satisfaction. The Mexico accord, which came out of this first set of talks, called for agreement on a schedule for implementation, compliance, and international verification of the accords. Both delegations were high-level and authorized to speak for their side, which was not always true in the past. The military officers present were veterans of antiguerrilla operations and were supporters of former Minister of Defense General Alejandro Gramajo's counterinsurgency approaches and his National Stability Doctrine.[62] Subsequent rounds of talks in June and July repeated the Salvadoran pattern of guerrilla unwillingness to lay down their arms and army unwillingness to negotiate until they did. There was also the same strong interest on both sides (more prevalent in the URNG) that any agreements be verified by the United Nations and include the presence of a preliminary UN human rights verification body similar to ONUSAL in El Salvador.[63]

Conservatives in Guatemala reacted predictably, but their target in the presidency was less vulnerable than Cerezo had been. (Two coup attempts against Cerezo were attributed in part to his willingness to talk with the Left.) Serrano's credibility was described as having a "Nixon-to-China element" in that he would be taken more seriously by both the URNG and the army.[64] Nevertheless, an anonymous group of army officers (believed to be young field commanders), calling themselves "Officers of the Mountain," attacked the talks and said they would not allow the peace process to proceed. They argued that they now had two sets of enemies: the terrorist subversives and the traitors within the Guatemalan military itself. The Officers of the Mountain, noting their own sacrifices in the field, also criticized the army leadership for their luxurious lifestyle, and were specially incensed over the fund that President Serrano was setting up to assist in the demobilization of the guerrillas.[65] The defense minister responded that members of this group were not officers at all, but rather civilian politicians out to damage the army and the government.

The role of the UN in the Guatemalan peace process in 1991 remained helpful and positive, but limited to observing and facilitating the initial talks. ONUCA had established a headquarters in Guatemala City, along with two verification centers in Esquipulas and Cuilapa, but their activities were severely circumscribed by political realities and limitations placed on their movements by the government. While the Secretary-General and his representative could be reasonably optimistic about the initial talks, it was clear that any greater UN involvement in the Guatemalan peace process would lag far behind that of Nicaragua and El Salvador.[66]

THE ESQUIPULAS SECURITY COMMISSION AND DISARMAMENT

Overshadowed by the more dramatic events in Nicaragua, and the tentative progress in peace talks in El Salvador and Guatemala, was the quiet work of the Security Commission established by the original Esquipulas agreement. Charged with exploring the possibilities for disarmament and confidence building in Central America—with a long-term goal of creating a zone of peace—it met several times in 1991 and presented reports at various high-level meetings of the Central American foreign ministers and presidents.

Its effectiveness was clearly a function of the political will and internal developments in each of the five nations.[67] Nicaragua was shrinking the size of its swollen military for a variety of economic and political reasons, but nevertheless claimed that it was doing it because of Esquipulas, took credit for this in the Security Commission, and proclaimed the virtues of the Nicaraguan example in matters of disarmament. Costa Rica somewhat smugly, but with justification, noted the value of its own historical example in matters of demilitarization and disarmament, while El Salvador and Guatemala argued that they could not contemplate reducing their military establishments while they were still fighting insurgencies. For its part, Honduras pushed in the Security Commission for parity, a position that cynics said was motivated by the fact that it had the smallest military (other than Costa Rica), and thus would hold at that level while the others drew down.

A typical meeting of the Central American Security Commission was held in Managua in mid-April 1991 with an agenda that included: a presentation of inventories of bases (only Costa Rica and Nicaragua did so), troops, and arms; a report from the technical subcommittee on armament inventory by types; measures to strengthen ONUCA; assistance in mine removal; and civilian disarmament. El Salvador and Guatemala declined to provide information on their armed forces inventories, giving as reasons the ongoing insurgencies and peace talks in their countries. There was, nevertheless, a general feeling that the Security Commission should continue to attempt to reach its goals because, as Nicaraguan Vice Foreign Minister Ernesto Leal commented: "In Central America it is no longer possible to return to the old concepts of regional security, nor take roads already covered. . . . Central America can become an example of efforts and persistence in favor of arms reduction and the creation of a new model of inter-state relations."[68]

The Hondurans turned in their arms inventory to the Assistant Secretary-General at the OAS General Assembly meeting in Santiago in June in a somewhat dramatic procedure under which their document would remain in a wax-sealed envelope that was not to be opened until all five Central American countries had also turned in their inventories. The OAS General Assembly praised the work of the Security Commission and its role in establishing confidence-building measures.[69]

At the July 1991 Central America summit, the Hondurans floated their comprehensive disarmament and confidence-building proposal (a Central American security treaty), which would set ceilings on military inventories and troops. These ceilings generally reflected the views of the "southern three" (Honduras, Costa Rica, and Nicaragua), which favored drawdowns, and went against the positions of the "northern cone" of Central America (El Salvador and Guatemala), which did not favor any military reductions until their insurgencies ended. The impact of UN peace observing in Central America emerged in one phrase in the preamble of the Honduran draft security treaty, which stated: "Persuaded that their [Central American] security rests principally on an international peacekeeping system. . . "[70] The Honduran proposal had a heavy emphasis on confidence-building measures as a way of diminishing the possibility of interstate conflicts. These confidence-building measures would include a pledge by the Central American nations to forsake the use of force to settle disputes and a commitment from the United States not to support irregular movements in Central America. The proposal also included suggestions of new tasks for the armed forces, such as involvement in the control of drugs and protection of natural resources.

There was a sharp reaction to the Honduran proposal, including the suggestion that it was self-serving and went against the work of both the Security Commission and the UN. In response, President Callejas of Honduras became so irritated he threatened to withdraw from the meeting.[71] Nevertheless, some of the Honduran ideas found an echo in the speeches made at the Ibero-American summit that followed immediately afterward, including Peruvian President Fujimori's proposal for a disarmed Latin America.[72]

The notion of confidence-building measures was now firmly imbedded in Central American thinking about disarmament and lowering of tensions. A number of confidence-building measures were included in the Honduran security proposal, and the commission mentioned several others in its various reports to the Central American presidents. For example, in June 1991 plans were announced for the establishment of a formal hot line that would provide secure and immediate telephone links between the presidents of the five Central American nations and Panama.[73] Thus, one of the features of the long Contadora/Esquipulas process was the way in which it greatly increased communications between the Central American countries, and especially its presidents, foreign ministers, and senior military officials. This confidence-building measure, along with many others, was an important legacy of the peace process of the 1980s.

NOTES

1. Much of the material in this chapter is based on interviews conducted during a research trip to Nicaragua in June 1991, and supplemented with interviews in Washington, D.C., Ottawa, and Toronto. Under the ground rules prevailing in many of the interviews (especially of government and international organization officials), the sources are only generally attributed, without names.

2. Discussion with ONUCA personnel, Managua and Estelí, June 1991.

3. Discussion with CIAV-OAS officials and others, Managua, June 1991.

4. *Barricada Internacional*, 6 October 1990, 4–5; *Excelsior*, Mexico, 7 October 1990, 2A.

5. *Central America Report*, 23 November 1990, 353–354.

6. Discussions with a U.S. journalist, Managua, June 1991.

7. *Barricada*, 8 January 1991, in Foreign Broadcast Information Service (FBIS), 11 January 1991, 14.

8. Managua Domestic Service, 18 January 1991, in FBIS, 22 January 1991, 22.

9. Discussions with UNAG and FSLN officials, Managua, León, and Matagalpa, June 1991.

10. Interview with Alejandro Bendaña, Managua, 18 June 1991.

11. Personal observation and discussion with OAS and CIAV officials, Managua, Matagalpa, and Estelí, June 1991.

12. The author served with General Sumner and Colonel Bermúdez on the IADB in this period.

13. Visit to "Enrique Bermúdez 3-80" Contra resettlement camp, Managua, June 1991.

14. *Excelsior*, Mexico, 6 May 1991, 2A; Panama, ACAN, 9 May 1991, in FBIS, 9 May 1991, 25; *Nuevo Diario*, 23 June 1991, 6.

15. *Barricada*, 13 May 1991, in FBIS, 21 May 1991, 12; *Nuevo Diario*, 25 May 1991, in FBIS, 30 May 1991, 19.

16. For example, see Radio Nicaragua, 30 May 1991, in FBIS, 3 June 1991, 21; or *La Prensa*, 25 June 1991, 3.

17. *Excelsior*, Mexico, 8 June 1991, 2A; *Central American Report*, 21 June 1991, 181.

18. *Barricada*, 11 June 1991, in FBIS, 13 June 1991, 14; FBIS, 16 June 1991, 2.

19. A piñata is a large, candy-filled, papier-mâché toy figure frequently used in Latin American celebrations and fiestas. In the Nicaraguan context, the term came to mean the "gift" of these lands, houses, and other privileges to loyal Sandinistas from their leaders, who frequently ended up with the most generous "piñatas" of all.

20. The author was with a LASA-sponsored research trip in Nicaragua in mid- and late June 1991, and with the group observed Sandinistas occupying the mayors' offices in Managua and Matagalpa. The LASA group was in peaceful Yalí

the day that a radio station in Managua claimed it had been taken over by 500 Recontras; none were seen. (Managua, Radio Ya, 20 June 1991, in FBIS, 21 June 1991, 11.) The group's scheduled meeting with Matagalpa UNO Mayor Frank Lanzas had to be moved to his palatial home because Sandinistas had taken over his downtown office; it was vacated that same day, with no damage other than a broken window and some stolen basketballs.

21. Interviews with CIAV officials, Managua and other locations in Nicaragua, June 1991.

22. *Washington Post,* 29 June 1991, A14; *El Nicaragüense,* 21 June 1991, 2–3.

23. Interviews at former Contra resettlement camps in Yalí and Managua, June 1991.

24. Managua, Radio Sandino, 27 August 1991, in FBIS, 28 August 1991; *Excelsior,* Mexico, 20 September 1991, 2A; *Los Angeles Times,* 26 November 1991, 1.

25. *Barricada,* Managua, 30 August 1991, in FBIS, 3 September 1991.

26. *Notimex,* Mexico, 4 September 1991, in FBIS, 4 September 1991.

27. *New York Times,* 12 September 1991, 4; *Barricada,* Managua, 15 September 1991, in FBIS, 17 September 1991.

28. Managua, Sistema Nacional de Televisión, 4 October 1991, in FBIS, 9 October 1991.

29. Managua, Radio Nicaragua, 26 September 1991, in FBIS, 1 October 1991.

30. Discussions with OAS and U.S. government personnel in Managua and Washington, D.C., 1991.

31. UN Document S/22543, 29 April 1991.

32. Ibid., 4, 7.

33. Ibid., 9; discussions with ONUCA officials, Managua and Estelí, June 1991.

34. *Barricada,* 8 June 1991, 3; 21 June 1991, 3; discussions with UN and CIAV personnel, Managua and Estelí, June 1991.

35. *Nuevo Diario,* Managua, 23 June 1991, 1.

36. *Washington Post,* 21 July 1990, A21.

37. *San Francisco Chronicle,* 4 December 1990, 13A.

38. San Salvador Domestic Service, 2 and 4 October 1990, in FBIS, 9 October 1990, 6–8, 13–16.

39. San Salvador, AFP, 5 October 1990, in FBIS, 5 October 1990, 6. For text of FMLN bulletin, see FBIS, 9 October 1990, 19.

40. Interviews with ONUCA personnel, Managua, June 1991.

41. *Miami Herald,* 19 January 1991, 11A.

42. *Notimex,* Mexico, 21 February 1991, in FBIS, 21 February 1991, 21–22.

43. Report of the Secretary-General, UN Document A/45/706 (S/21931), 8 November 1990, 6–8, 10–13.

44. *Miami Herald,* 15 March 1991, 20A.

45. Discussions with Iqbal Riza at various International Peace Academy workshops (Cancún, Mexico, 1983, et al.). Riza was familiar with the intricacies of UN peacekeeping as well as the Latin American environment.

46. Radio Venceremos, 16 March 1991, in FBIS, 22 March 1991, 17.

47. *Washington Post,* 7 April 1991, A24.

48. *Central America Report,* 19 April 1991, 107–108; *Pensamiento Propio,* May 1991, 23–25.

49. Discussions with Salvadoran Army officers, Washington, D.C., 1990, 1991.

50. *Times of the Americas,* 15 May 1991, 1.

51. Radio Farabundo Martí, 21 May 1991, in FBIS, 22 May 1991, 9; and FBIS, 23 May 1991, 9–10; 24 May 1991, 11–15.

52. Discussions with UN personnel in Nicaragua, June 1991; *Excelsior,* Mexico, 7 June 1991, 2A; and Panama ACAN, 16 July 1991, in FBIS, 16 July 1991, 10.

53. San Salvador, Canal Doce Televisión, 26 July 1991, in FBIS, 29 July 1991; *Central America Report,* 16 August 1991, 247; *New York Times,* 13 August 1991, A5.

54. San Salvador, Radio Cadena, 25 September 1991, in FBIS, 26 September 1991.

55. *Central America Report,* 27 September 1991, 282.

56. *Washington Post,* 26 September 1991, A1; 27 September 1991, A25; *New York Times,* 27 September 1991, 6.

57. *Times of the Americas,* 11 December 1991, 2.

58. *El Mundo,* San Salvador, 1 November 1991, in FBIS, 4 November 1991. For ONUSAL response, see *Diario Latino,* San Salvador, 8 November 1991, in FBIS, 12 November 1991.

59. Text in FBIS, 2 April 1990, 30.

60. Guatemala Domestic Service, 8 April 1991, in FBIS, 9 April 1991, 11–15; *Central America Report,* 12 April 1991, 97–104.

61. *New York Times,* 25 May 1991, 4; *Pensamiento Propio,* May 1991, 14–15; interview with Alejandro Bendaña, Managua, June 1991.

62. *Excelsior,* Mexico, 27 April 1991, 2A; *Central America Report,* 3 May 1991, 121–122; discussions with General Gramajo, Washington, D.C., May 1989, June 1990.

63. *Times of the Americas,* 7 August 1991, 1; Commission on U.S.–Latin American Relations, "Memorandum on the Guatemala Peace Talks," 27 June 1991.

64. *Washington Post,* 17 May 1991, 6.

65. *Excelsior,* Mexico, 21 June 1991, 2A.

66. Report of the Secretary-General, UN Document S/21931, 8 November 1990, 8–9, 14–16.

67. Discussion with Alejandro Bendaña, Managua, 18 June 1991.

68. *Central America Report,* 26 April 1991, 119.

69. OAS Document AG/CG/doc. 12/1991, 6 June 1991.

70. Draft Central American Security Treaty, State Department Translation Division, no. 135433, 1991, 2; and Voz de Honduras, 5 July 1991, in FBIS, 8 July 1991.

71. *Excelsior,* Mexico, 15 July 1991, 10A; *Notimex,* Mexico, 16 July 1991, in FBIS, 17 July 1991, 2–3.

72. *Washington Post,* 20 July 1991, A16; *Times of the Americas,* 7 August 1991, 1.

73. *La Prensa,* Managua, 17 June 1991, 5.

PART 5
CONCLUSIONS

9

ASSESSMENT AND IMPLICATIONS

THE SIGNIFICANCE OF THE CONTADORA PROCESS

The importance and impact of the Contadora process varied for the different actors involved:

For Central America the main impact was the direct effect the process had on diminishing the ravages of years of conflict. In creating the conditions for peace through mediation, dialogue, and compromise, the process greatly increased the Central American nations' knowledge of each other and multiplied their contacts at many levels. As we have seen, the Contadora process was an important milestone for Central America in that it introduced the concepts of "confidence-building measures" and "zones of peace" to that geographic area. While it is still utopian, the idea of Central America as a zone of peace is now deeply rooted in the ideals and aspirations of those who have lived with Central American conflict for so long. Until the goal of a zone of peace is achieved, the confidence-building measures that began with Contadora can help the Central Americans work in practical and immediately achievable ways to make conflict less likely to break out again due to misunderstandings, accidents, or miscommunication of intentions.

For Latin America the Contadora process represented an attempt to find a Latin American solution to a Latin American problem involving the United States. Although this was not the only such attempt in this period, the magnitude and scope of the Contadora process, and its clash with U.S. interests and policies, made it a major benchmark in U.S.–Latin American relations. The four Contadora nations, Mexico, Venezuela, Colombia, and Panama, were the initial leaders in this process, but with the creation of the Lima Group, Peru, Argentina, Brazil, and Uruguay, and the widespread support for Contadora beyond the Lima Group, it became obvious that the process could count on the goodwill of almost all the Latin American nations, and many others outside the hemisphere as well. The involvement of this many Latin American nations also changed their dealings with each other and their relationship with the United States and the relevant international organizations. The survival of Contadora, and the success of the following Esquipulas process, led many of the Latin American nations to re-examine the hemisphere's security arrangements, which had been seriously undermined by a number of events occurring before and during the Contadora process, such as the Falklands/Malvinas war and the U.S. invasions of Grenada and Panama.

For the United States Contadora represented at best a well-meaning initiative that would eventually converge with U.S. goals in the region and at worst a serious challenge to U.S. influence and hegemony, not only in Central America but in the Western Hemisphere as a whole. The Reagan administration was hard pressed to come up with a consistent policy toward the Contadora process. Because of the widespread support it garnered, and the awkwardness of seemingly objecting to peace, the U.S. government rarely criticized Contadora publicly. However, there was much U.S. government opposition to the Contadora process, and this opposition frequently found its public outlet through the issue of verification of any agreements. This focus on verification thus became a way of blocking the Contadora process without seeming to, and especially without appearing to be against peace as an overriding good. U.S. policymakers recognized early on that Contadora was going to undermine the Reagan administration's goals in Central America— most significantly the goal of bringing down the Sandinista regime in Nicaragua, through covert or military means if necessary. They also recognized the broader implications for the Inter-American Security System and for the creation of interlinked zones of peace in the Western Hemisphere, which they perceived to be against long-range U.S. interests. Contadora, in effect, was the channel through which the principal nations of Latin America (with considerable outside support) were delivering to the world in general and the United States in particular the message that they wished to assume greater responsibility for their regional security in an arrangement markedly different from the one the United States had dominated for so long.[1]

For Canada the Contadora process was the beginning of a very new and historic role in the Western Hemisphere. It was, in effect, the coming-out of the hemisphere's perennial great absentee, and it is noteworthy that one important vehicle for this emergence was Canada's major contribution to the Contadora process: its previous experience as a helpful fixer in numerous UN peacekeeping and peace-observing operations.[2] Canada had to play a delicate game, being careful not to annoy its powerful neighbor (and important trade and security partner) to the south, while at the same time helping the Central American peace process in ways that were clearly not pleasing to the Reagan administration. Canada's involvement in the peace process was multifaceted, although this book has concentrated on the contribution it made by moving the Contadora verification problem from vague generalities to the realities of what it took to do it on the ground, culminating with the major Canadian role in the United Nations peacekeeping presence, ONUCA.[3]

For the United Nations the Contadora/Esquipulas process was important because it was its first involvement in Western Hemisphere peacekeeping and election monitoring. Coming at a time when UN peacekeeping was reaching unprecedented global popularity and effectiveness, it was one more step in the revival of the organization. It also changed the way many Latin Americans perceived the UN, and opened up the possibility of greater UN involvement in hemispheric security affairs. The role of several Latin American nations (plus Spain) in UN peacekeeping gave these countries the kind of practical experience the UN could very well call on in the future in the hemisphere and elsewhere.

For the Organization of American States, and the Inter-American System, Contadora/Esquipulas was both a threat and an opportunity. In the early years of the process, the threat involved frequent accusations that the OAS (and many of its instruments, such as the Rio Treaty) was inefficient and inoperative, especially after the debacle of the Falklands/Malvinas war. Indeed, one of the often heard explanations for the need to create the ad hoc Contadora Group was the inability of the OAS to confront the Central American crisis. As noted in Chapter 1, the OAS historically had dealt fairly effectively with Central American conflicts. But clearly the crisis of the 1980s was of a different kind, seemingly well beyond its ability to cope.[4] Furthermore, the Nicaraguans demonstrated a strong preference for bilateral contacts, or for the UN if multilateral solutions were necessary. The OAS, they felt, was under excessive U.S. influence. With time, the survivability and success of the Contadora process was seen by some as signaling an OAS without the United States or even the end of the OAS, although in the long run these views did not prevail.[5] The opportunities Contadora offered for the Organization of American States were not evident until the end of the process in late 1986, as it shifted to become Arias/Esquipulas. Surprisingly, at that point the OAS became a partner with the UN in the verification process and assumed a major role in the resettlement of the Contras in 1990 and 1991. However, as noted in Chapter 8, the controversy surrounding this role for the OAS suggested that this involvement with the Contras might be more a negative than a positive element in the recovery of the prestige and efficiency it lost in the early 1980s.

For conflict resolution approaches the Contadora process represented the beginning of a successful application of some basic principles to an area where they had previously been relatively unknown, or used under a very special set of circumstances characterized by heavy U.S. influence. As indicated in Chapter 1, the hemisphere's prior experiences with peacekeeping were negative ones stemming from, among other things, the 1965–1966 Inter-American Peace Force in the Dominican Republic and the ill-fated U.S. attempt to insert a peacekeeping presence in Nicaragua during the final decline of Somoza in 1979. The sensitivity toward the term "peacekeeping" in Latin America led to a de-emphasis of the concept and a new set of terms stressing the verification and technical facets of the process. There was an initial lack of realism on the part of the Contadora and Central American nations as to what kind of force would be required to do what in the verification process, and it is to the credit of the UN and the Canadians that realism was slowly, tactfully, and steadily stressed until it was accepted by the parties involved.[6]

The end result was what has accurately been called a minimalist operation that respected the Latin American wish for as few military personnel as possible and used the labels "observer" and "verifier."[7] When the occasion required it (as in the demobilization of the Contras in mid-1990), there was a reluctant and brief move up the spectrum to peacekeeping with the possibility of peace enforcement if essential.

Although confidence-building measures had always existed in traditional Western Hemisphere diplomacy and military-to-military contacts, the Contadora process marked the beginning of the deliberate use of confidence-building measure terminology, theory, and practice.[8] From 1983 on, it became increasingly common to see confidence-building ideas appear in articles, speeches, and proposals dealing with international and intermilitary relations in Latin America.

The Central American peace process also allowed the Latin American nations to further develop and apply their special notion of a "zone of peace." Linked to the broader Latin American push for zones of peace in Antarctica, the South Atlantic, and the Pacific, as well as the Caribbean, it potentially could be one of the most significant legacies of the process.[9]

THE EVOLUTION FROM CONTADORA TO ARIAS/ESQUIPULAS

The Arias/Esquipulas peace plan marked a turning point in both the Central American peace process and in important aspects of verification and confidence building. While Arias/Esquipulas was obviously different from Contadora, there were also important continuities, and Esquipulas would not have been possible without the groundwork laid and time gained by Contadora.

The shift from Contadora to Arias/Esquipulas also reflected some of the political and psychological undercurrents at work in the Central American peace process, as well as in the history of relations between Central America and the rest of the hemisphere. From the beginning of the Contadora process in 1983, there was always some irritation and even resentment among the Central American nations over the fact that a group of outside and, with the exception of Panama, much larger nations was becoming increasingly involved in Central American affairs. When the Lima Group joined the original four, the eight helper nations represented over two-thirds of Latin America's population, and the weight of their involvement in Central America was even more obvious. Thus, one of the characteristics of the Arias/Esquipulas process was that it was a *Central American* initiative, not one imposed or suggested from the outside.

One element that was dropped in the shift from Contadora to Esquipulas was the specificity of the verification measures and mechanisms. The Arias/Esquipulas documents do refer back to the draft Contadora Act on matters of security, verification, and control, but in such a way as to make it clear that these old provisions were to be the subject of negotiation and would undergo modification. With Esquipulas the five Central American nations took greater initiative, but also recognized that the demands of verification would require outside resources. Initially wishing to employ neither the Contadora nations nor the OAS, they turned to the global organization. The UN Secretary-General, and the nations that might be involved in carrying out the UN verification function, repeatedly made it clear that UN peace verification would not be easy or inexpensive, if it were to be carried out seriously.

Because of the ties to what went before, the Central Americans could feel that Arias/Esquipulas was the final stage of Contadora,[10] but it was now their own creation, which led to a much greater concern for addressing internal problems—such as pacification, reconciliation, *concertación,*[11] and democratization—with a schedule and procedures that *they* established and felt comfortable with. The United States made a major contribution to the Esquipulas process by lowering its profile and meddling less. In part, this was a natural function of the distractions of the Iran-Contra scandals; but ultimately it was due to the discrediting of the hard-liners in the Reagan administration, and then finally the different perspective (and views on the role of the disintegrating Soviet Union in Central America) held by the far more pragmatic Bush administration.

IMPLEMENTING AND VERIFYING ARIAS/ESQUIPULAS

In Chapter 1, fundamental peacekeeping principles were identified, based on an analysis of a wide range of peacekeeping experiences in the United Nations and regional international organizations. These basic principles of effective peacekeeping are applied here to the implementation and verification of the Esquipulas peace plan by ONUCA, and to a lesser extent CIAV-OAS.

1. *Consent of the principal parties:* All parties to the Central American crisis indicated their consent to peacekeeping in principle, but one could question the sincerity of the commitment by some of the parties involved. In particular, effective peacekeeping and verification of two key border areas (Nicaragua-Honduras and Nicaragua-Honduras–El Salvador along the Gulf of Fonseca) would affect the capacity of irregular groups to operate in Nicaragua and El Salvador. This affected the Contras far more than the FMLN, but was an element in the opposition to peacekeeping by the United States, and to a lesser degree the supporters of the FMLN in El Salvador.

2. *Impartiality and neutrality of the contingent:* ONUCA's impartiality and neutrality were rarely questioned, and its role, which focused on cross-border operations by irregular forces, generally kept it out of controversy. In the period during and after Contra resettlement, CIAV-OAS was not so fortunate because its basic role made it suspect in the eyes of the Sandinistas and their sympathizers.

3. *Balance:* In a similar fashion, the makeup of ONUCA reinforced its image of neutrality. The three major contributors included one Latin American nation (Venezuela—an original Contadora member and a major player in the peace process), one European nation (Spain—an ally of the United States with a special relationship to Latin America), and an even closer North American ally of the United States (Canada). Others involved in ONUCA, but to a lesser degree, were Germany, Ireland, Sweden, Brazil, Colombia, Ecuador, India, and Argentina. There were no nations closely allied to the Soviet bloc, but given the cooperative approach to the Esquipulas process taken by the United States and the Soviet Union, and the diversion caused by internal events in the latter, this posed few problems. As has been noted, the strong Argentine element in CIAV-OAS was perceived by the Sandinistas as contributing to its alleged tilt to the Contras, and can be seen as a violation of the principle of balance.

4. *Approval of the major powers:* Although the United States under the Reagan administration attempted to block the Contadora/Esquipulas process, by the time of the creation of ONUCA (December 1989), there was a high degree of understanding on Central American issues between the United States and the Soviet Union, which greatly facilitated the peacekeeping process.

5. *Freedom of movement and access within the area:* This basic requirement was met by the use of helicopters and a substantial fleet of four-wheel-drive vehicles, light aircraft, and patrol boats in the Gulf of Fonseca. There was concern at certain times that irregular forces might attempt to impede access to key areas by the verification groups, but this was not a major problem. Once the critical stage of Contra demobilization in 1990 passed, the cost of the helicopters led to a reduction in their numbers, which did in fact limit the coverage by ONUCA to symbolic levels only.

6. *Non-use of force:* This is a difficult but necessary condition for the professional soldiers on any peacekeeping contingent to accept, and in the Central American context, it could have been made more complicated by the fact that the contingent would be likely to encounter armed guerrilla groups that were not under the effective control of any nation and might fire at the peacekeepers for their own motives. However, this turned out not to be a significant problem for ONUCA because of the way its presence was generally accepted by all concerned. (CIAV-OAS personnel, of course, were all civilians and carried no weapons). The riskiest period for ONUCA was during the Contra demobilization in mid-1990 when it became necessary to bring in an armed Venezuelan parachute infantry battalion. It is to the credit of the UN peacekeepers, as well as those being demobilized, that there were no incidents involving the use of firearms. The observers in ONUCA were generally unarmed and operated under instructions to avoid situations in which arms would be necessary. The fact that two major groups of irregular forces, the Contras and the FMLN, had surface-to-air missiles caused some legitimate concern, but they were apparently never fired at ONUCA aircraft.

7. *Voluntary participation by a broad spectrum of states:* This principle, which closely parallels the balance principle, also did not prove to be a problem for ONUCA, despite the absence of representation from states allied to the Soviet Union. They were distracted by the disintegration of the Soviet state, which occurred about the time Esquipulas came to fruition. The problems stemming from CIAV-OAS's heavy representation from Argentina have been noted.

8. *The use of peacemaking to parallel peacekeeping:* This was perhaps the key to the success of the Esquipulas effort. The political will to reach peace was already in place when ONUCA arrived, and the mechanisms for effective peacemaking were already functioning. In hindsight, this confirmed the wisdom of the United Nations (and the Canadians as a key element in the UN approach) in avoiding premature commitment of a third-party neutral contingent.

9. *Centralized management of the administrative and logistical support:* An ad hoc group such as Contadora would probably have had major problems with this aspect of peacekeeping and verification. As noted in previous chapters, the Canadians were insistent on this point and, given their past experience with UN peacekeeping, strongly preferred that body's involvement. Centralized UN management made the Esquipulas process different from prior hemispheric peacekeeping or peace-observing efforts, in which the United States controlled logistics and administration. Given the U.S. position in Central America in the 1980s, this old arrangement was clearly not possible under Contadora or Esquipulas.

10. *A clear political mandate:* As suggested previously, peacekeeping

contingents in the field need an unambiguous set of rules under which they can operate and an available political body that can provide timely clarification if needed. The ad hoc nature of the Contadora process tended to violate this principle, and the worst case situation would have been a frustrated verification contingent caught in the middle of a touchy situation on the ground with no access to a higher body that could give it appropriate instructions. As with the centralized management principle, the Canadians quite correctly insisted on a clear political mandate from an established international organization, preferably the UN.

11. *Freedom of expression:* Under this principle the peacekeeping contingent must be able to freely report and make public, through the responsible oversight authority, any violations it finds. Neither ONUCA nor CIAV-OAS had any difficulty with this, although the partisan press in Nicaragua on occasion distorted news stories on CIAV-OAS for political purposes.

12. *Adequate financing:* Even when modest in scope and duration, peacekeeping is expensive. The complex nature of the Central American conflict environment and the logistical requirements imposed by the terrain and the variety of regular and irregular forces meant that even the relatively modest size of ONUCA was costly. This was a factor in reducing the size of ONUCA to symbolic dimensions after the key period of Contra demobilization ended. In the case of CIAV-OAS, there were constant complaints that the United States was not providing enough funds, and the very source of CIAV-OAS funds (the U.S. Agency for International Development) caused the Sandinistas in Nicaragua to suspect (and charge) that CIAV-OAS was an instrument of U.S. policy in supporting the Contras.

CENTRAL AMERICA AS A ZONE OF PEACE

The concept of a "zone of peace" was introduced in Chapter 1 when the basic concepts of "peacekeeping" and "confidence building" were explored. The zones were defined as extensive geographic areas in which explicit confidence-building measures had reached a point where the various parties in the region had significantly reduced their levels of armaments, while external military powers had been persuaded to reduce their military influence in the area to a minimum.

A zone of peace also implies that the parties accept a number of other commitments, including:

- Renouncing the use of force to solve problems and accepting established procedures to find peaceful solutions to conflicts and tensions;

- Strengthening mutual confidence and cooperation between states in the region;
- Moving toward arms reductions and cutting military spending;
- Establishing economic cooperation and integration arrangements;
- Denuclearizing the region;
- Respecting established norms regarding nonintervention;
- Persuading outside powers to limit their geopolitical influence in the region; and
- Removing foreign military bases.[12]

The possibility that the Central American peace process from 1983 to 1991 might lead to a zone of peace builds on these commitments and on a number of different but relevant situations in which the principles for creating zones of peace have been applied. Although none of these zones has achieved all of the elements listed above, each in its own way has strengthened the foundations on which other zones of peace, such as one in Central America, could be established.

The Antarctic Treaty system is perhaps the oldest of these zones of peace, although it was not called that when the treaty was signed in 1959.[13] But the treaty—and the large body of conventions, agreements, and resolutions stemming from numerous meetings—has established Antarctica as the world's first nuclear-free zone, as well as the largest demilitarized zone ever created. In Antarctica scientific cooperation has been an effective confidence-building measure, even between the bitterest of Cold War adversaries, or between warring states such as Argentina and the United Kingdom in 1982.

In a similar vein, global treaties to limit nuclear testing and proliferation, while not universally accepted, have also contributed to the establishment of regional denuclearized zones, such as those envisioned by the Western Hemisphere's Treaty of Tlatelolco.

Various subregions of the continent have been the subject of attempts to establish zones of peace. These have included the Caribbean (sometimes including Central America, and sometimes not), the South American landmass, and the South Atlantic.[14] The United Nations resolution establishing this latter area as a zone of peace was the result of post–Malvinas/Falklands war attempts to minimize the possibilities for further conflict in that area.

At various stages in the lengthy Contadora/Arias/Esquipulas peace process, the idea of making Central America a zone of peace has appeared. At times this has been implicit, and can be seen in the collective body of measures to reduce tensions, cut arms expenditures, limit the influence of foreign powers, and establish confidence-building measures among the regional states. But the peace process has also resulted in explicit calls for a zone of peace, such as at the December 1990 summit in Puntarenas, where there was discussion of a Nicaraguan initiative for a "Declaration of Central America as a Zone of Peace, Democracy and Cooperation." Discussion of the declaration indicated that a much broader notion of a "zone of peace" was being considered that would embrace the equally wide economic, political, and social measures imbedded in Contadora/Arias/Esquipulas.[15] In addition to the basic elements of a zone of peace described above, the proposed declaration would also require commitments to regional economic integration, demilitarization, effective verification, internal reconciliation, education for peace, democracy through periodic free and supervised elections, eradication of drug trafficking, and the creation of a New Ecological Order in the region.

As indicated, the creation of a zone of peace relies heavily on the contribution made by confidence-building measures, to the extent that authors have spoken of the Central American peace process as creating "a confidence-building regime" or "an arms control regime."[16] One of the notable aspects of the Central American peace process is the way in which the basic notion and vocabulary of confidence-building measures was introduced into the various documents and the extended discourse of the peace process. Discussion of CBMs was very limited in Latin America prior to 1983, and the term, when used at all, was restricted to the European (NATO–Warsaw Pact) or superpower conflict environment. Academics and practitioners who study the Central American peace process have noted this phenomenon, and have prepared extensive lists of actual or possible confidence-building measures that could be applied to Central America or other conflict situations in the Western Hemisphere.[17]

The sweeping scope of these topics makes clear the utopian nature of many of the proposals for a zone of peace, which have to be seen as hortatory goals rather than immediately achievable objectives. Nevertheless, the lesson of the Central American peace process is that a process that started out in the early 1980s as a collection of vaguely and imperfectly formulated ideals did in fact achieve many of its objectives and continues to show promise.

IMPLICATIONS FOR OTHER
HEMISPHERE CONFLICT SITUATIONS

There is a widely held perception that, with the exception of Central America and the brief 1982 Falklands/Malvinas war, interstate relations in Latin America are generally peaceful. However, a closer look indicates that there are a number of long-standing, simmering, and unresolved conflict situations in the hemisphere. While few of these have erupted into armed confrontations, they represent areas of tension that could conceivably escalate into military conflict. They also represent fitting subjects on which to bring to bear the lessons learned from the Central American peace process. A number of authors have attempted typologies or summaries of these conflicts. Table 9.1 represents one such effort.

One measure of the significance of the Central American peace process is that many of these potential conflict situations are amenable to amelioration using some of the techniques applied to Central America from 1983 to date. The combination of peacemaking, peace building, peacekeeping, peace observing, treaty verification, and confidence-building measures offers powerful tools, especially when used in symbiotic ways.

These tools, of course, were always available to countries committed to resolving conflicts and reducing tensions in the Western Hemisphere. But their effectiveness was diminished by deep suspicions regarding the historical use of some of them by the United States to further its own goals. In particular, peacekeeping and peace observing were discredited and indeed delegitimized by improper use in situations such as the Dominican Republic in 1965.

As a result, a major contribution of the Contadora/Arias/Esquipulas peace process has been to restore the legitimacy of these concepts by delinking them from U.S. policy goals and giving them a more Latin American tone. This process has also involved shifting the emphasis away from large-scale peacekeeping and down the conflict resolution spectrum toward peace observing and treaty verification. In addition, the concept of a "zone of peace" has been introduced and given viability, despite U.S. opposition in several instances. The vocabulary of many of the conflict resolution concepts introduced in Central America since the birth of Contadora in 1983 is now commonly found in popular and scholarly analyses of tensions in Latin America. This phenomenon is especially noteworthy with regard to concepts associated with peacekeeping, treaty verification, confidence building, and zones of peace.[18]

The Central American peace process has another major implication for other conflict situations in the hemisphere because of the new actors introduced, most notably Canada, Spain, and the United Nations. These actors had not previously played a significant role in hemispheric conflict resolution, and there is every hope that their invaluable contribution in the Central American peace process can be applied to other potential conflicts in the Western Hemisphere.

This optimistic view is buttressed by a series of other realities in the decade of the 1990s: there has been a decline in some of the more aggressive and chauvinistic forms of geopolitical thinking as the military regimes that predominated in Latin America in the 1970s and 1980s have given way to more democratic and representative governments. Several of the conflicts listed in Table 9.1 have been resolved or ameliorated, such as the Beagle

158 CONCLUSIONS

Table 9.1 Potential Interstate Conflicts in Latin America

Location	Parties	Type of Conflict
The Caribbean Basin Cluster		
Mexico-U.S.	Mexico, U.S.	Migratory, border
Caribbean	Caribbean states, U.S	Ideological, influence, migratory
Central America	Central America, U.S., Contadora nations	Ideological, influence, migratory, border
Hispaniola	Dominican Republic, Haiti	Border, migratory
Honduras– El Salvador	Honduras, El Salvador	Territorial, migratory
Belize-Guatemala	Belize, Guatemala, U.K.	Territorial
Panama-U.S.	Panama, U.S	Territorial, resource
The Northern South American Cluster		
San Andrés islands	Nicaragua, Colombia	Territorial
Gulf of Venezuela	Colombia, Venezuela	Territorial, resource, border
Essequibo	Venezuela, Guyana	Territorial, resource
New River Triangle	Guyana, Suriname	Territorial, resource
Litani River	Suriname, French Guiana	Territorial
Northern Andes	Ecuador, Peru	Territorial, resource
Maritime claims	Coastal states	Territorial, resource
The Southern Cone/Antarctica Cluster		
Central Andes	Peru, Bolivia, Chile	Territorial, resource (Bolivia)
Southern Andes	Chile, Argentina	Territorial, resource, border
Argentina-Brazil	Argentina, Brazil	Influence, resource
Bolivia-Paraguay	Bolivia, Paraguay	Territorial, resource
Maritime claims	Coastal states	Territorial, resource
Falklands/Malvinas	Argentina, U.K.	Territorial, resource
South Atlantic	Argentina, Brazil, outside powers	Resource, influence
Antarctica	Treaty signatories, Third World, ecologists	Territorial, resource

Source: Jack Child, "Interstate Tensions in the Western Hemisphere," *International Journal,* Canada, 43 (Summer 1988): 383. Reprinted with permission.

Channel dispute and the possibility of tensions over mineral exploitation in Antarctica.

But this optimism must be tempered by the fact that most of the conflicts do remain in the background, available to irresponsible demagogues or ardent nationalists eager to seize upon an issue that will unify their nation behind them. It is to these situations that the peacekeepers, peacemakers, confidence builders, and architects of zones of peace should apply the lessons of Central America.

One must also recognize that these conflict resolution approaches tend to focus on nation-states as the primary actors and offer few solutions to conflicts in which some of the actors are not nation-states, such as insurgents, terrorists, and drug traffickers.

IMPLICATIONS FOR THE
INTER-AMERICAN SECURITY SYSTEM AND THE MILITARY

The Central American peace process also has implications for the Inter-American Security System (IASS) and for the changing role of the hemisphere's military establishments.

In the early 1990s the Inter-American Security System could be described as a mix of an old anachronistic set of institutions and a series of new initiatives and arrangements that seriously challenge the old structures. The old anachronistic set of institutions is the formal Inter-American Military System, established under U.S. initiative and heavy control in World War II and the years of the Cold War.[19] Its original rationale was hemispheric defense—first against the Axis, and then the Soviet bloc—but this shifted to counterinsurgency after the Cuban Revolution in 1959. The system consists of weak multilateral institutions, nominally subsumed under the Rio Treaty and the OAS, and a series of fairly strong bilateral links (the military assistance programs) between the United States and most of the Latin American nations. The more notable institutions include U.S. military assistance groups and liaison offices, mobile training teams, the Inter-American Defense Board and College, located in Washington, D.C., the School of the Americas, originally in Panama then moved to Fort Benning, Georgia, a regional U.S. military headquarters, the Southern Command in Panama, periodic conferences of the chiefs of the armies, navies, and air forces of the hemisphere, and a network of military attachés and communications facilities.

The traditional Inter-American Security System was considerably weakened in the late 1970s when, under U.S. President Jimmy Carter, the providing of military assistance was conditioned on acceptable human rights performance. This coincided with a period in which many of the Latin American militaries, equipped with the doctrine of national security, took power under the rationale that a very real subversive threat required them to take violently draconian measures against their own people. The combination of the U.S. emphasis on human rights and the Latin American military's crusade against leftist subversives produced great strains in the Inter-American Security System and led to the termination of many of the old patterns and institutions of military assistance. Even so, some of the multilateral institutions remained in place, although their sense of purpose and energy were seriously weakened.

In the early 1980s several crises cast serious doubts on the viability of the Inter-American Security System and launched the series of initiatives and new directions that are the essence of the challenge of the early 1990s. Among the crises were: the enduring Central American conflict, the South Atlantic war in 1982 over the Malvinas/Falklands, and the Grenadan and Panamanian invasions/liberations in 1983 and 1989, respectively. During this period, many of the national security military regimes of the 1970s began to turn power over to elected civilian governments. The security panorama of the 1980s was further influenced by the attempts of South American nations to reduce the tensions stemming from historical bilateral strains (Brazil-Argentina, Argentina-Chile, Chile-Peru, Peru-Ecuador, Colombia-Venezuela, Venezuela-Guyana). This produced a sharp contrast to the tense Central American situation in the 1980s, when tensions increased between the Nicaraguan Sandinistas, the neighboring states, and the Contra insurgents backed by the United States. The hemispheric security policies of the United States became "Centralamericanized" as this region received high priority in Washington while South America was generally ignored. The end result was to create two separate and distinct subregional security environments (Central American–Caribbean and Southern Cone), and to seriously undermine the rationale for any overarching regional military institutions, for the Inter-American Security System as a whole, and even for the diplomatic and political bodies of the Inter-American System.

In the late 1980s the larger and more sophisticated military establishments of South America increasingly focused their attention on the concept of Latin American military and geopolitical integration. Although not necessarily antagonistic to the United States, this emphasis on Latin American integration clearly recognized that the United States was devoting its hemispheric strategic attention almost exclusively to Central America, and that the multilateral Inter-American Security System and its associated juridical instruments, primarily the Rio Treaty, were essentially irrelevant. However, the proponents of Latin American military integration recognized that they could not remain isolated from other alliances and strategic arrangements, and several of the proposals included ideas such as links to NATO via Spain and Portugal and cooperation with other nations in the South Atlantic and Antarctica.

The late 1980s and early 1990s was a difficult period for the Latin American military. As military regimes returned power to elected civilian governments in most of the nations of the hemisphere, there was a sense among civilians and military personnel alike that there had to be a reassessment of the military's traditional roles.[20] One of the suggestions made in this connection was that they could become more active in the peacekeeping and confidence-building field.

The implications of the Central American peace process for the Inter-American Security System and the Latin American military reside in this possibility: that both the IASS and the Latin American military establishments might indeed assume a role in which they develop military confidence-building measures and prepare for participation in UN or OAS peacekeeping or peace-observing missions. These could be either in the hemisphere under OAS or UN auspices, or in other regions of the world under UN aegis. The experiences of a number of Latin American military personnel in the Central American peace process provide a solid foundation for these possibilities; in addition to the 800-strong Venezuelan paratrooper battalion, there were numerous Latin American military observers who served with ONUCA.

This possibility would require a certain re-orientation of mind-sets among the military and the institutions of the Inter-American Security System. As was indicated in earlier chapters, the Inter-American Defense Board was at one point mentioned as a possible verifier of Central American peace agreements. It was proposed for this role because of its multilateral international nature and the presence of 21 different hemispheric nations in its membership. However, because of the high U.S. profile on the board and its location in Washington, it is generally perceived as being under too much U.S. influence to be an objective third-party neutral. Its effective role in this field would thus require the lowering of that profile, and perhaps a move of its headquarters to a Latin American nation.

The professional orientation of the Latin American military would also require a change if the opportunities suggested by the Central American peace process are to become a reality. Peacekeeping and confidence building are suspect among many Latin American officers, who generally show little enthusiasm for it. (It should be noted, however, that peacekeeping tends to be enthusiastically supported by those officers actually involved in such missions.) The reasons for military suspicion of peacekeeping and confidence building lie in the fact that these missions fall outside of the heroic tradition of the military as the forgers and guardians of a nation. They tend to take them physically away from the centers of national power and are generally not seen as professionally rewarding. There is also resistance to any outside suggestions that they should adopt roles that might diminish their traditional political roles and privileged socioeconomic status. In its more extreme form, this viewpoint holds that peacekeeping and confidence-building missions are part of a neo-Marxist plot to weaken the military and thus make Communist revolution more likely.[21]

The change in traditional thinking about security and the role of the military was underscored at the June 1991 General Assembly of the OAS, when a resolution (titled "Cooperation for Security in the Hemisphere") was approved, calling for the Permanent Council of the OAS to set up a committee to study new approaches to hemispheric security. The nontraditional thrust of this committee's work can be seen from a working document prepared in early 1992:[22]

> DEFINITION OF SECURITY: Security, in the broadest sense, is the result of cooperation and coordination of the actions carried out by states and international organizations which tend to achieve, maintain and guarantee the existence and integral development of their peoples, taking into consideration for that end the following principles (among others):
> 1. Sovereign equality.
> 2. Democratic stability.
> 3. Representative democracy.
> 4. Non-use of force or threat of force.
> 5. The peaceful resolution of disputes.
> 6. The respect for human rights and fundamental freedoms.
> 7. Cooperative security.
> 8. Integral development.
> 9. Protection of the environment.
> 10. Limits on the proliferation of the instruments of war and weapons of massive destruction.
> 11. Drug traffic.

The Inter-American Defense Board reacted to the OAS committee's work in 1991 and 1992 by drafting its own set of "Tasks for the IADB," by making informal contact with the OAS committee, and by holding a series of discussion groups and panel sessions with diplomats and academics.[23] However, an examination of the two approaches favored by the OAS committee and the IADB suggests that there are major differences in the concept of "hemisphere security" held by these two organizations, and that the board runs the serious risk of having its funds from the OAS cut back so severely that it might cease to exist.[24]

CONCLUSION

The Contadora/Esquipulas Central American peace process has traveled a long and difficult road in the years since four concerned Latin American nations met on a Panamanian island in January 1983. From broad, overarching, holistic, and even utopian initial approaches, the process has been forced to come to terms with the reality that peace will not come easily or quickly simply because many people want it. The original Contadora documents now serve as ideals, and in the early 1990s the activities of the peacekeepers and peacemakers are focusing on much more limited, but more realistic goals. Implementation of the full scope of early Contadora would require either massive blind faith or more verification and monitoring resources than the world community could muster. In terms of peace verification, the process has moved from not addressing the problem at all, to proposing (with Canadian assistance) a detailed and complex ad hoc organization (the CIVS), which became moot when the Contadora effort gave way to Esquipulas. With Esquipulas the five Central American nations took greater initiative, but also recognized that the demands of verification would require outside resources. Their reluctance to use the Contadora nations or the OAS for verification support led them to rely on the United Nations.

The creation of a zone of peace in Central America— supported by a CBM regime in which communications were effective, and in which any hostile intent would be transparent—has not been realized, nor is it likely to be in the foreseeable future. But the validity of this concept as a goal has been recognized, and the small but significant steps taken in this direction give one hope for the future.

In the long run, the ultimate confidence-building measure and guarantor of a zone of peace in Central America is the venerable ideal of Central American integration in all its important dimensions: economic, cultural, and strategic. No treaty can make this happen at the stroke of a pen, and the logic of functionalism suggests that more important than the overarching formal agreements are the small things of daily life that tie individuals and nations together.

The use of a United Nations peace verification mission in the Western Hemisphere is unprecedented and occurred at a time when the UN was enjoying a renaissance of prestige and effectiveness. This did not come without risks, however, and if the effort fails in the long run in Central America, some of the blame, fairly or unfairly, will fall on the peacekeepers and the international organization that gave them their mandate. On the other hand, successful verification and monitoring of the Central American peace process by the UN mission will suggest to many that a similar approach could be used in other hemispheric conflict situations.

The increased role for the UN tends to further diminish the credibility of the regional international organization that in the past would have mounted the peace verification mission. Efforts early on by the United States to involve the OAS in verification were met with suspicions that the United States would attempt to use the OAS as an instrument of its policy, as happened in past hemispheric peacekeeping efforts. However, in the late 1980s there was an interesting turnabout in which the Secretary-General of the OAS was repeatedly invited to participate in the Central American process along with his UN counterpart, frequently over U.S. objections. This suggests that the OAS might finally be freeing itself from its historical domination by the United States and in the process become more truly representative of the hemisphere. One key element in this new OAS role in conflict resolution was the Peruvian nationality of the UN Secretary-General, and it remains to be seen if this enhancement of the role of the OAS will survive the retirement of Javier Pérez de Cuéllar. Another factor in the evolution of the OAS was the addition of Canada in 1989. The long-term Canadian role in the OAS is still undefined, although there is the intriguing possibility that Canada might help the OAS get more involved in realistic approaches to peacekeeping that are not under excessive U.S. influence. Canada, in effect, may be able to play the role of helpful balancer of the United States in the OAS as well as that of helpful fixer.

The Central American peace process from 1983 to date has also affected the relationship between the nations involved and the United States. Historically under heavy U.S. influence, Central America has become less so, and the evolution of the relationship is not simple for any of the parties. For the Esquipulas process to reach fruition, it was necessary to "let Central America be Central America," and this in turn required a reduction of U.S. influence and presence.

A number of caveats must be added. Peace verification—or peacekeeping or peace observing—can only create space and gain time for the peacemakers and peace builders. This time and space must be used wisely by the diplomats and politicians if peace is to endure. The potentially negative effects of international peacekeeping must also be considered. Among such effects is the possibility that third-party neutral peacekeeping may in fact only serve to prolong the conflict if the underlying causes of the conflict are not addressed through dialogue and political, social, and economic channels. It is not enough to simply establish a surface peace based on stability if underlying social and economic injustices and political oppression remain.

The considerations addressed in this book lead to the conclusion that like almost everything else surrounding Central America in the last quarter of the twentieth century, the verification of peace accords and the establishment of confidence-building measures will not be simple, inexpensive, or easy.

Nevertheless, if an enduring, peaceful way out of the Central American crisis is found, it seems apparent that the helpful fixers, the confidence builders, the crafters of zones of peace, the peacekeepers, and the peacemakers of the Contadora/Esquipulas process will have effectively used the techniques and experiences described in this book. In that process they will have left the enduring legacies of a change in U.S.–Latin American relations, an increase in Latin American self-confidence, new roles for key actors such as Canada and Spain, and an invigorated mandate for the peacekeeping instruments of multilateral international organizations.

NOTES

1. Aguilar Zinzer, *Negotiation in Conflict*, 97.
2. Roundtable on Negotiation, *Interim and Confidence-Building Measures*, 30.
3. Klepak, *Security Considerations*, especially 38–48, 55.
4. Lecture (and subsequent conversation with) Carlos Andrés Pérez, Washington, D.C., 30 April 1984; and Mercado Jarrín, *Sistema*, 32–33.
5. *El Tiempo*, Bogotá, 18 August 1983; *Excelsior*, Mexico, 2 February 1986.
6. Klepak, *Security Considerations*, 38–48.
7. North, *Between Peace and War*, 190.
8. Child, *Conflict in Central America*, especially Chapter 8 and 157–158; Child, "U.S. Security and Contadora," 54–59.
9. Heraldo Muñoz, "La Agenda de Seguridad," in Somavía and Insulza, *Seguridad Democrática*, 175.
10. Interview with Guillermo Ungo at the Roundtable for Peace in Central America, Ottawa, 5 May 1989.
11. The term "concertación" became closely associated with this aspect of Esquipulas. It translates poorly, but is derived from the notion of "acting in concert," and thus can be best rendered as "harmonization" or "reconciliation."
12. For a discussion of zones of peace, see "América del Sur: Zona de Paz," *Nueva Sociedad* 91 (October 1987): 99–102; Mercado Jarrín, *Sistema*; Serbín, "La Paz en el Caribe"; *Nuestra América Latina*, February–July 1989, 380–393; and Portales, "Zona de Paz, 113–127.
13. Ramaciotti de Cubas, "La Antártida como Zona de Paz"; and Child, *Antarctica and South American Geopolitics*.
14. Goldblat, "Zone of Peace," 404–408; Carlos Portales, "South American Regional Security," in Varas, *Hemisphere Security*, 172–178; Somavía, *Seguridad Democrática*.
15. Mauricio Herdocia, "The Esquipulas Accords and the Declaration of Central America as a Zone of Peace, Democracy and Cooperation," *Centro de Estudios Internacionales* (Nicaragua) 1 (May 1991): 27–34.
16. Child, "A Confidence-Building Approach to Resolving Central American Conflicts," in Child, *Conflict in Central America*; Klepak, *Security Considerations*, especially 34–37.
17. Child, "A Confidence-Building Approach," 125–129; Palma, "Cooperation and Confidence-Building Measures," especially 92–94.
18. Varas, *Política de Armas*; Félix Calderón, "Verificación y Medidadas de Confianza Mutua," in Varas, *Limitaciones de Armamentos*, 103–109; Mercado Jarrín, "Doctrina Sudamericana de Defensa y Seguridad," in Somavía and Insulza, *Seguridad Democrática*.
19. Child, *Unequal Alliance*.
20. Goodman, *The Military and Democracy*; and conversation with U.S. OAS Ambassador Luigi Einaudi, State Department, June 1991. See also interview with Ambassador Einaudi, *Times of the Americas*, 20 March 1991.
21. The generalizations made in this paragraph are based on numerous discussions with Latin American military officers; the notion of peacekeeping as

a neo-Marxist plot was articulated by a senior Salvadoran officer in Washington, D.C., 1991.

22. OAS, Permanent Council, Grupo de Trabajo sobre Cooperación para la Seguridad Hemisférica, *Nuevo Concepto de Seguridad,* OAS Document CP/GT/CSH-13/92, 12 February 1992, 3–5.

23. The author participated in several of these IADB-sponsored discussions, including one session in which heated words were exchanged between a Latin American OAS ambassador and a Central American colonel. The colonel accused the ambassador, and civilians in general, of wanting to destroy the military by severely cutting back defense budgets; the ambassador replied that there was no real justification for a Latin military (beyond self-perpetuation of a repressive institution), and that their budgets should be cut so as to reduce them to essentially police forces.

24. Lieutenant Colonel Michael J. Dziedzic, "Latin American Regional Security and the New World Order," paper presented to the 1991 Annual Meeting of the American Political Science Association, Washington, D.C., August 1991. Also discussions with senior officials of the IADB and ambassadors who were members of the OAS committee, January–April 1992.

APPENDIXES

APPENDIX 1: CHRONOLOGY

This chronology traces the principal benchmarks in the Contadora/Esquipulas peace process from January 1983 to December 1991. The emphasis is on those events with special significance for verification, monitoring, and confidence building. For the location of the principal sites mentioned, see the map at the beginning of the book.

1983

January 8–9: The first Contadora meeting (foreign ministers of Mexico, Venezuela, Colombia, Panama); the Contadora Declaration.

April 12–13: Contadora observer mission visits Honduras and Costa Rica.

July 17: Cancún (Mexico) Summit; the Cancún Declaration.

September 7–9: Panama Contadora foreign ministers' meeting; the 21 Objectives document.

1984

January 8: Panama Contadora foreign ministers' meeting; the "Principles for the Implementation of the Commitments Undertaken in the Document of Objectives."

June 9: First draft Contadora Act ("Contadora I").

August: Canadian input to security and control aspects of Contadora begins.

September 7: The draft "Contadora Act on Peace and Co-operation in Central America, revised version" ("Contadora I revised").

October 15: La Palma meeting between President Duarte and the FMLN.
October 20: The "Revised Tegucigalpa draft of the Contadora Act."

1985

April 11–12: Contadora and Central American representatives meet in Panama to discuss verification and implementation procedures for Contadora; Statute of Verification and Cooperation.
July 27: Lima Declaration; formation of the Contadora Support Group (Argentina, Brazil, Peru, Uruguay).
September 12: Second draft Contadora Act.

1986

January 12: Contadora and Support Group nations meet in Venezuela and issue "The Caraballeda Message for Peace, Security and Democracy in Central America."
June 5–7: Panama meeting; final draft Contadora Act.
November 18: Secretaries-General of UN and OAS offer their good offices.

1987

February 15: San José *"Una hora para la paz"* Summit; Arias peace plan floated.
August 7: Esquipulas II (Arias) peace plan.
December 10: President Arias receives Nobel Peace Prize.

1988

January 14: CIVS report critical of several Central American nations. Presidents end CIVS's mandate and replace it with an Executive Commission made up of their foreign ministers..
March 21–23: Sandinista and Contra representatives meet in Sapoá.
April 7: Technical Advisory Group created (Canada, the Federal Republic of Germany, Spain, and later Venezuela).
September 29: UN peacekeepers win Nobel Peace Prize.

1989

February 12–14: Summit in Costa del Sol, El Salvador (Tesoro Beach).
March 23: U.S. congressional Democratic leaders reach agreement with Bush administration on a bipartisan Central American policy.

August 5–7: Summit in Tela, Honduras, calls for further UN help; CIAV (International Commission of Support and Verification) created.

September: UN reconnaissance mission to Central America to prepare for ONUCA.

November 7: UN Security Council approves ONUCA with Resolution 644.

December 7: ONUCA deployed to Central America to monitor borders under its first limited mandate.

December 12: San Isidro de Coronado (Costa Rica) Summit; Coronado Declaration asking that ONUCA's mandate be expanded to include Contra demobilization.

1990

February 25: Elections in Nicaragua. Violeta Chamorro defeats President Daniel Ortega of the incumbent Sandinista government.

March 15: UN Secretary-General requests that ONUCA be expanded to include an infantry battalion for Contra demobilization.

March 27: Toncontín (Honduras) Accord: Sandinistas agree to transfer power to Chamorro on schedule.

March 27–29: Guatemalan URNG guerrillas and representatives of the National Reconciliation Commission meet in Oslo.

April 1–3: Montelimar "Farewell" Summit.

April 4: Salvadoran government and the FMLN meet in Geneva under UN auspices in the presence of the Secretary-General.

April 5: First contingent of 170 armed Venezuelan soldiers arrives in Honduras to begin disarming the Contras.

May 30: Protocol on Disarmament signed in Managua by the Contras and the Chamorro government.

May 31: URNG and Guatemala government representatives sign the El Escorial Accord.

June 18: Antigua (Guatemala) Summit.

July 5: ONUCA's Venezuelan battalion returns from Central America.

December 15–17: Puntarenas (Costa Rica) Summit.

December 28: Creation of ONUSAL (UN Observer Group in El Salvador).

1991

January 10–11: Tuxtla (Mexico) Summit.

March 17: San José VII Summit.

April 27: Preliminary agreement between El Salvador government and FMLN.

July 15: San Salvador Summit.

July 25: Querétaro Accord between Guatemalan National Reconciliation Commission and the URNG.

July 26: ONUSAL begins operations in El Salvador under limited mandate of observing human rights compliance while waiting for a cease-fire agreement.

September 25: Preliminary New York agreement at UN between Salvadoran government and FMLN.

November 15: Disarmament brigade created by President Chamorro to lower tensions between Recontras and Recompas.

December 31: After intense last-minute talks at the UN, Act of New York (cease-fire) signed by the Salvadoran government and the FMLN after midnight of the day Pérez de Cuéllar's tenure as Secretary-General ends.

APPENDIX 2: ORGANIZATION OF ONUCA

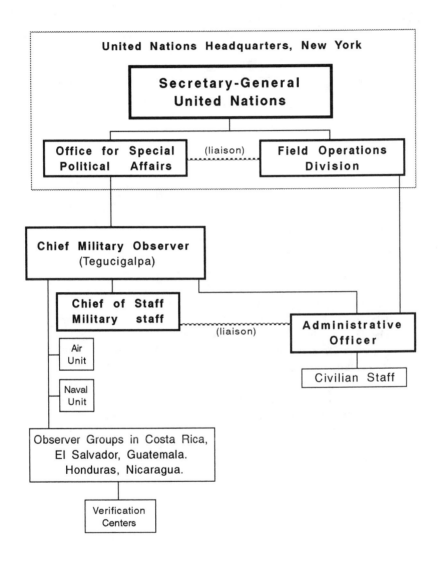

Source: Adapted from United Nations, *The Blue Helmets: A Review of UN Peacekeeping,* 2nd ed. New York: UN, 1990, 418.

APPENDIX 3: THE 21 OBJECTIVES DOCUMENT, 9 SEPTEMBER 1983

Considering:

The situation prevailing in Central America, which is characterized by an atmosphere of tension that threatens security and peaceful coexistence in the region, and which requires, for its solution, observance of the principles of international law governing the actions of States, especially:

The self-determination of peoples;
Non-intervention;
The sovereign equality of States;
The peaceful settlement of disputes;
Refraining from the threat or use of force;
Respect of the territorial integrity of States;
Pluralism in its various manifestations;
Full support for democratic institutions;
The promotion of social justice;
International cooperation for development;
Respect for and promotion of human rights;
The prohibition of terrorism and subversion;

The desire to reconstruct the Central American homeland through progressive integration of its economic, legal and social institutions;

The need for economic cooperation among the States of Central America so as to make a fundamental contribution to the development of their peoples and the strengthening of their independence;

Adopted on September 9, 1983, by the Contadora countries of Mexico, Panama, Colombia, and Venezuela and the Central American nations of Guatemala, Honduras, El Salvador, Nicaragua, and Costa Rica.
Source: U.S Department of State.

The undertaking to establish, promote or revitalize representative, democratic systems in all the countries of the region;

The unjust economic, social, and political structures, which exacerbate the conflicts in Central America;

The urgent need to put an end to the tensions and lay the foundations for understanding and solidarity among the countries of the area;

The arms race and the growing arms traffic in Central America, which aggravate political relations in the region and divert economic resources that could be used for development;

The presence of foreign advisers and other forms of foreign military interference in the zone;

The risks that the territory of Central American States may be used for the purpose of conducting military operations and pursuing policies of destabilization against others;

The need for concerted political efforts in order to encourage dialogue and understanding in Central America, avert the danger of a general spreading of the conflicts, and set in motion the machinery needed to ensure the peaceful coexistence and security of their peoples.

Declare Their Intention of Achieving the Following Objectives

To promote detente and put an end to situations of conflict in the area, restraining from taking any action that might jeopardize political confidence or obstruct the achievement of peace, security and stability in the region;

To ensure strict compliance with the aforementioned principles of international law, whose violators will be held accountable;

To respect and ensure the exercise of human, political, civil, economic, social, religious and cultural rights;

To adopt measures conducive to the establishment and, where appropriate, improvement of democratic, representative, and pluralistic systems that will guarantee effective popular participation in the decision-making process and ensure that the various currents of opinion have free access to fair and regular elections based on the full observance of citizens' rights;

To promote national reconciliation efforts wherever deep divisions have taken place within society, with a view to fostering participation in democratic political processes in accordance with the law;

To create political conditions intended to ensure the international security, integrity and sovereignty of the States of the region;

To stop the arms race in all its forms and begin negotiations for the control and reduction of current stocks of weapons and on the number of armed troops;

To prevent the installation on their territory of foreign military bases or any other type of foreign military interference;

To conclude agreements to reduce the presence of foreign military advisers and other foreign elements involved in military and security activities, with a view to their elimination;

To establish internal control machinery to prevent the traffic in arms from the territory of any country in the region to the territory of another;

To eliminate the traffic in arms, whether within the region or from outside it, intended for persons, organizations or groups seeking to destabilize the Governments of Central American countries;

To prevent the use on their own territory by persons, organizations or groups seeking to destabilize the Governments of Central American countries and to refuse to provide them with or permit them to receive military or logistical support;

To refrain from inciting or supporting acts of terrorism, subversion or sabotage in the countries in the area;

To establish and coordinate direct communication systems with a view to preventing or, where appropriate, settling incidents between States of the region;

To continue humanitarian aid aimed at helping Central American refugees who have been displaced from their countries of origin and to create suitable conditions for the voluntary repatriation of such refugees, in consultation with or with the cooperation of the United Nations High Commissioner for Refugees (UNHCR) and other international agencies deemed appropriate;

To undertake economic and social development programs with the aim of promoting well being and an equitable distribution of wealth;

To revitalize and restore economic integration machinery in order to attain sustained development on the basis of solidarity and mutual advance;

To negotiate the provision of external monetary resources, which will provide additional means of financing the resumption of intraregional trade, meet the serious balance-of-payments problems, attract funds for working capital, support programs to extend and restructure production and promote medium- and long-term investment projects;

To negotiate better and broader access to international markets in order to increase the volume of trade between the countries of Central America and the rest of the world, particularly the industrialized countries; by means of a revision of trade practices, the elimination of tariff and other barriers, and the achievement of the price stability at a profitable and fair level for the products exported by the countries of the region;

To establish technical cooperation machinery for the planning, programming, and implementation of investment and trade promotion projects.

The Ministers for Foreign Affairs of the Central American countries, with the participation of the countries in the Contadora Group, have begun negotiations with the aim of preparing for the conclusion of the agreements and the establishment of machinery necessary to formalize and develop the objectives contained in this document, and to bring about the establishment of appropriate verification or monitoring systems. To that end, account will be taken of the initiatives put forward at the meetings convened by the Contadora Group.

Panama City, 9 September 1983.

APPENDIX 4: THE CENTRAL AMERICAN PEACE AGREEMENT, 7 AUGUST 1987

Preamble

The Presidents of the Republics of Guatemala, El Salvador, Honduras, Nicaragua, and Costa Rica, meeting in Guatemala City on August 6 and 7, 1987, encouraged by the vision and continuing desire of Contadora and the Support Group in favor of peace, strengthened by the constant support of all the governments and peoples of the world, their principal international organizations, and especially by the European Economic Community and His Holiness John Paul II, inspired by Esquipulas I, and having gathered together in Guatemala in order to discuss the peace plan presented by the Government of Costa Rica, have agreed to:

- Assume fully the historic challenge to forge a destiny of peace for Central America;
- Undertake to fight for peace and eliminate war;
- Make dialogue prevail over violence and reason over rancor;
- Dedicate these peace efforts to the youth of Central America, whose legitimate aspirations for peace and social justice, for freedom and reconciliation, have been frustrated for many generations;
- Establish the Central American Parliament as a symbol of freedom and independence of the reconciliation to which we in Central America aspire.

We ask for the respect and assistance of the international community in our efforts. Central America has its own pathways to peace and development, but we need help to make them a reality. We ask for an international

---

Source: U.S. Department of State.

agreement that would ensure development so that the peace we seek may be a lasting one. We firmly reiterate that peace and development are inseparable.

We express our appreciation to President Vinicio Cerezo Arevalo and to the noble people of Guatemala for having served as the host for this meeting. The generosity of the Guatemalan people and their leader has been vital in creating the climate in which the peace agreements were adopted.

Procedure for Establishing a Stable and Lasting Peace in Central America

The Governments of the Republics of Costa Rica, El Salvador, Guatemala, Honduras, and Nicaragua, having undertaken to achieve the objectives and develop the principles established in the United Nations Charter, the Charter of the Organization of American States, the Document of Objectives, the Caraballeda Message for Peace, Security, and Democracy in Central America, the Guatemala Declaration, the Punta del Este Communique, the Panama Message, the Esquipulas Declaration, and the draft Contadora Act for Peace and Cooperation in Central America of June 6, 1986, have agreed upon the following procedure for establishing a stable and lasting peace in Central America.

1. National Reconciliation
(a) Dialogue

To carry out urgently, in those cases in which deep divisions have occurred within a society, actions of national reconciliation to allow the people to participate, with full guaranties, in authentic political processes of a democratic nature, on the basis of Justice, freedom, and democracy, and, for that purpose, to establish mechanisms for dialogue with opposition groups, in accordance with the law.

To that end, the respective governments shall initiate dialogue with all domestic political opposition groups that have laid down their arms and with those that have accepted the amnesty.

(b) Amnesty

In each Central American country, except in those where the International Evaluation and Follow-up Committee determines that it is not necessary, decrees of amnesty shall be issued, which shall establish all the provisions to guarantee the inviolability of life, freedom in all its forms, property, and the security of the persons to whom such decrees apply. Simultaneously with the issue of the amnesty decrees, the irregular forces in the respective country shall release any persons they may be holding.

(c) National Reconciliation Committee

In order to verify the fulfillment of the commitments undertaken by the five Central American governments upon signing this document, with regard to amnesty, cease-fire, democratization, and free elections, a National Reconciliation Committee shall be created. Its function shall be to determine whether the process of national reconciliation is actually under way, and whether there is absolute respect for all the civil and political rights of Central American citizens guaranteed herein.

The National Reconciliation Committee shall be composed of one regular delegate and one alternate from the Executive Branch and one regular member and one alternate suggested by the Episcopal Conference and selected by the government from a slate of three Bishops to be submitted within 15 days of receipt of the formal invitation. This invitation shall be extended by the governments within 5 working days of the signing of this document. The same nomination procedure shall be used to select one regular member and one alternate from the legally registered opposition political parties. The three-person slate shall be submitted in the same time period as mentioned above. Each Central American government shall also select to serve on the committee one outstanding citizen who is not part of the government and does not belong to the government party, as well as one alternate. Copies of the agreements or decrees creating each National Committee shall be transmitted immediately to the other Central American governments.

2. Urging a Cessation of Hostilities

The governments vehemently urge that a cessation of hostilities be arranged in those states in the area currently experiencing the action of irregular or insurgent groups. The governments of such states undertake to carry out all actions necessary to achieve an effective cease-fire within a constitutional framework.

3. Democratization

The governments undertake to provide the impetus for an authentic democratic process, both pluralistic and participatory, which entails the promotion of social justice, respect for human rights, sovereignty, territorial integrity of the states, and the right of all nations to choose, freely and without any outside interference whatsoever, their economic, political, and social system. Furthermore, the governments shall adopt in a verifiable manner measures conducive to the establishment and, where appropriate, improvement of democratic, representative, and pluralistic systems that will guarantee the organization of political parties and effective participation by the people in the decision-making process and ensure that the various currents of opinion have free access to fair and regular elections based on the full observance of citizens' rights. To ensure good faith in the development of this process of democratization, it shall be understood that:

(a) There must be complete freedom for television, radio, and the press, which shall encompass the freedom for all ideological groups to open and maintain in operation communications media, and the freedom to operate such media without prior censorship.

(b) There shall be complete pluralism of political parties. In this respect, political groups shall have broad access to the communications media and full enjoyment of the rights of association and the ability to hold public demonstrations in the unrestricted exercise of the right to publicize their ideas orally, in writing, and on television, as well as freedom of mobility for the members of the political parties in their campaign activities.

(c) Similarly, the Central American governments that are maintaining in effect a state of siege or emergency shall abolish it and bring about the rule of law in which all constitutional guarantees are in effect.

4. Free Elections

Once the conditions inherent in any democracy have been created, free, pluralistic, and fair elections shall be held.

As a joint gesture of the Central American states toward reconciliation and lasting peace for their peoples, elections shall be held for the Central American Parliament, which was proposed in the Esquipulas Declaration of May 25, 1986.

To that end, the Presidents have expressed their wish to move forward with the organization of the Parliament. The Preparatory Committee of the Central American Parliament shall therefore conclude its deliberations and deliver the respective draft treaty to the Central American Presidents within 150 days.

These elections shall be held simultaneously in all the countries of Central America during the first 6 months of 1988 on a date to be agreed upon in due course by the Presidents of these states. They shall be subject to monitoring by the appropriate electoral bodies, and the respective governments agree to extend an invitation to the Organization of American States and to the United Nations, as well as to governments of third states, to send observers to attest to the fact that the electoral procedures have been governed by the strictest rules of equal access for all political parties to the communications media, as well as extensive opportunities for holding public demonstrations and engaging in any other type of campaign propaganda.

In order that the elections for membership in the Central American Parliament may be held within the time period indicated in this section, the treaty establishing that body shall be submitted for approval or ratification in the five countries.

As soon as elections for membership in the Central American Parliament have been held, equally free and democratic elections shall be held in each country, with international observers and the same guarantees and within the established intervals and the timetables to be proposed under the present political constitutions, to select the people's representatives in the municipalities, congresses, and legislative assemblies, as well as the Presidents of the Republics.

5. Cessation of Aid to Irregular Forces and Insurgent Movements

The governments of the five Central American states shall request governments in the region or those outside it that are providing, either overtly or covertly, military, logistic, financial or propagandistic aid or assistance in the form of troops, weapons, munitions, and equipment to irregular forces or insurgent movements to cease such aid as an essential requirement for achieving a stable and lasting peace in the region.

The foregoing does not include assistance used for repatriation, or, if that does not occur, relocation, and assistance needed to accomplish the reintegration into normal life of those persons who have belonged to the above-mentioned groups or forces. Similarly, the irregular forces and insurgent groups active in Central America shall be asked to refrain from receiving such aid for the sake of a genuine Latin Americanist spirit. These requests shall be made in fulfillment of the provisions of the Document of Objectives as regards elimination of the traffic in weapons within the region or from outside sources to persons, organizations, or groups attempting to destabilize the Central American governments.

6. Non-use of Territory To Attack Other States

The five countries signing this document reiterate their commitment to prevent the use of their own territory and to neither furnish nor allow logistical military support for persons, organizations, or groups seeking to destabilize the governments of the Central American countries.

7. Negotiations on Security, Verification, Control, and Limitation of Weapons

The governments of the five Central American states, with participation by the Contadora Group in the exercise of its function as mediator, shall proceed with negotiations on the points on which agreement is pending in matters of security, verification, and control under the draft Contadora Act for Peace and Cooperation in Central America.

These negotiations shall also cover measures for the disarmament of those irregular forces that are willing to accept the amnesty decrees.

8. Refugees and Displaced Persons

The Central American governments undertake to address, with a sense of urgency, [the problem of] the flow of refugees and displaced persons caused by the regional crisis, by means of protection and assistance, especially with regard to health, education, employment, and security and, furthermore, to facilitate their repatriation, resettlement, or relocation, provided that it is of a voluntary nature and takes the form of individual cases.

They also undertake to arrange for aid from the international community for the Central American refugees and displaced persons, whether such assistance is direct under bilateral or multilateral agreements or obtained through the United Nations High Commissioner for Refugees (UNHCR) or other organizations and agencies.

9. Cooperation, Democracy, and Freedom for Peace and Development

In the climate of freedom guaranteed by democracy, the Central American countries shall adopt such agreements as will permit them to accelerate their development in order to achieve societies that are more egalitarian and free from misery.

The consolidation of democracy entails the creation of an economy of well-being and economic and social democracy. In order to attain those objectives, the governments shall jointly seek special economic assistance from the international community.

10. International Verification and Follow-up
(a) International Verification and Follow-up Committee

An International Verification and Follow-up Committee shall be created, composed of the Secretaries General of the Organization of American States and the United Nations, or their representatives, as well as by the foreign ministers of Central America, the Contadora Group, and the Support Group. The functions of this committee shall be to verify and follow up on the fulfillment of the commitments contained herein.

(b) Support and Facilities for Mechanisms of Reconciliation and of Verification and Follow-up

In order to reinforce the efforts of the International Verification and Follow-up Committee, the governments of the five Central American states shall issue statements of support for its work. All nations interested in promoting the cause of freedom, democracy, and peace in Central America may adhere to these statements.

The five governments shall provide all necessary facilities for the proper conduct of the verification and follow-up functions of the National Reconciliation Committee in each country and of the International Verification and Follow-up Committee.

11. Timetable for Implementing the Commitments

Within 15 days of the signing of this document, the Central American foreign ministers shall meet as an Executive Committee to regulate and promote the agreements contained herein and to make their application feasible. They shall also organize the working committees so that, as from this date, the processes leading to the fulfillment of the commitments entered into within the intervals stipulated may begin through consultations, negotiations, and any other mechanisms deemed necessary.

When 90 days have elapsed from the date of the signature of this document, the commitments with regard to amnesty, cease-fire, democratization, cessation of aid to irregular forces or insurgent movements, and the non-use of territory to attack other states, as defined in this document, shall simultaneously begin to govern publicly.

When 120 days have elapsed from the date of the signature of this document, the International Verification and Follow-up Committee shall analyze the progress made in the fulfillment of the agreements provided for herein.

When 150 days have elapsed, the five Central American Presidents shall meet and receive a report from the International Verification and Follow-up Committee and shall make pertinent decisions.

Final Provisions

The points included in this document form a harmonious and indivisible whole. Signing it entails the obligation, accepted in good faith, to comply simultaneously and within the established time limits with the provisions agreed upon.

The Presidents of the Five Central American states, with the political will to respond to our people's yearnings for peace, hereby sign this document in Guatemala City on August 7, 1987.

Oscar Arias Sánchez
    President
    Republic of Costa Rica

Vinicio Cerezo Arévalo
    President
    Republic of Guatemala

José Napoleón Duarte
    President
    Republic of El Salvador

José Azcona Hoyo
    President
    Republic of Honduras

Daniel Ortega Saavedra
    President
    Republic of Nicaragua

ACRONYMS

ARENA (Alianza Republicana Nacionalista): Nationalist Republican Alliance, right-wing party in El Salvador.

CBMs: Confidence-building measures.

CIAV (Comisión Internacional de Apoyo y Verificación): International Commission of Support and Verification.

CIAV-OAS (Comisión Internacional de Apoyo y Verificación-OAS): The OAS portion of the International Commission of Support and Verification.

CIAV-UN (Comisión Internacional de Apoyo y Verificación-UN): The UN portion of the International Commission of Support and Verification.

CIVS (Comisión Internacional de Verificación y Seguimiento): International Commission for Verification and Follow-up.

CMO: Chief Military Observer (of a UN peace-observing mission).

CONDECA (Consejo de Defensa Centroamericano): Central American Defense Council.

COPAZ: National Commission for the Consolidation of Peace.

CVC (Comisión de Verificación y Seguimiento): Control and Verification Commission.

ECOMOG: The military arm of ECOWAS.

ECOWAS: Economic Committee of West African States.

EPS (Ejército Popular Sandinista): Sandinista People's Army.

FBIS: Foreign Broadcast Information Service.

FDR: Frente Democrático Revolucionario.

FMLN (Frente Farabundo Martí de Liberación Nacional): Farabundo Martí National Liberation Front of El Salvador.

FPM (Frente Patriótico Morazanista): Morazán Patriotic Front of Honduras.

FSLN (Frente Sandinista de Liberación Nacional): Sandinista National

Liberation Front of Nicaragua.

IADB: Inter-American Defense Board, Washington.

IAPF: Inter-American Peace Force.

IASS: Inter-American Security System.

ICJ: International Court of Justice, Geneva.

IIC: International Inspector Corps.

IPA: International Peace Academy, New York.

LASA: Latin American Studies Association.

MFO: Multinational Force and Observers.

NATO: North Atlantic Treaty Organization.

NRC: National Reconciliation Commission.

NSC: National Security Council.

OAS: Organization of American States.

OGELS: Observer Group in El Salvador.

ONUCA: UN Observer Group in Central America.

ONUSAL: UN Observer Group in El Salvador.

ONUVEH: UN Election Verification Mission in Haiti.

ONUVEN: UN Observer Group for the Verification of Elections in Nicaragua.

PAHO: Pan American Health Organization.

TAG: Technical Advisory Group.

UN: United Nations.

UNAVEM: UN Angola Verification Mission.

UNDP: United Nations Development Program.

UNHCR: United Nations High Commissioner for Refugees.

UNMO: UN Military Observer.

UNO (Unión Nacional Opositora): National Opposition Union.

URNG (Unidad Revolucionaria Nacional Guatemalteca): Literally "Guatemalan National Revolutionary Unity," but the sense is better rendered as "Guatemalan United National Revolutionary Front."

USAID: U.S. Agency for International Development.

USIP: United States Institute of Peace.

VC: Verification Center.

BIBLIOGRAPHY

Aguilar Zinzer, Adolfo. "Negotiation in Conflict: Central America and Contadora." In *Crisis in Central America,* edited by Nora Hamilton. Boulder, Colo.: Westview, 1988.

Aguilera, Gabriel. "Contadora, Realidad o Ilusión?" *Panorama Centroamericano* (Guatemala) 2/86 (March–April 1986).

———. "Centroamérica: la Crisis sin Fin." *Revista de Ciencias Sociales* (Costa Rica) 36 (1987).

———. "Esquipulas y el Conflicto Interno en Centroamérica." *Anuario de Estudios Centroamericanos* 14 (1988): 131–141.

———. "Centroamérica: Concertación y Conflicto, una Exploración." *Nueva Sociedad* 102 (July–August 1989).

———. *El Fusil y el Olivo.* San José: FLACSO, 1989.

Alford, Jonathan. *Confidence-Building Measures.* Adelphi Papers, no. 149. London: International Institute for Strategic Studies, 1979.

———, ed. *The Future of Arms Control: Part III—Confidence Building Measures.* London: The International Institute for Strategic Studies, 1979.

Allen, Captain John R. "Peacekeeping and 'Local Presence' Missions: Capabilities and Challenges." *Defense Science* (December 1985–January 1986 and February–March 1986).

Alvarez, Oscar. "El Proceso de Esquipulas." *Relaciones Internacionales* (San José) (January–March 1989).

Arias, Oscar. "Only Peace Can Write the New History." *Transnational Perspectives* 14, no. 1 (1988).

———. *El Camino de la Paz.* San José: Editorial Costa Rica, 1989.

Arnson, Cynthia. *Crossroads: Congress, the Reagan Administration and Central America.* New York: Pantheon, 1989.

Bagley, Bruce. *Contadora and the Central American Peace Process.* Vol. 1, documents. Boulder, Colo.: Westview, 1985.

———. *Contadora and the Diplomacy of Peace in Central America.* Boulder, Colo.: Westview, 1987.

Bagley, Bruce, and Juan G. Tokatlian. *Contadora: The Limits of Negotiation.* Lanham, Md.: University Press of America, 1987.

Baradini, Roberto. "Centroamerica: Otro Año de Esperanzas Frustradas." *Nueva Sociedad* 99 (February 1989).

Baranyi, Stephen. "Canadian Foreign Policy Towards Central America, 1980–84: Independence, Limited Public Influence, and State leadership." *North-South* 10 (1985): 23–57.

———. *Peace in Central America?* Ottawa: Canadian Institute for International Peace and Security, 1986.

———. *Promoting Peace and Demilitarization in Central America.* Toronto: York University Center for Strategic Studies, 1988.

Barros, Alexandre de S.C. "Confidence-Building Measures in South America: Some Notes on Opportunities and Needs." In *Confidence-Building Measures,* edited by Karl Kaiser, 185–200. Bonn: FDDGFAP, 1983.

Barton, David. "The Sinai Peacekeeping Experience: A Verification Paradigm for Europe." Chap. 16 in *SIPRI Yearbook.* Stockholm: SIPRI, 1985.

Bekarevich, Anatoly. "El Pensamiento Político Nuevo y los Problemas del Arreglo del Conflicto Centroamericano." *Nuestra América Latina* (Puerto Rico) 6 (February–July 1989).

Bendaña, Alejandro. "El Sandinismo ante el 'Colapso del Comunismo.'" *La Avispa* 2 (December 1990–January 1991).

Bermúdez, Enrique. "The Nicaraguan Resistance at a Crossroads." *Strategic Review* (Spring 1989).

Blachman, Morris, and William Leogrande, eds. *Confronting Revolution: Security through Diplomacy in Central America.* New York: Pantheon, 1986.

Bloomfield, Richard J., and Gregory F. Treverton, eds. *Alternative to Intervention: A New U.S.–Latin American Security Relationship.* Boulder, Colo.: Lynne Rienner, 1990.

Bricker, Calvin. *Central America and Peacekeeping: A Workshop Report.* Toronto: Canadian Institute of Strategic Studies, 1986.

Bulichov, Ilia. "El Grupo Contadora: Intricada Ruta Hacia la Paz." *America Latina* (USSR) (January 1985).

Buvollen, Hans Petter. "Low-Intensity Warfare and the Peace Plan in Central America." *Bulletin of Peace Proposals* (September 1989): 314–334.

Byers, R. B., ed. *Canada and Peacekeeping: Prospects for the Future.* Toronto: York University, 1983.

Calderón, Félix. "Verificación y Técnicas de Confianza." In *Limitación de Armamentos y Confianza Mutua en América Latina,* edited by Augusto Varas. Santiago: CLADDE-RIAL, 1988.

Calloni, Stella. *La "guerra encubierta" contra Contadora.* Panama: Centro de Capacitación Social, 1984.

Camacho, Daniel. *La Crisis Centroamericana.* San José: EDUCA/FLACSO, 1984.

Canada. House of Commons. *Peace Process in Central America, Minutes of Proceedings,* 27 April 1988, 4 May–29 June 1988.

———. *Supporting the Five.* Ottawa, 1988.

CAPA. *Report Card on Canada's First Year in the OAS.* Toronto: CAPA, 1991.

Center for International Policy. *International Policy Report.* Various Issues. Washington, D.C.: CIP, 1986–1991.

Centro de Estudios Internacionales (Managua). *Cuadernos del CEI,* no. 1, May 1991.

Cepeda Ulloa, Fernando. *Contadora: Desafío a la Diplomacia Tradicional.* Bogotá: Universidad de los Andes, 1985.

———. *Democracia y Desarrollo en América Latina.* Buenos Aires: GEL, 1985.

Cepeda, Fernando, and Rodrigo Pardo. *Negociaciones de Pacificación en América Central*. San José: FLACSO, 1987.

Cerdas Albertazzi, Ana Luisa. *La Abolición del Ejército en Costa Rica*. San José: Imprenta Nacional, 1988.

Certad Mejía, Aquiles. "El Grupo de Contadora y la Paz en Centroamérica." *Relaciones Internacionales* (Costa Rica) 6 (1983).

Child, Jack. *Unequal Alliance: The Inter-American Military System, 1938–1978*. Boulder, Colo.: Westview, 1980.

Child, Jack. "Peacekeeping and the Inter-American System." *Military Review* (October 1980): 40–54.

———, ed. *Conflict in Central America: Approaches to Peace and Security*. New York: St Martin's, 1986.

———, ed. *Regional Cooperation for Development and the Peaceful Settlement of Disputes in Latin America*. Boston: Martinus Nijhoff, 1987.

———. "U.S. Security and the Contadora Process: Toward a CBM Regime in Central America." In *Contadora and the Diplomacy of Peace in Central America*. Vol. 1, edited by Bruce Bagley, 50–68. Boulder, Colo.: Westview, 1987.

———. *Antarctica and South American Geopolitics*. New York: Praeger, 1988.

Chumakova, Marina. "De Contadora a Caraballeda." *América Latina* (USSR) 10 (1986).

Comisión Sudamericana de Paz. "América del Sur: Zona de Paz." *Nueva Sociedad* 91 (October 1987).

———. "Seguridad Democrática Regional: una Concepción Integral de Seguridad." *Relaciones Internacionales* (Costa Rica) 23 (1988).

Dallanegra Pedraza, Luis. *Proceso de Desmovilización de la Resistencia Nicaragüense*. Buenos Aires: Ministry of Foreign Affairs, 1990.

Daremblum, Jaime. *Centro América, Conflicto y Democracia*. San José: Libro Libre, 1985.

Darling, Jonathan. "The 1969 War Between El Salvador and Honduras: a Case Study in Central American Peace-keeping." Paper delivered at the annual conference of Middle Atlantic Council of Latin American Studies (MACLAS), April 1991.

De Gonzalo, Marisol. "La Significación del Grupo Contadora como Actor Internacional." *Política Internacional* (Venezuela) 3 (July–September 1986): 16–23.

Diaz-Callejas, Apolinar. *Contadora: Desafío al Imperio*. Bogotá: La Oveja Negra, 1985.

Dickey, Christopher. *With the Contras*. New York: Simon & Schuster, 1987.

Dosman, Edgar J. *Latin America and the Caribbean: The Strategic Framework—A Canadian Perspective*. Ottawa: ORAE, Department of National Defence, 1984.

Duran, Esperanza. "La Solución de Contadora para el Logro de la Paz en Centroamérica." *Estudios Internacionales* (October 1984).

Duran, Esperanza. "Pacification, Security and Democracy: Contadora's Role in Central America." In *The Central American Security System*, edited by Peter Calvert. Cambridge: Cambridge University Press, 1988.

Escalante Herrera, Elizabeth. "La Propuesta de Paz del Presidente Arias: Un Caso de Autonomía Relativa?" *Relaciones Internacionales* (Costa Rica) 26 (1989).

Ethell, Lt. Col. D. S. "Central American Peacekeeping Observation Organization." Canadian Ministry of Defence staff paper, 1987.

Fagen, Richard, ed. *Forging Peace: The Challenge of Central America*. New York: Basil Blackwell, 1987.

190 BIBLIOGRAPHY

Falcoff, Mark. "Regional Diplomatic Options in Central America." *AEI Foreign Policy and Defense Review*, 5, no. 1 (1984): 54–60.

FLACSO. *Informe Blanco sobre los Avances en el Proceso de Cumplimiento del Acuerdo de Paz para Centroamérica, Esquipulas II.* San José: FLACSO, 1988.

Flores Pinel, Fernando. "De Esquipulas a Tela." *ECA-Estudios Centroamericanos* 492 (October 1989): 809–833.

Fouquet, David. "Counting the Cost of UN Peacekeepers." *Jane's Defense Weekly* 24 (December 1988): 1589.

Frambes-Buxeda, Aline. "El Proceso de Paz en Centroamérica." *Homines* (Puerto Rico) 5 (1988).

Frohman, Alicia. "De Contadora al Grupo de los Ocho." *Estudios Internacionales* (July 1989): 385–427.

Goldblat, Jozef. "Zone of Peace in the South Atlantic." Chap. 11 in *SIPRI Yearbook.* Stockholm: SIPRI, 1987.

Gomariz, Enrique. *Balance de una Esperanza, Esquipulas II, Un Año Después.* San José: FLACSO, 1988.

Goodman, Louis, ed. *The Military and Democracy: the Future of Civil-Military Relations in Latin America.* Lexington, Mass.: DC Heath, 1990.

Gorostiaga, Xabier. *Geopolítica de la Crisis Regional.* Managua: INIES, nd.

———. "Peace with no Losers." *NACLA* (July 1987): 6–10.

Gutman, Roy. *Banana Diplomacy: the Making of American Policy in Nicaragua, 1981–1987.* New York: Simon & Schuster, 1988.

Hackel, Jay, ed. *In Contempt of Congress: The Reagan Record on Central America.* Washington, D.C.: Institute for Policy Studies, 1985.

Haglund, David. "The Missing Link: Canada's Security Interests and the Central American Crisis." *International Journal* 52, no. 4 (Autumn 1987).

Hamilton, Nora, ed. *Crisis in Central America.* Boulder, Colo.: Westview, 1988.

Hanning, Hugh, ed. *Peacekeeping and Confidence-Building Measures in the Third World.* New York: International Peace Academy, 1985.

Harbottle, Michael. *The Blue Berets.* Harrisburg, Pa.: Stackpole Books, 1971.

Harrelson, Max. *Fires All Around the Horizon.* New York: Praeger, 1989.

Hepburn, Davidson. "Cooperation and CBMs in Latin America and the Caribbean." *Disarmament* (Autumn 1989).

Herrera Cáceres, Roberto. *Democracia, Desarrollo y Paz en Centroamérica.* Tegucigalpa: Guaymuras, 1989.

Hirst, Monica. *Desarme y Desarrollo en América Latina.* Buenos Aires: Fundación Arturo Illia, 1990.

Holland, Stuart. *Kissinger's Kingdom (A Counter Report on Central America).* Nottingham, U.K.: Spokesman, 1984.

Houghton, Robert. *Multinational Peacekeeping in the Middle East.* Washington, D.C.: Foreign Service Institute, 1985.

Ichikawa, Akira. *The "Helpful Fixer": Canada's Persistent International Image.* Toronto: Canadian Institute of International Affairs, 1979.

Instituto Centroamericano de Estudios Políticos. *La Crisis Centroamericana: Tres Enfoques de Actualidad.* Guatemala City: ICEP, 1986.

Inter-American Defense Board. *Basic Norms for the Organization and Employment of an Inter-American Peacekeeping Force.* IADB Document T-369, 9 November 1979.

———. *Guide for the Performance of Military Observers.* IADB Document C-2044/T-373, 21 January 1981.

International Peace Academy. *Peacekeeper's Handbook.* New York: IPA, 1978.

———. *Weapons of Peace: How New Technology Can Revitalize Peacekeeping.* New York: IPA, 1980.

———. *Peace-keeping and Technology: Concepts for the Future.* New York: IPA, 1983.

Joly, Colonel John. "ONUCA—A Story of Success in the Quest for Peace." *Canadian Defence Quarterly* (June 1991): 12–19.

Jones, Peter. *Peacekeeping: An Annotated Bibliography.* Kingston, Ontario: Frye, 1989.

Keesing's International Studies. *Conflict in Central America.* London: Longman, 1987.

Kissinger, Henry A. *Kissinger Commission Report.* New York: Macmillan, 1984.

Klepak, H. P. *Verification of a Central American Peace Accord.* Ottawa, Canada: External Affairs, Arms Control and Disarmament Division, 1989.

———. "The Application of the Sinai Model to Central American Peace Initiatives." In *Back to the Future: Lessons from Experience for Regional Arms Control and Verification,* edited by Brian S. Mandell. Ottawa, Canada: Carleton University, 1989.

———. *Security Considerations and Verification of a Central American Arms Regime.* Ottawa, Canada: External Affairs, Arms Control and Disarmament Division, 1990.

Krehbiel, Carl. *Confidence- and Security-Building Measures in Europe.* New York: Praeger, 1989.

Krepon, Michael. *Verification and Compliance.* Cambridge: Balinger, 1988.

Labastida, Jaime, et al. *Centroamérica: Crisis y Política Internacional.* Mexico City: Siglo XXI, 1982.

Latin American Studies Association. *Electoral Democracy Under International Pressure (1990 Nicaraguan Elections).* Pittsburgh: LASA, 1990.

Leary, Brig. Gen. B. V. "Principles of Peace Observation." *Marine Corps Gazette* (June 1986): 40–41.

Leiken, Robert S., ed. *Central America: Anatomy of Conflict.* New York: Pergamon, 1984.

Lemco, Jonathan. "Canada and Central America: A Review of Current Issues." *Behind the Headlines* 43 (May 1986).

———. "Canadian Foreign Policy Interests in Central America." *Journal of Interamerican Studies* 28, no. 2 (Summer 1986): 119–146.

———. *Canada and the Crisis in Central America.* New York: Praeger, 1991.

Leogrande, William M. "Rollback or Containment." In *Contadora and the Diplomacy of Peace in Central America,* edited by Bruce M. Bagley. Boulder, Colo.: Westview, 1987.

Lernoux, Penny. *Fear and Hope: Toward Political Democracy in Central America.* New York: The Field Foundation, 1984.

Liu, F. T. *UN Peacekeeping: Management and Operations.* New York: International Peace Academy, 1990.

Macintosh, James. *Confidence (and Security) Building Measures in the Arms Control Process: A Canadian Perspective.* Ottawa, Canada: Department of External Affairs, 1985.

Maira, Luis, ed. *La Política de Reagan y la Crisis en Centroamérica.* San José: Editorial Universitaria Centroamericana, 1982.

Manwaring, Max G. *El Salvador at War: An Oral History.* Washington, D.C.: National Defense University, 1988.

Maza, Emilio. *Centroamérica: el Nuevo Escenario.* Guatemala City: Sofarma, 1983.

McDonald, Brian, ed. *Canada, the Caribbean and Central America*. Toronto: Canadian Institute of Strategic Studies, 1986.

McNeil, Frank. *War and Peace in Central America*. New York: Scribner's, 1988.

Melendez, Guillermo. *Queremos la Paz*. San José: DEI, 1984.

Mendez Asensio, Luis. *Contadora: las Cuentas de la Diplomacia*. Mexico City: Plaza y Janés, 1987.

Mercado Jarrín, Edgardo. *Un Sistema de Seguridad y Defensa Sudamericano*. Lima: CEPEI, 1989.

Morris, Michael A., and Victor Millán. *Controlling Latin American Conflicts: Ten Approaches*. Boulder, Colo.: Westview, 1983.

Multinational Force and Observers. *The Multinational Force and Observers*. Annual Reports. Rome: MFO, 1987–1990.

North, Liisa. *Negotiations for Peace in Central America*. Ottawa, Canada: Canadian Institute for International Peace and Security, 1985.

——. *Between Peace and War in Central America: Choices for Canada*. Toronto: CAPA, Between the Lines, 1990.

ONUCA. *ONUCA Observer*. Tegucigalpa: ONUCA, 1990.

Ortega Durán, Oyden. *Contadora y su Verdad*. Madrid: R. G. Blanco, 1985.

Ortega, Daniel. *Combatiendo por la Paz*. Mexico City: Siglo XXI, 1988.

Palma, Hugo. "Confidence Building: Present Situation and Future Prospects." In *Peacekeeping and Confidence-Building Measures in the Third World*, edited by Hugh Hanning, 53–56. New York: International Peace Academy, 1985.

——. *América Latina: Limitación de Armamentos y Desarme en la Región*. Lima: CEPEI, 1986.

——. "Co-operation and Confidence-Building Measures in Latin America and the Caribbean." *Disarmament* (Autumn 1989).

——. "Medidas de Confianza Reciproca." In *Seguridad Democratica Regional: Una Concepción Alternativa*, edited by Juan Somavía. Caracas: Nueva Sociedad, 1990.

Pellegrini Delgado, Carlos. *Las Industrias Bélicas, las Medidas de Confianza y el Proceso de Limitación de Gastos en Armamentos en el Cono Sur*. Lima: CEPEI, 1989.

Pensamiento Propio. "Informe de la CIVS: La Verdad que se Quiso Ocultar." *Pensamiento Propio* (January 1988): 7–11.

Portales, Carlos. "Zona de Paz: Una Alternativa a los Desafíos Estratégicos de América Latina." *Cuadernos Semestrales* 15 (1984).

Purver, Ron, ed. *The Guide to Canadian Policies on Arms Control, Disarmament and Conflict Resolution*. 4 vols. Ottawa, Canada: Canadian Institute for International Peace and Security, 1987–1990.

Ramaciotti de Cubas, Beatriz. "La Antártida como Zona de Paz." *Themis* 10 (1988).

Rico, Carlos. "La Experiencia de Contadora y el Futuro Potencial de una Acción Latino Americana Conjunta en Asuntos de Seguridad." In *Desarme y Desarrollo en America Latina*, edited by Monica Hirst. Buenos Aires: Fundacion Arturo Illia, 1990.

Rikhye, Indar Jit. *The Theory and Practice of Peacekeeping*. London: Hurst, 1984.

——. *The UN and Peacekeeping: Results, Limitations and Prospects*. London: Macmillan, 1990.

Rochlin, James. "Aspects of Canadian Foreign Policy Towards Central America, 1979–1986." *Journal of Canadian Studies* 22, no. 4 (1987–1988).

Rojas Aravena, Francisco. *Relaciones Internacionales en Centroamérica*. San José: Instituto de Documentación e Investigación Social, 1986.

———. *El Proceso de Esquipulas: El Desarrollo Conceptual y los Mecanismos Operativos*. Heredia, Costa Rica: Universidad Nacional, Escuela de Relaciones Internacionales, 1989.

———. "Centroamérica: Dos Años de Trabajo por la Paz." *Relaciones Internacionales* (Costa Rica) 30 (1990).

———. *Costa Rica: Política Exterior y Crisis Centroamericana*. Heredia, Costa Rica: Universidad Nacional, 1990.

Roundtable on Negotiations for Peace in Central America. *Interim and Confidence-Building Measures*. Toronto: The Roundtable, 1987.

Schmitz, Gerald. *Canadian Foreign Policy in Central America*. Ottawa, Canada: Library of Parliament, 1986.

Serafino, Nina. "The Contadora Initiative, the US, and the Concept of a Zone of Peace." In *Hemisphere Security and US Policy in Latin America,* edited by Augusto Varas. Boulder, Colo.: Westview, 1989.

Serafino, Nina. *The Contadora Initiative: Implications for the Congress*. Congressional Research Service Issue Brief, 22 September 1985.

———. *Nicaraguan Elections and Transition: Issues for U.S. Policy*. Congressional Research Service Report for Congress, no. 90-187-F, 26 March 1990.

———. *Nicaragua Chronology Since the February 25, 1990, Elections*. Congressional Research Service Report for Congress, no. 90-423-F, 5 September 1990.

Serbín, Andrés. *¿El Caribe, Zona de Paz?* Caracas: Nueva Sociedad, 1989.

———. "La Paz en el Caribe: Una Utopia Posible?" *Nuestra América Latina* (Puerto Rico) 6 (February–July 1989).

———. *Caribbean Geopolitics: Toward Security Through Peace?* Boulder, Colo.: Lynne Rienner, 1990.

Silva Michelena, Jose A., ed. *Paz, Seguridad y Desarrollo en América Latina*. Caracas: Editorial Nueva Sociedad, United Nations University, 1987.

———. *Los Factores de la Paz*. Caracas: Nueva Sociedad, 1987.

Sklar, Holly. *Washington's War on Nicaragua*. Boston: South End, 1988.

Sohr, Raul. *Centroamérica en Guerra*. Mexico City: Alianza Estudios, 1988.

Solis Rivera, Luis Guillermo. "La Paz y el Futuro de Centroamérica." *Relaciones Internacionales* (Costa Rica) 21 (1987).

Somavía, Juan, and José Miguel Insulza. *Seguridad Democrática Regional: Una Concepción Alternativa*. Caracas: Nueva Socieded, 1990.

Sosa, Ignacio. *Centroamérica: Desafíos y Perspectivas*. Mexico City: Universidad Nacional Autónoma, 1984.

Tinoco, Victor Hugo. *Conflicto y Paz: El Proceso Negociador Centroamericano*. Mexico City: Editorial Mestiza, 1988.

Toro Hardy, Alfredo. "El Por Qué de Contadora." *Política Internacional* (Venezuela) 1 (January 1986).

Torres Rivas, Edelberto. *Crisis del Poder en Centroamérica*. San José: EDUCA, 1981.

———. *América Central hacia el 2000: Desafíos y Opciones*. Caracas: Nueva Sociedad, 1989.

Treleaven, Michael. "Canada, U.S., Vietnam, and Central America." *International Perspectives* (September–October 1986): 10–13.

U.S. Congress. Subcommittee on Western Hemisphere Affairs. *Hearing and Markup: Recent Events Concerning the Arias Peace Proposal*. Washington, D.C.: GPO, July 9, 15, 28, 1987.

U.S. Department of State. *Resource Book: The Contadora Peace Process.* Washington, D.C., 1985.

———. *Negotiations in Central America (Chronology).* Washington, D.C., 1987.

———. *Regional Brief: Central America.* Washington, D.C., 1988.

United Nations. *The Blue Helmets: A Review of UN Peacekeeping.* 2d ed. New York: UN, 1990.

Valenta, Jiri, and Esperanza Durán. *Conflict in Nicaragua.* Winchester, Mass.: Allen & Unwin, 1987.

Varas, Augusto. *Militarization and the International Arms Race in Latin America.* Boulder, Colo.: Westview, 1985.

———. *La Autonomía Militar en América Latina.* Caracas: Nueva Sociedad, 1988.

———. *La Política de las Armas en América Latina.* Santiago: FLACSO, 1988.

———, ed. *Limitaciones de Armamentos y Confianza Mutua en América Latina.* Santiago: CLADDE-RIAL, 1988.

———. *Hemispheric Security and US Policy in Latin America.* Boulder, Colo.: Westview, 1989.

Wall, James T. "Costa Rica and Contadora: A Narrative." 1991.

Wiseman, Henry. *Peacekeeping: Appraisals and Proposals.* New York: Pergamon, 1983.

York University Centre for International and Strategic Studies. *Central America and Peacekeeping: A Workshop Report.* Toronto: CISS, 1986.

INDEX

Ortega, Humberto, 89, 100, 109, 122; and
  assassination of Enrique Bermúdez,
  122

Panama, invasion of December 1989, 160
Panama Foreign Ministers' Meeting,
  September 1983, 18–19; April 1984,
  25–26; January 1984, 21
Peace building, 3
Peace dominoes, 4
Peace enforcement, 2–3, 126, 150
Peace observing, 3, 8–9, 33
Peace parks, 114
Peace verification, 4, 8–9, 15–16, 19, 22–
  23, 25–6, 31, 33, 38, 48–50, 148, 157,
  164; Centers (ONUCA), 84; and
  Esquipulas, 61–77, 151–154
Peaceful settlement of disputes, 3
Peacekeeping, 2, 8–9, 33, 161
Peacemaking, 3
Pérez, Carlos Andrés, 91–92
Pérez de Cuéllar, Javier, 64, 77, 128, 136,
  164
Piñata (1990), 123, 142
Poles of Development, 106–109
Political mandate (peacekeeping principle),
  153–154
Principles for Implementation (of
  Contadora), 21
Principles of peacekeeping, 5–8, 151–154
Protocol on Disarmament (Contras-
  Chamorro), 103
Puntarenas summit, December 1990, 156

Quesada Gómez, Agustín, 82, 84, 91, 95,
  118

Reagan administration, 15, 18–19, 21–23,
  31, 46, 61, 148, 151
Reagan-Wright peace plan, 46–47
Recompas, 124–126
Recontras, 1990–91, 120–127
Resettlement of Contras, 119
Resistance, Nicaraguan. See Contras
Revised Contadora Act, September 1984,
  30–32
Rio Group, 39–40
Rio Treaty, 8, 16, 149, 159
Riza, Iqbal, 134, 136

Sandinista People's Army (EPS), 113, 126
Sandinistas, 20, 37, 47, 124; and Poles of
  Development, 107; and Sapoá
  Agreement, 53–55
Sapoá Agreement, March 1988, 53–55
Security Commission, Esquipulas. See
  Esquipulas Security Commission

Security definition, 162
Security treaty, Central American, 141–
  142
Security zones (for Contra resettlement),
  95–97; in El Salvador, 133
Serrano, Jorge, 138–140
Shultz, George, 24, 61
Simultaneous peacekeeping and
  peacemaking (peacekeeping principle),
  8, 153
Soares, Joao Baena, 40, 54
Somoza, Anastacio, 62, 150
South American Peace Commission, 5
Soviet Union, and Central American peace,
  19, 67–69, 151
Spain, 46, 57, 149, 152; and Esquipulas
  Technical Advisory Group (TAG),
  57
Strains between ONUCA and CIAV, 129–
  130
Suanzes Pardo, Victor, 118
Sumner, Gordon, 22, 122, 142
Surface-to-air missiles, 74, 106, 128
Swordsmen's metaphor, 3–4

Technical Advisory Group (TAG), 55
Technical group, 21
Tegucigalpa Draft Contadora Act, October
  1984, 32–33
Tela Summit, August 1989, 69–72
Tesoro Beach Summit (Costa del Sol),
  February 1989, 65–67
Tinoco, Víctor Hugo, 33, 66, 101
Tlatelolco Treaty (proscription of nuclear
  weapons), 4, 155
Truth Commission, El Salvador, 135
Twenty-one Objectives Document,
  September 1983, 18–19, 30; text, 174–
  177

UN Election Verification Mission in Haiti
  (OUNVEH), 127
UN High Commissioner for Refugees
  (UNHCR), 86, 117
UN Military Staff Committee, 10, 69
UN Observer Group for the Verification of
  Elections in Nicaragua (ONUVEN),
  February 1990, 70, 75, 88–89
UN Observer Group in Central America
  (ONUCA), 23, 66, 75–77; attack on
  Honduras headquarters, June 1990, 130;
  and Contra demobilization (1990), 95–
  114; Demobilization Report, June 1990,
  106; early implementation phase (1989–
  1990), 81–92; expanded mandate (1990),
  82–83, 89–91; initial deployment,
  December 1989, 83–85; in late 1990,

ABOUT THE BOOK AND AUTHOR

The Contadora peace process and the Arias/Esquipulas II Peace Plan that evolved from it represent a historic turning point for Central America and its relationship with both the inter-American system and the United Nations. The creation of UN peacekeeping and treaty-verification operations in Central America was unprecedented, as was the cooperation between the UN and the OAS in supervising the demobilization and resettlement of guerrilla forces.

Child examines the peace process from the first Contadora meeting, in January 1983, through the signing of the breakthrough agreement between the government of El Salvador and the FMLN in late 1991. His principal focus is on the verification of the Central American peace accords, the peacekeeping operation mounted by the United Nations, and the use of confidence-building measures to create trust between the parties to the various conflicts. Of particular interest is his conclusion that the approaches to conflict resolution taken in Central America have considerable relevance for the search for solutions to other conflicts and for the slowly evolving movement to create zones of peace in the Western Hemipshere.

JACK CHILD is professor of Spanish and Latin American Studies in the Department of Language and Foreign Studies of the American University. He was born of American parents in Buenos Aires, and lived in South America until he came to the United States in 1955 to attend Yale University. Following graduation, he entered the U.S. Army, and served as Latin American Specialist until his retirement as a lieutenant colonel in 1980. While on active duty he earned his master's and doctoral degrees in the international relations of Latin America from the School of International Service of the American University.

In 1980 Child joined the School of International Service as assistant dean. Two years later he moved to the Department of Language and Foreign Studies, where he teaches a variety of courses (in both English and Spanish) dealing with translation, conflict, and Latin American studies (international relations, history, art, and literature).

Child's principal research interests have focused on conflict and its resolution in Latin America and Antarctica. He has worked with the International Peace Academy (associated with the United Nations) on issues dealing with peacekeeping and confidence-building measures in Central and South America, and has edited three books on Latin American conflict resolution for the academy. In July 1989 he was awarded a grant from the U.S. Institute of Peace to research peacekeeping and confidence-building aspects of the Central American peace process, 1983–1991.